TOOLS

FOR THOUGHTFUL ASSESSMENT

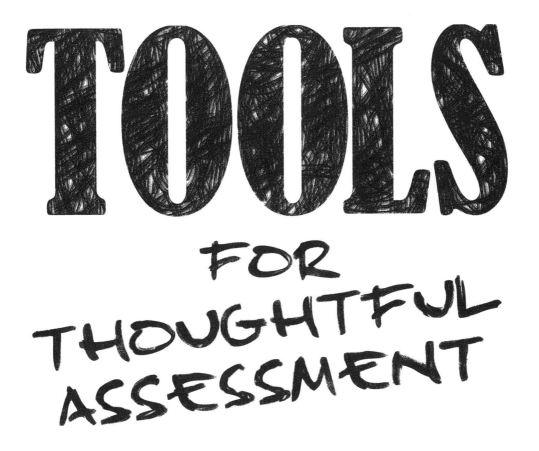

TOOLS FOR THOUGHTFUL ASSESSMENT

Classroom-Ready Techniques for Improving Teaching and Learning

Over 75 tools for

- Establishing learning targets
- Checking for understanding
- Providing effective feedback
- Using writing as an assessment tool
- Differentiating assessment practices
- Building self-assessment and goal-setting skills

Abigail L. Boutz | Harvey F. Silver | Joyce W. Jackson | Matthew J. Perini

Silver Strong & Associates
Thoughtful Education Press

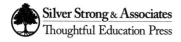 **Silver Strong & Associates**
Thoughtful Education Press

227 First Street, Ho-Ho-Kus, NJ 07423
Phone: 800-962-4432 or 201-652-1155
Fax: 201-652-1127
Website: www.ThoughtfulClassroom.com
Email: questions@thoughtfulclassroom.com

Quantity discounts are available. For information, call 800-962-4432.

ISBN: 978-1-58284-200-4

President: Harvey F. Silver
Director of Publishing: Matthew J. Perini
Design and Production Directors: Bethann Carbone & Michael Heil
Proofreader: Susan T. Landry

Tools Series Developer: Harvey F. Silver
Tools Series Editor: Matthew J. Perini

Printed in the United States of America

20 19 18 17 16 15 14   5 6 7 8 9 10

Acknowledgments

The authors would like to acknowledge the contributions of the schools, teachers, and individuals whose assistance has made this book possible. First and foremost, we would like to thank the teachers and researchers whose work and ideas have influenced our philosophy as educators and our commitment to developing this series of practical and teacher-friendly classroom tools. We are particularly grateful to Barbara Heinzman for her input on addressing the needs of primary-grade teachers, to Ellen Silver for providing and reviewing classroom examples, to John Brunsting for letting us pick his mathematician's brain, to Sherry Gibbon for her thoughtful review of the manuscript, to Christopher and Claudia Geocaris for their assistance with A Test Worth Taking, and to the late Richard W. Strong, whose work and dedication to teachers continues to inspire us.

Other educators who deserve special thanks include Kimberly Zeidler-Watters and her group of Regional and Appalachian Teacher Partners from the P–12 Math and Science Outreach Unit of the University of Kentucky's Partnership Institute for Mathematics & Science Education Reform (PIMSER), who inspired this book of assessment tools; the teachers and administrators from Marquardt School District 15 (Illinois), Community Consolidated School District 93 (Illinois), and the P–12 Math and Science Outreach Unit of PIMSER's 2011 Meeting the Challenge Conference, whose feedback and ideas influenced the direction of this book; the educators and administrators from Durand Area Schools (Michigan) who provided tools ideas and the classrooms to test them in; and the teachers, principals, and students who kindly contributed samples of work for us to use—especially Brenda Donahue and Jessica Salvesen from Circle Center Grade School in Yorkville, IL; Katherine Beery and Max Chernick from Hinsdale Central High School in Hinsdale, IL; James Kenneth Mattingly and Becky Smith from Rockcastle County Schools (Kentucky); and Mary Claire Lewis from Errick Road Elementary School in North Tonawanda, NY.

Finally, we would like to thank Justin Gilbert for his assistance with permissions and production issues, and Paul Boutz and Kimberly Nunez for their help and support throughout the writing and production process.

For copies of the reproducibles
and other downloadable "extras" noted in the text,
visit **www.ThoughtfulClassroom.com/Tools**.

Contents

SECTION THREE: Assessment Tools to Use When Deepening and Reinforcing Learning

SECTION FOUR: Assessment Tools to Use When Having Students Apply and Demonstrate Their Learning

SECTION FIVE: Assessment Tools to Use When Inviting Students to Reflect On and Celebrate Their Learning

Introduction

Assessment: A Continuous Journey Toward Improved Learning

Over the last two decades, the meaning of the word *assessment* in education has been changing—and for the better. Today's educators know that assessment means much more than assigning and grading student work. They know assessment is an ongoing process that involves regularly gathering information about student learning, using that information to make better instructional decisions, and inviting students to take responsibility for monitoring and improving their learning.

This shift in assessment priorities goes by various names, most notably *formative assessment* and *assessment for learning*. Jan Chappuis, Rick Stiggins, Steve Chappuis, and Judith Arter (2011), who helped popularize the term assessment for learning, describe the overall approach as one of helping students ask and answer three questions:

- Where am I going? (What learning targets am I trying to achieve?)
- Where am I now? (What is my current level of understanding or mastery?)
- What can I do to close the gap? (How can I use feedback, self-assessment data, and learning opportunities to reach my learning targets?)

To do this well—to take students on a continuous journey toward improved learning and higher achievement—teachers need a collection of effective assessment techniques that will integrate seamlessly into their overall instructional design. This book is that collection of techniques.

We call the techniques in this book *tools* because, in the most general sense, a tool is something designed to make work easier and more effective. And what this book does is provide teachers with more than seventy-five tools that can help them more easily accomplish the many jobs associated with the assessment-for-learning journey—jobs like establishing clear learning targets, teaching students how to assess their own learning, and helping students understand how to produce quality work. It also includes tools that can be used to evaluate student learning at the end of a learning episode.

In developing the content and structure of this book, we've been influenced by three groups of experts. The first includes the educational researchers who have shown, beyond a shadow of a doubt, that using assessment to advance rather than simply evaluate student learning leads to very real gains in achievement. Paul Black and Dylan Wiliam's (1998a) review of nine years' worth of data from hundreds of studies spanning the full range of grade levels and subject areas revealed that formative assessment leads to dramatic gains in achievement, "amongst the largest ever reported for educational interventions" (p. 61). More recently, Robert Marzano (2006) surveyed the major research on classroom assessment and concluded that "formative classroom assessment is one of the most powerful tools a classroom teacher might use" (p. 11).

The second group of experts whose work has informed ours includes authors and scholars like Rick Stiggins, Jan Chappuis, Anne Davies, Susan Brookhart, Connie Moss, and W. James Popham, who have helped teachers translate the research on assessment for learning into effective classroom practice. These important experts have helped us—and the larger field of education—understand how to harness the power of assessment so that students become active participants in their own learning.

The third group of experts is the most important group of all: the teachers who are charged with making assessment work in their classrooms. In developing this book, we invited hundreds of teachers to review, test-drive, and help us refine our collection of tools. From these teachers, we learned four key lessons.

Four Lessons About Assessment Tools

Lesson One: Make sure the tools respond to the challenges that teachers face. So what are these challenges? To find out, we asked teachers from around the country to identify the key challenges associated with making assessment work in their classrooms. We then cross-referenced their responses against the major literature on assessment for learning and assessment in general. Out of this work, we identified twelve critical challenges. Finally, we turned each challenge into a question, and we made these twelve questions the chapters in our book. Here are the twelve questions:

1. How will I identify and communicate learning goals to students?

2. How will I use pre-assessments to inform and enhance instruction?

3. How will I prepare students to produce high-quality work?

4. How will I check for understanding *while* presenting new information?

5. How will I check for understanding *after* presenting new information?

6. How will I help students review, practice, and check their grasp of the material?

7. How will I help students improve their work through feedback and self-assessment?

8. How will I help students monitor their learning and establish goals and plans for moving forward?

9. How will I use writing tasks to help students synthesize and show what they know?

10. How will I develop high-quality culminating assessment tasks and evaluation frameworks?

11. How will I differentiate assessment to promote success for all students?

12. How will I help students reflect on, learn from, and celebrate their achievements?

Lesson Two: Make the tools practical. When it came time to create a standard design for the tools in this book, the overwhelming theme in teachers' feedback was *make each tool as practical and classroom-ready as possible.* And so we created a common format that provides the precise information teachers need to decide if a tool meets their purpose and put the tool to work in the classroom. This common, recurring format also makes it easy for teachers to find what's important to them within each tool. Using the 3-2-1 tool as an example, Figure 1 shows how every tool answers four crucial questions.

Figure 1: The Four Questions Every Tool in This Book Answers

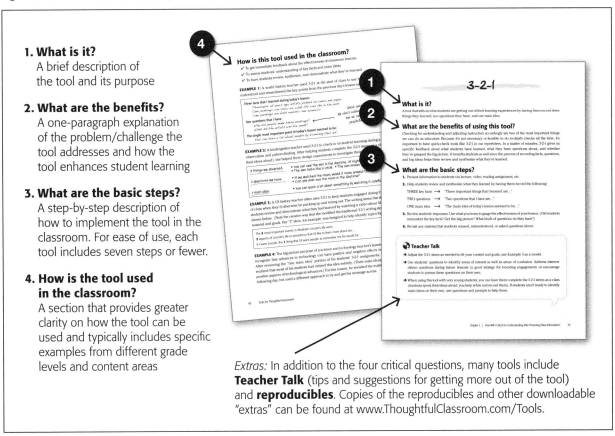

1. What is it?
A brief description of
the tool and its purpose

2. What are the benefits?
A one-paragraph explanation
of the problem/challenge the
tool addresses and how the
tool enhances student learning

3. What are the basic steps?
A step-by-step description of
how to implement the tool in the
classroom. For ease of use, each
tool includes seven steps or fewer.

**4. How is the tool used
in the classroom?**
A section that provides greater
clarity on how the tool can be
used and typically includes specific
examples from different grade
levels and content areas

Extras: In addition to the four critical questions, many tools include
Teacher Talk (tips and suggestions for getting more out of the tool)
and **reproducibles**. Copies of the reproducibles and other downloadable
"extras" can be found at www.ThoughtfulClassroom.com/Tools.

Because the tools are organized around crucial challenges (Lesson One) and follow a common
format (Lesson Two), this book offers educators an entirely flexible approach to enhancing classroom
assessment. *Tools for Thoughtful Assessment* is not meant to be read cover to cover, and there is no need
to implement the tools in any particular order. Instead, we encourage you to identify the challenges that
resonate most with you and then skim to find the tools that will be the best fit for your goals, content, and
students. We also encourage you to adapt the tools as needed to make them work in your classroom (e.g.,
feel free to simplify existing language to make a tool more primary-grade appropriate).

Lesson Three: Don't forget the Common Core. Just as we were about to move from development
into production, something happened. That something was the Common Core State Standards. What
had been a whisper in the wind, a "thing that was coming" became a reality for teachers across the
country. And so a new and very important question popped up: How is all of this connected to the
Common Core State Standards? In response to this question, we went back through all the tools and
looked for connections. Many of these connections were natural and merely had to be documented.
Others required us to make revisions, add variations, or even include some new tools that did a better
job of helping teachers address the new standards. The result of these changes is that many of the tools
in this book now feature Common Core applications and connections. As you read and use these tools,
keep an eye out for these Common Core connections, which are highlighted in different sections of the
individual tools.

Lesson Four: Highlight the connections between instruction and assessment. Many teachers asked us to address the relationship between instruction and assessment. Responding to this request was an easy one since assessment and instruction go hand in hand. They *need* each other, in the same way that Romeo and Juliet need each other, which is to say, quite desperately. Using the information that we and our students derive from classroom assessments, we can adjust our plans—slow down, speed up, take a step back, try a new approach—so as to improve teaching and learning.

The tools in this book have been organized in support of this intimate relationship between instruction and assessment. In thinking through this relationship, we relied heavily on our "Five Episodes of Effective Instruction" model (Silver Strong & Associates, 2012), which synthesizes the preeminent instructional design models (Hunter, 1984; Wiggins & McTighe, 2005; Marzano, 2007) into a single, universal design. This model, which is illustrated in Figure 2, outlines five "episodes" that every well-designed instructional unit includes.

Figure 2: The Five Episodes of Effective Instruction

	Preparing students for new learning During this episode, teachers establish purpose, spark interest, and help students activate prior knowledge.	
Deepening and reinforcing learning During this episode, teachers help students solidify their understanding of the content and practice new skills.	**Presenting new learning** During this episode, teachers present new material and help students engage with/acquire the content.	**Reflecting on and celebrating learning** During this episode, teachers help students look back on, learn from, and celebrate their learning.
	Applying and demonstrating learning During this episode, teachers challenge students to synthesize, apply, and demonstrate their learning.	

So how does assessment fit into this instructional model? During each of these five episodes, there are specific assessment questions that teachers should ask themselves. By asking yourself these questions throughout the instructional process, you can seamlessly integrate assessment into your larger instructional design.

When you're **preparing students for new learning**, these are the key assessment questions:

1. How will I identify and communicate learning goals to students?

2. How will I use pre-assessments to inform and enhance instruction?

3. How will I prepare students to produce high-quality work?

When you're **presenting new learning**, these are the key assessment questions:

4. How will I check for understanding *while* presenting new information?

5. How will I check for understanding *after* presenting new information?

When you're **deepening and reinforcing student learning**, these are the key assessment questions:

6. How will I help students review, practice, and check their grasp of the material?

7. How will I help students improve their work through feedback and self-assessment?

8. How will I help students monitor their learning and establish goals and plans for moving forward?

When you're asking students to **apply and demonstrate their learning**, these are the key assessment questions:

9. How will I use writing tasks to help students synthesize and show what they know?

10. How will I develop high-quality culminating assessment tasks and evaluation frameworks?

11. How will I differentiate assessment to promote success for all students?

When you're helping students **reflect on and celebrate learning**, this is the key assessment question:

12. How will I help students reflect on, learn from, and celebrate their achievements?

If you take a peek at the Table of Contents, you'll notice not only that these twelve assessment questions correspond to the twelve chapters in this book, but also that these twelve questions are organized around the Five Episodes of Effective Instruction (each episode gets its own section). As a result, you can quickly select tools based on your immediate assessment objectives *and* based on where you are in your instructional sequence.

Thoughtful Assessment—Now More Than Ever

With the Common Core State Standards shaping the national landscape in education, it might be tempting for some to dismiss assessment for learning as too far removed from the day's concerns, as a "nice thing" to get to if time allows. This would be a terrible mistake. If we want our students to read more rigorous texts, produce more powerful writing, create engaging multimedia presentations, develop sophisticated mathematical practices, and, in general, develop the skills and habits needed for success in the 21st century, then we'll need to redouble our commitment to assessment for learning. We'll need to create clear learning targets derived from our standards. We'll need to use pre-assessment before instruction begins to find out what students know and how they think. We'll need to use formative assessment throughout the instructional process to monitor and advance student learning. We'll need to teach students how to distinguish average work from exemplary work. We'll need to give students feedback they can use to improve their work. We'll need to teach them how to become quality-control managers who can use self-assessment and reflection to grow and get better. We'll need to design high-quality culminating assessment tasks that require the same kinds of higher-order thinking as those found in the Common Core State Standards. And to do all of this well, we'll need a trusty set of tools.

How Will I Identify and Communicate Learning Goals to Students?

If you don't know where you're going, you might not get there.

—Yogi Berra

What is the intended learning? That one question should drive all planning and assessment in schools today.

—Rick Stiggins, Judith Arter, Jan Chappuis, and Stephen Chappuis, *Classroom Assessment for Student Learning: Doing It Right—Using It Well*

Good teaching and good learning start with well-defined outcomes. These outcomes go by various names in the assessment literature, most commonly *learning goals* and *learning targets*. Regardless of what we call these outcomes, one thing is certain: In order for the assessment and instruction processes to work, both teachers and students need to be unmistakably clear about where the learning is headed and what its ultimate results will be.

In this chapter, we present five tools that help teachers establish learning goals/targets and share them with students:

1. **Learning Window** helps teachers unpack and convert their standards into four distinct types of learning goals.

2. **Student-Friendly Learning Targets** helps teachers ensure that learning targets are clear and easy for students to understand.

3. **Vocabulary Knowledge Rating (VKR)** introduces students to the critical vocabulary terms that they will encounter and need to master over the course of an upcoming unit.

4. **Review/Preview** helps students see where they are within an instructional sequence by highlighting what's been covered (review) and what's coming next (preview).

5. **Backwards Learning** has students analyze culminating assessment tasks at the start of a unit to determine what they'll need to know and be able to do by the end of that unit.

Learning Window

What is it?

A framework for transforming complex standards into classroom-level learning goals—specifically, knowledge goals, understanding goals, skill-acquisition goals, and dispositional goals/habits of mind

What are the benefits of using this tool?

Standards are often too broad and complex to provide a clear focus for instruction and assessment. This is why it's so important to "unpack" and convert them into smaller, more specific learning goals/targets. A Learning Window facilitates this unpacking process by helping us determine what our students will need to know, understand, be able to do, and be like in order to achieve the standards in question. It does this by having us respond to five simple questions, each of which is framed within a pane or sill of a window-shaped organizer like this one:

What will students need to KNOW?	What HABITS OF MIND will I try to foster?
What will students need to UNDERSTAND?	What SKILLS will students need to develop?
What TERMS will students need to know?	

What are the basic steps?

1. Identify the standards that you intend to address during an upcoming lesson or unit.

2. Begin to unpack them by scanning for useful information. Underline words or phrases that point to knowledge, understandings, skills, and habits of mind that students will need to acquire.

3. Use the questions on the reproducible Learning Window (p. 11) to help you complete the unpacking process. For help with the Habits of Mind pane, download the Habits of Mind Reference Page at www.ThoughtfulClassroom.com/Tools.

   Note: The Skills pane is typically reserved for *general* thinking/learning skills (see the upper panel of Figure 4 on p. 198 for examples). Content-specific (procedural) skills like adding fractions or using a pH meter should be listed in the Knowledge pane.

4. Refer to your completed Learning Window as you map out your lesson or unit. Use it to guide the development of assessments, assignments, and activities. (If you want, you can record lesson-planning ideas directly on your window.)

5. *Optional:* Use your completed Learning Window to generate a list of student-friendly learning targets. See the Student-Friendly Learning Targets tool (p. 12, especially Step 2) for guidance.

How is this tool used in the classroom?

✔ To unpack standards, identify learning goals, and focus instruction/assessment

Teachers use Learning Windows to help them unpack their standards and design their lessons and units. Two sample windows are shown here; additional samples are available for download at www.ThoughtfulClassroom.com/Tools.

EXAMPLE 1: Prior to developing a lesson on the interdependence of living things, a third-grade teacher used a Learning Window to unpack the standards that she wanted to address. She then used her completed Learning Window to develop and focus her lesson plans.

Standards that I intend to address:

- Science Standard, Big Idea 17A: <u>Plants and animals</u>, including humans, <u>interact with and depend upon each other</u> and their environment to satisfy their basic needs.*

- Common Core Reading Standard RI.3.2: <u>Determine the main idea of a text</u>; <u>recount the key details</u> and <u>explain how they support the main idea</u>.

- Common Core Writing Standard W.3.2: <u>Write informative/explanatory texts</u> to examine a topic and <u>convey ideas and information clearly</u>.

LEARNING WINDOW

Lesson title: Honeybees, Ants, and Plants...Oh, My!

Purpose: 1. To have students practice main idea identification skills while acquiring critical content knowledge

2. To address the Common Core's call for reading in all content areas (lesson is organized around an informational text called "Animals and Plants Working Together")

What will students need to KNOW?	**What HABITS OF MIND will I try to foster?**
• Animals depend on plants for food and shelter. • Plants depend on animals for pollination, seed dispersal, and access to nutrients. (Students should be able to give specific examples for each point.)	• <u>Communicating with clarity and precision</u> I'll encourage students to focus on clarity and accuracy while writing their paragraphs. • <u>Thinking about thinking</u> I'll have students reflect on and describe the processes that they use to identify main ideas.
What will students need to UNDERSTAND?	**What SKILLS will students need to develop?**
• That living things help and depend on each other (the main idea of the lesson/reading assignment) • That good readers try to identify main ideas both as AND after they read something — and that they look for details/examples to support those ideas	• <u>Identifying important information within a text</u> • <u>Writing an explanatory paragraph</u> I'll have students write a paragraph about how living things help each other (main idea should be supported with details/examples from the text).

What TERMS will students need to know?

basic needs, shelter, pollinate, interdependent, main idea, seed dispersal, explanatory paragraph

---

*Next Generation Sunshine State Standards: http://www.floridastandards.org

EXAMPLE 2: After identifying the standards that she wanted to address during an upcoming exploration unit, a history teacher used a Learning Window to unpack those standards and design her unit. Before beginning the unit, she converted the information on her Learning Window into a list of student-friendly learning targets (not shown) and then shared those targets with students.

EXPLORATION OF THE AMERICAS

Content standards:

- Understand the <u>causes and effects</u> of <u>European overseas exploration</u> and expansion in the 15th and 16th centuries.
  - <u>Analyze</u> the <u>conditions/factors/motives</u> (political, economic, social, technological, religious) that stimulated exploration.
  - <u>Understand</u> the <u>consequences and significance</u> of European expansion (e.g., the impact on <u>Native Americans</u>).

Common Core Standards:

- <u>Write arguments</u> focused on discipline-specific content (WHST.6-8.1).
- <u>Analyze</u> a case in which <u>two or more texts provide conflicting information</u> on the same topic (RI.8.9).
- <u>Conduct research</u> to answer a question (W.8.7) and <u>gather information from multiple print and digital sources</u> (W.8.8).

LEARNING WINDOW

What will students need to KNOW?

- Conditions/factors (political, economic, etc.) that stimulated exploration
- Technological advances (navigation, map making, naval engineering) that facilitated exploration and conquest
- Consequences of expansion, including impact on Native Americans
- Names, nationalities, motivations, and accomplishments of principal explorers

What HABITS OF MIND will I try to foster?

- Seeking out reasons, explanations, and evidence
- Considering different perspectives and viewpoints
- Evaluating the quality of ideas and information

What will students need to UNDERSTAND?

- That one person's explorer can be another person's conqueror
- How technological innovations can impact the course of history
- That periods of exploration happen for a reason
  - Why did the Age of Exploration happen when it did?
  - Why was the time right for Columbus in 1492?

What SKILLS will students need to develop?

- <u>Justifying positions with evidence</u>
  Task: Did the times make Columbus, or did Columbus make the times? Take a position and support it in writing.

- <u>Researching and reporting</u>
  - Gather relevant information from multiple sources.
  - Take accurate notes, summarize key points.
  - Quote or paraphrase properly; avoid plagiarism.

- <u>Comparing and hypothesizing</u>
  Task: Compare the account of Columbus's character, actions, and achievements from our textbook with that in Howard Zinn's "A People's History of the United States." What are the differences? Why might they exist?

What TERMS will students need to know?

cartography, mariner's astrolabe, caravel, New World, imperialism, Age of Exploration, Inca, Aztecs, 1492, conquistadors, colonialism, Columbus, de Soto, Cortez, de Leon, Pizarro, Prince Henry the Navigator

Title/topic: _____

Purpose: _____

Learning Window

What will students need to KNOW?

(terms,* facts, formulas, events, procedures, etc.)

What HABITS OF MIND will I try to foster?

*Record key terms in the "windowsill" portion of the organizer.

What will students need to UNDERSTAND?

(big ideas, concepts, principles, "hows & whys")

What SKILLS will students need to develop?

(general thinking and learning skills like summarizing, note taking, justifying with evidence, analyzing)

What TERMS will students need to know?

Student-Friendly Learning Targets

What is it?

A tool that helps students see where they're going by ensuring that classroom learning targets are both specific and student friendly

What are the benefits of using this tool?

Letting students in on where they're going and what they're expected to learn can boost motivation and achievement. Sharing a list of learning targets can help, but that list is only useful if the targets are both understandable and assessable by students. This tool explains how to create just such a list. It also reminds us that targets can't be posted and then forgotten about; rather, they need to be revisited, reinforced, and assessed throughout the course of instruction.

What are the basic steps?

1. Generate a list of learning targets for an upcoming lesson or unit. To do this, ask yourself what you want students to know, understand, and be able to do by the end of the lesson or unit.

   Tip: Be sure to list *targets* (what you want students to know, understand, and be able to do) rather than *activities* (the things students will be doing in class).

2. Make your list of targets student friendly. To do this,

   • Write the targets in "I will" or "I can" format. ("I will know/understand/be able to _____.")
   • Frame the targets in simple, age-appropriate language that students will understand.
   • Be specific. A well-written target should tell students what they're trying to achieve and let them assess their ability to achieve it.

   Note: Because *understanding* can be hard to define and assess, you may want to replace the word *understand* with something more specific when framing your targets (e.g., "I will be able to *explain*..." instead of "I will *understand*...").

3. Post the list in a prominent location and leave it there throughout the lesson or unit. Discuss the targets with students so that they're clear about what they're aiming for and why it's worthwhile (e.g., "We'll be learning how to use a book's index. This is important because...").

   Note: Alternative methods of sharing learning targets are discussed in Teacher Talk.

4. Refer to the list regularly to show students how the things they're doing in class (tasks, activities, assignments) relate to the things they're supposed to be learning (targets).

   For example: Today, you'll be examining *yes* and *no* examples of prime numbers (activity). The goal of this activity is for you to understand and be able to define what a prime number is (target).

5. Remind students to revisit the list of targets throughout the lesson or unit to gauge their progress.

How is this tool used in the classroom?

✔ To make students aware of the intended learning targets

✔ To enable students to assess and monitor their learning

EXAMPLE: A state science standard transformed into a list of student-friendly learning targets

---

Standard that I intend to address:

4-5 LS2C: Plants and animals are related in food webs with producers (plants that make their own food), consumers (animals that eat producers and/or other animals), and decomposers (primarily bacteria and fungi) that break down wastes and dead organisms, and return nutrients to the soil.[*]

Student-friendly learning targets

• I will be able to define the following terms in my own words and give an example of each: food web, producer, consumer, decomposer, ecosystem, population, organism.

• I will be able to compare and contrast the roles of producers, consumers, and decomposers.

• I will know what a food web is, what it illustrates, and how to create one of my own.

• I will be able to explain and give specific examples of how plants and animals in an ecosystem depend on one another for survival.

• I will be able to predict how a change in the population of one organism might affect the population of other organisms in the same ecosystem.

---

*Washington State K–12 Science Learning Standards, Version 1.2: http://www.k12.wa.us/science/pubdocs/WASciencestandards.pdf

🜂 Teacher Talk

→ When you describe classroom learning targets using everyday language, you make those targets accessible to parents as well as students. This, in turn, prepares parents to better support their children's learning efforts.

→ Primary-grade teachers can make their targets even more student friendly by expressing them using pictures as well as words. Here's an example:

I can listen quietly when others are talking.

→ Learning targets are often introduced at the start of a lesson or unit to guide the learning process, but they can be shared at other points in an instructional sequence as well—and in a number of different ways. Instead of *telling* students the targets, for example, you could invite them to uncover the targets for themselves by having them analyze a culminating assessment task ("What will you need to know and be able to do in order to complete this task successfully?") or complete an activity ("What did we learn by creating a plot of temperature vs. elevation?"). And instead of simply posting targets on the board, you could use an engaging "hook" or activity to concretize and give context to the targets. ("What's the difference between the subtraction problems we learned to solve yesterday and the new ones on the board? Today, we're going to learn how to use a technique called 'borrowing' to tackle these new problems.")

Ultimately, the time and method that you use to share your targets should be determined by the content and purpose of your lesson. Regardless of how and when you share your targets, students should be able to explain what they're supposed to be learning long before that learning is assessed. Check their ability to do this by posing questions like these: "Why are we doing this?" or "What's our goal?"

Vocabulary Knowledge Rating (VKR)

What is it?

A technique (adapted from Blachowicz, 1986) that prepares students to become more self-directed vocabulary learners by introducing them to critical terms before instruction begins—and by training them to assess and improve their knowledge of these terms over time

What are the benefits of using this tool?

The Common Core State Standards emphasize the importance of helping students learn and accurately use a wide range of content-specific vocabulary terms (Language Anchor Standard 6). Vocabulary Knowledge Rating uses a simple "double-assessment process" (Silver, Brunsting, & Walsh, 2008) to help students deepen their understanding of key concepts/terms from a unit of study. Students rate their knowledge of these terms at the start of the unit, which focuses their attention on what they'll need to learn. They then rate their knowledge again at the end of instruction to see how their understanding has grown.

What are the basic steps?

1. Record the critical vocabulary terms for an upcoming unit on a Vocabulary Knowledge Rating Organizer (p. 16).

Note: If specific people, places, or things (proper nouns like Iroquois, Peru, or Nobel Prize) are critical to the content that you're teaching, be sure to include them on the organizer.

2. Introduce the terms to students by having students see, hear, and say them (*look* at the terms on their organizers, *listen* to the terms as you read them aloud, *say* the terms as a class).

3. Explain that these are the terms they'll encounter and need to master during the upcoming unit.

4. Instruct students to assess and indicate their familiarity with each term by circling the appropriate number on the four-point scale. Have them add up their points to get their initial (pre-instruction) vocabulary knowledge rating.

5. Throughout the unit, encourage students to reflect on how their understanding of the terms has grown and changed.

Optional: Ask students to recalculate their vocabulary knowledge ratings.

6. Ask students to reassess their understanding of each term at the end of the unit. Have them compare their final knowledge ratings with their initial ones.

7. Help students reflect on and celebrate their progress. Encourage them to develop plans for shoring up their understanding of terms they haven't yet mastered.

How is this tool used in the classroom?

✔ To activate and assess students' prior knowledge of critical vocabulary terms

✔ To have students monitor their understanding of key terms over time

✔ To have students reflect on their learning at the end of instruction

EXAMPLE 1: The VKR Organizer below was completed by a student at the start of a unit on fractions. This student reassessed his knowledge of these same terms again at the end of the unit (not shown).

LIST OF TERMS	I've never seen or heard of this term.	I've seen or heard of this term, but I don't know what it means.	I know this term, but I can't fully explain it in my own words.	I can explain this term in my own words and give an example of it.
		Fractions		
fraction	1	2	(3)	4
numerator	1	2	3	(4)
denominator	1	2	3	(4)
proper fraction	(1)	2	3	4
improper fraction	(1)	2	3	4
equivalent fractions	1	(2)	3	4
mixed numbers	(1)	2	3	4
whole	1	2	3	(4)
part	1	2	3	(4)

Initial vocabulary knowledge rating __24__ Date: __3/12__

Final vocabulary knowledge rating _____ Date: _____

EXAMPLE 2: A first-grade teacher uses this simpler three-column VKR Organizer with her students:

Vocabulary word	I have never seen or heard of this.	I know a little bit about this.	I know this really well! I can explain it in my own words.
calendar	1	2	3
month	1	2	3

🛑 Teacher Talk

→ To avoid vocabulary overload, limit the terms that you include on your VKR Organizer to people, places, things, and concepts that are central to your content (i.e., "need to know" terms rather than "nice to know" terms). Consider grade level as well (select fewer terms for younger students).

→ Have students use different colored pens—or different VKR forms—to do their initial and final ratings. This will make it easier for them to distinguish and tally their before-and-after scores.

→ If you want, add a definition/explanation column to the basic VKR Organizer. Use this column to have students define the terms in their own words at the end of the unit.

→ Use this tool to help students "expand their vocabulary in the course of studying content" as called for by the Common Core State Standards (National Governors Association Center for Best Practices, Council of Chief State School Officers [NGA Center/CCSSO], 2010, p. 25).

Name: _____ Date: _____

Lesson/unit topic: _____

Vocabulary Knowledge Rating Organizer

Instructions: Indicate your familiarity with each term by circling the appropriate number. Add the numbers together to get a vocabulary knowledge rating. Assess your progress by comparing your initial rating with your end-of-unit rating.

Term	I've never seen or heard of this term.	I've seen or heard of this term, but I don't know what it means.	I know this term, but I can't fully explain it or give an example of it.	I can explain this term in my own words, use it in context, and give an example if appropriate.
	1	2	3	4
	1	2	3	4
	1	2	3	4
	1	2	3	4
	1	2	3	4
	1	2	3	4
	1	2	3	4
	1	2	3	4
	1	2	3	4
	1	2	3	4
	1	2	3	4
	1	2	3	4

Initial vocabulary knowledge rating: _____ Date: _____   Final vocabulary knowledge rating: _____ Date: _____

Review/Preview

What is it?

A tool that helps students understand where they are within an instructional sequence by pointing out what they've already covered ("review") and what's coming up next ("preview")

What are the benefits of using this tool?

When we begin an instructional unit, *we* know exactly what we plan to cover and in what order. Our students, on the other hand, don't have the benefit of this big-picture vision—and without it, they can easily get lost. This tool keeps them oriented by giving them a road map for instruction and helping them track their progress. (What topics and learning targets have we already addressed? Where are we going next?)

What are the basic steps?

1. Create a road map for an upcoming unit by listing the topics and learning targets you plan to address. If you'll be covering these topics/targets in a specific order, your map should reflect that.

   Note: Your map can be as simple or creative as you want—anything from a list of learning targets to a drawing that looks like an actual road map. Here are a few examples:

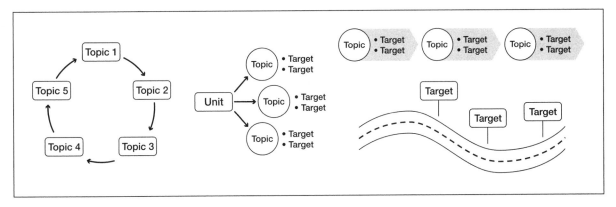

2. Share the map with students before instruction begins. Keep a copy on display throughout the entire unit so you can refer to it.

3. Stop at various times throughout the course of instruction to point out where you are on the map. ("At this point, we've already covered ____ and ____. Next, we're going to be learning ____.")

4. Help students improve their big-picture understanding of the material by pointing out how the topics, targets, and lessons within your unit connect to one another. A web or flowchart-style map can make these connections easier for students to see.

How is this tool used in the classroom?

   ✔ To give students a road map of the learning to come
   ✔ To help students keep track of where they are within an instructional sequence

Backwards Learning

What is it?

A learning-with-the-end-in-mind technique that has students analyze culminating assessment tasks *before* instruction begins to identify the knowledge and skills they'll need to complete those tasks successfully

What are the benefits of using this tool?

Thanks to Grant Wiggins and Jay McTighe's *Understanding by Design* (2005), many educators are familiar with backward design, or the process of designing instruction with learning outcomes and assessments in mind. But thinking backwards is hardly the exclusive domain of lesson designers. In fact, thinking backwards is what gives our most successful students their self-direction. Successful students regularly ask themselves what assigned tasks will demand of them and what they can do to meet those demands. This tool teaches all students to do the same by giving them a step-by-step process for analyzing a task, breaking it down into *knowing* and *doing* goals, and devising a plan for success.

What are the basic steps?

1. Examine the learning goals/targets for an upcoming lesson or unit. Develop a culminating assessment task that is consistent with these goals/targets.

2. Introduce your lesson or unit, then present the assessment task to students.

3. Download copies of the Backwards Learning Organizer (www.ThoughtfulClassroom.com/Tools) or let students draw their own organizers using the ones on pp. 19–20 as models.

4. Use the organizer to walk students through the steps in the Backwards Learning process. Specifically,

   • Check (and help students check) that they understand the given task by asking them to explain it in their own words. Examine students' responses and clarify or re-explain the task if needed.

   • Ask students to determine what they'll need to *know and understand* in order to complete the task successfully (e.g., "I'll need to know the difference between an acid and a base").

   • Ask students to determine what they'll need to *be able to do* (skills) in order to complete the task successfully (e.g., "write a comparative essay" or "create a picture graph").

   • *Optional:* Help students spell out their plans for acquiring the requisite knowledge and skills. Sample action plan: "I'll consult a dictionary, Wikipedia, and my text to see what I can learn about allegory."

How is this tool used in the classroom?

✔ To have students analyze a task and determine what it will require of them

✔ To teach students to establish goals and plans for completing assigned tasks

✔ To help students become more self-directed learners

Organizers from different grade levels and content areas are shown below (additional examples are available for download at www.ThoughtfulClassroom.com/Tools). The optional "create an action plan" portion of Step 4 is illustrated in Example 1.

EXAMPLE 1: A fourth grader's analysis of the culminating assessment task for a poetry unit

What is my task?

Write about something I love using three kinds of poems.

The three kinds of poems are called haiku, limerick, and cinquain.

KNOWING GOALS

What will I need to know and understand?

What a haiku is
What a limerick is
What a cinquain is

DOING GOALS

What will I need to be able to do?

I will need to know how to write my own haiku, limerick, and cinquain. It sounds like fun!

What is my plan for completing this task successfully? What steps will I take?

I will decide what to write about. I think I am going to write about cats.

I will look at example poems to learn from them.

I will listen carefully and make some notes when we learn about the kinds of poems.

I will write some poems for practice before writing my real ones.

I will ask my friend Giada if she wants to work on our poems together after school.

EXAMPLE 2: A high school student's analysis of a task on renewable/nonrenewable energy

What is my task?

Write an editorial that explains the difference between renewable and nonrenewable energy and that takes a position on how to address the energy crisis.

What will I need to know?

• Differences between renewable and nonrenewable energy

• Causes and effects of the energy crisis

• Options for addressing the energy crisis and the pros/cons of each

What will I need to be able to do?

• Conduct a comparison

• Research different options for addressing the energy crisis

• Write a persuasive editorial

EXAMPLE 3: A middle school student's analysis of a physical-chemistry design task

> **At the end of this unit, I'll be asked to…**
> *Design a container that has the least amount of heat loss.*
>
> | **Here's what I'll need to know:** | **Here's what I'll need to be able to do:** |
> |---|---|
> | · *How heat moves*
· *What materials slow down heat loss*
· *What factors affect heat loss*
· *If the material in the container is a solid or a liquid* | · *Design containers*
· *Measure temperature*
· *Calculate heat loss*
· *Compare heat loss of different designs* |

EXAMPLE 4: An organizer that first-grade students completed as a class with some help from their teacher (note that the task was designed to target Common Core Standard RL.1.5)

> **What is my task?**
> Make a poster that could teach someone the differences between books that tell stories and books that give information. The poster should show examples of both kinds of books.
>
> | **What do I need to know?** | **What do I need to be able to do?** |
> |---|---|
> | • I need to know what a book that tells a story is.
• I need to know what an information book is. | • Explain the difference between books that tell stories and books that give information.
• Find examples of both kinds of books.
• Make a poster. |

🌑 Teacher Talk

→ Here are some scaffolding tips:

- Before using the tool, discuss the difference between knowing goals (goals that involve acquiring and making sense of declarative knowledge) and doing goals (goals that require mastering specific skills, procedures, or behaviors). Use concrete examples to help students understand the distinction.

- Familiarize students with the kinds of questions they should ask themselves when developing their action plans (optional portion, Step 4). Then help them brainstorm some possible answers.

  Sample questions and answers: Where will I look for information? (textbook, Internet, notes); Who can help me? (librarian, teacher, friend, parent); What learning or study strategies will I try? (text previewing, Interactive Note Making, mnemonic devices)

  Note: The questions above are printed on the downloadable organizer for easy reference.

- Let students complete a Backwards Learning Organizer as a class before having them complete one on their own. *Note:* Very young students can complete the organizer as a class every time.

How Will I Use Pre-assessments to Inform and Enhance Instruction?

The same man cannot be skilled in everything; each has his special excellence.

—Euripides

To teach a student well, a teacher must know that student well.

—Carol Ann Tomlinson and Marcia B. Imbeau, *Leading and Managing a Differentiated Classroom*

Figuring out where students are before instruction begins is an important phase in the assessment process. We call this phase "pre-assessment." The tools in this chapter are all pre-assessment tools designed to help teachers learn about their students and optimize instruction so that it suits the needs of individuals and the class as a whole. These tools are divided into two groups:

Group One: Tools for Pre-assessing Students' Academic Readiness. What do students already know about the content to come? What misconceptions do they have? What prerequisite skills do they have under their belts, and which skills will need extra attention? David Ausubel (1968), a pioneer in educational psychology, makes the case for this kind of pre-assessment in absolute terms: "If I had to reduce all of educational psychology to just one principle, I would say this: The most important single factor influencing learning is what the learner already knows. Ascertain this and teach him accordingly" (p. vi).

The following tools are designed to help teachers determine what students know at the outset of instruction:

1. **A & Q** tests students' background knowledge by turning the traditional question-and-answer (Q & A) format on its head; instead of giving students questions and asking for answers, it gives students answers and asks them to generate possible questions.

2. **Pretest** prepares teachers to teach more effectively by making them aware of students' existing knowledge and skills.

3. **What Comes to Mind?** gives teachers a quick and easy way to assess students' background knowledge, questions, and feelings about a topic.

Group Two: Tools for Pre-assessing Students' Talents, Interests, Attitudes, and Learning Profiles. Pre-assessment has a heart as well as a mind. If the first group of tools is for learning what students know and can do (assessing their minds), then the second group is for learning about who students are, how they learn, and where their passions and talents lie (assessing their hearts):

4. **Attitude ACE** helps teachers create customized surveys to assess students' attitudes about a specific content area.

5. **Best Foot Forward** helps teachers gather information about students' strengths, talents, and self-perceptions.

6. **From Topics to "Top Picks"** enables students to preview upcoming topics and identify those that interest them most.

7. **Hand of Knowledge** encourages students to think about and share their interests, talents, and goals for the future.

A & Q

What is it?

A tool that tests students' knowledge of a given topic by giving them an answer (e.g., "Henry VIII") and having them generate possible questions ("Who was an English king? Who had lots of wives?")

What are the benefits of using this tool?

In order to teach our students effectively, we need to determine what they already know and understand about the material we're planning to cover. Involving students in an A & Q session *(answer and question, as opposed to *question and answer)* is a fun and engaging way to do this. The A & Q format encourages students to exercise their creative thinking skills and interact with their classmates. It also prepares them for the learning to come by helping them activate their prior knowledge.

What are the basic steps?

1. Explain the A & Q format to students. (You'll give them an answer and they'll come up with as many possible questions for that answer as they can in a given amount of time.)

2. Before engaging students in an A & Q session about your content, let them practice as a class using a familiar topic like pets, food, or music; see sample dialog below.

   Teacher: If "dog" is the answer, what are some possible questions?

   Students: What's a four-legged animal with fur? What do police use to locate explosives? What is a Dalmatian an example of? What's a popular pet that's not a cat? What's an animal that helps blind people "see"? What's man's best friend? What kind of animal is the main character in *Old Yeller*?

3. Use the A & Q format to assess students' knowledge of a topic you're planning to teach (or a topic you've already taught):
   - Give students an answer that relates to the topic in question.
   - Challenge them to think creatively and jot down as many questions for that answer as they can.

4. Invite students to share their responses with the class, and encourage them to build off each other's ideas.

5. Collect and review students' responses to determine what students already know and understand about the given topic. Design your instruction accordingly.

How is this tool used in the classroom?

✔ To assess students' knowledge of a given topic and design instruction accordingly

✔ To help students access their prior knowledge at the start of instruction

✔ To help students review (and let us assess) what they've learned at the end of a lesson or unit

A & Q sessions are typically used to assess students' prior knowledge *before* instruction begins (see Example 1), but they work just as well for assessing student learning *during* or *at the end of* instruction (see Example 2).

EXAMPLE 1: Before beginning a graphing unit targeting Common Core Standard 3.MD.B.3, a third-grade teacher used the following question to assess students' background knowledge: "If 'bar graph' is the answer, what are some possible questions?" She used students' responses (see box below) to help her determine how much reviewing she needed to do (less than she thought!), to identify any misconceptions that she might need to address (e.g., the idea that the bars on a bar graph are always vertical), and to help her segue into her new material: "Believe it or not, each box on a bar graph can actually represent more than one thing. Later this week, we'll see how!"

What is one kind of graph?	What is a graph you can use to solve more than or less than problems?
What is a kind of graph that's not a picture graph?	What is a graph you can use to count how many of something there are?
What is a graph where the bars go up and down?	What is a graph where each box stands for one of the things you counted?
What is a graph you can see in a newspaper or book?	What is a way to show amounts using a drawing instead of numbers?

EXAMPLE 2: A world history teacher used an A & Q session instead of a traditional Q & A session to assess (and help his students review) what they had learned about the Renaissance prior to an end-of-unit test. He hung pieces of poster paper around the room, recorded a different "answer" on each piece of paper, and invited students to move around and record questions for each answer. At the end of the session, students regrouped to discuss their responses and identify topics that needed further review. Some of the answers that they were asked to respond to are shown here:

- If "Leonardo da Vinci" is the answer, what are the possible questions?
- If "humanism" is the answer, what are the possible questions?
- If "factors that led to the start of the Renaissance" is the answer, what are the possible questions?
- If "Renaissance architecture" is the answer, what are the possible questions?

🎭 Teacher Talk

→ Avoid basing instructional decisions solely on students' verbal responses (just because one student knows something doesn't mean that all students do). Review students' written responses or survey the class before deciding how to proceed. ("Did anyone other than Tim know that Henry VIII was excommunicated from the Catholic Church? Who knows what it means to be excommunicated?")

→ For a change of pace, try breaking students into teams and challenging each team to outdo the other in terms of the number, quality, and creativity of their responses. This kind of friendly competition has been linked to significant gains in learning and achievement (Marzano, 2010).

Pretest

What is it?

A tool that prepares us to teach more effectively by telling us what our students already know about the material we're planning to cover

What are the benefits of using this tool?

Before treating you, a doctor listens to what you have to say, reviews your medical history, and performs an examination. This kind of pre-assessment is just as important in the educational realm as it is in the medical one since it's impossible to prescribe the right kind of instruction for our students without examining their existing knowledge. Administering pretests prepares us to initiate instruction at a level that works for our students—not too hard (which can lead to frustration), not too easy (which can lead to boredom), but just right. It lets us differentiate instruction as well by making us aware of each student's individual needs and readiness level.

What are the basic steps?

1. Determine what students should know, understand, and be able to do by the end of an upcoming lesson or unit. (What are the learning goals/targets?)

2. Develop questions or activities (a pretest) that will help you determine what students *already* know and understand about the material you're planning to teach. See p. 28 for design tips.

3. Clarify the purpose of the pretest before administering it. ("This will help *me* teach you more effectively by showing me what you have and haven't yet learned. It will help *you* visualize your progress by letting you compare what you know at the end of the unit with what you knew at the start.")

4. Administer the pretest. Explain that it won't be graded, and that students shouldn't worry if they can't answer many (or any) of the questions at this point in time. Clarify that the goal is for them to be able to answer these questions by the *end* of the lesson or unit.

5. Analyze the results of the pretest. Use what you learn to determine an appropriate entry point for instruction. (Where should I begin teaching?)
   - *If the pretest reveals gaps in essential background knowledge or skills*, back up and fill them in before starting on new material. Work with individuals, groups, or the entire class.
   - *If students already know what you were planning to teach them*, skip ahead to something new—or teach the same material, but at a deeper level.

6. Accommodate different readiness levels by providing "catch-up instruction" or "jump-ahead instruction" for students (or groups of students) who need it.

7. *Optional:* Re-administer the pretest at the end of the lesson or unit so that you and your students can see how far they've come.

How is this tool used in the classroom?

✔ To assess students' background knowledge at the start of a lesson or unit

✔ To gather data that can help us differentiate instruction by readiness level

EXAMPLE 1: A second-grade teacher administers a spelling pretest at the start of each week. Her goal is to show her students where they're going (what words will they need to know how to spell?) and where they are now (which words can they already spell?) so they can work to close the gap.

EXAMPLE 2: A third-grade teacher begins the year by asking students to correct the capitalization, punctuation, and grammar errors in a writing sample that he gives them. His goal is to determine which elements of Common Core Language Standards 1 and 2 his students have mastered and which they need to work on. Rather than waste time teaching students skills they already know, he groups students based on their pretest performance (students who need to work on subject-verb agreement, students who need help using quotation marks, etc.) and works with each group separately.

EXAMPLE 3: A seventh-grade mathematics teacher uses her unit learning goals as a guide when crafting the questions for her pretests. She also consults the Tips for Designing a Pretest form (p. 28) to remind herself of the different kinds of questions she might want to include. In the case of her three-dimensional figures pretest (below), which was designed to assess students' readiness for a geometry unit on volume, she chose to include a *comparison* question, a *drawing* question, a *definition* question, a *real-world connection* question, and a *calculation* question.

PRETEST: Three-dimensional figures

Instructions: The questions on this pretest are ones that you'll learn how to answer during the upcoming unit. If you know (or think you know) any of the answers already, that's a bonus—go ahead and jot them down. Don't worry about getting things wrong since this test won't be graded.

---

1. What's the difference between two-dimensional and three-dimensional figures?

2. Do you know anything at all about the three-dimensional figures below? Can you sketch any of them?

rectangular prism	triangular prism	cylinder
rectangular pyramid	triangular pyramid	cone

3. What is volume? (Think math, not how loudly you play your music!)

4. Why might people want to know the volume of something?

5. How might we calculate the volume of any of the figures in question 2? Any ideas?

EXAMPLE 4: A health teacher designed her respiratory-system unit around three central questions: *What do we breathe? Why do we breathe? How do we breathe?*

She posed these three questions on her pretest (below) to see what students knew at the start of instruction. She included these same questions on her end-of-unit test as well so that she and her students would be able to see how far they had come.

RESPIRATION PRETEST (3 questions total; this test won't be graded)

We'll be investigating the three questions below during our upcoming unit on respiration. In the meantime, jot down anything you think you already know.

What do we breathe?   Why do we breathe?   How do we breathe?

Variation: Range Finder

A Range Finder is a specific type of pretest. To use the Range Finder format, identify a skill that you'll be helping students develop during an upcoming lesson or unit, and design three different tasks to test their proficiency at that skill—each at an increasing level of difficulty. Present the three tasks to students, instruct them to complete the most challenging one they can, and use their choices to gather information about individual readiness levels (who needs Level 1 instruction, who needs Level 2, etc.). Design lesson plans that will accommodate the needs of students at each level.

🎧 Teacher Talk

→ Ideally, pretests should be administered at least a week before instruction begins so that you have time to analyze the results and design your lesson plans accordingly.

→ Clarify that pretest scores are a reflection of what students have already learned—*not* how smart they are. ("Your score on a pretest is simply a reflection of your prior knowledge and experiences. Since all of you have had different experiences, all of you will know different things about different topics—more about some, less about others.")

→ With all that we're expected to do, it can be tempting to pass on pretests and get right to teaching. While it's true that skipping pretests can save time up front, pretests actually save time in the end by letting us teach more effectively—no wasting time teaching things that students already know, no getting halfway through a unit only to realize that students are lost because we failed to identify and correct gaps in background knowledge, and so on.

→ Try not to be discouraged if pretest results reveal that students lack background knowledge and skills that they "should have already acquired." Instead of dwelling on these gaps, do as Chapman and King (2008) suggest and use "this valuable time and energy…to design plans and activities that fill the gaps" (p. 39).

→ Questions like the ones in Example 4, which are general enough for students to be able to respond to in some way before instruction begins, and which should elicit increasingly sophisticated responses as instruction progresses, are ideal pretest questions. (Essential questions often meet these criteria.)

Tips for Designing a Pretest

Include questions that will assess prerequisite knowledge as well as upcoming knowledge.

- Create pretest questions that will tell you whether students have the background knowledge and skills they'll need to understand the material you're planning to teach them.

  Before teaching a lesson on DNA replication, for example, check if students understand the basic structure of DNA. Before beginning a unit on three-digit multiplication, check if students have mastered one- and two-digit multiplication.

- Create pretest questions that will test students' command of the material you're planning to teach them. (Have they already learned any or all of this material in another class?)

Consider different types of questions and tasks. *(Think: What is the best way to gather the information that I need?) Among other things, you could ask students to*

- Fill in blanks or mix and match.

- Complete multiple-choice questions.

- Define. *(What is a prime number?)*

- Give examples. *(What are some examples of amphibians?)*

- List facts. *(List anything you think you already know about the French Revolution.)*

- Calculate. *(Convert these from molar to millimolar.)*

- Locate. *(Can you find Canada on a map? Can you locate an example of irony in this story?)*

- Identify. *(Which of these is an example of Gothic architecture? Can you identify the picture of a cello?)*

- Label. *(Label the following parts of the human body.)*

- Draw. *(Can you represent these fractions using pictures? Can you draw any of these types of arches?)*

- Compare. *(What is the difference between a fact and an opinion?)*

- Analyze. *(Based on the data, which player would you choose to send to the free-throw line?)*

- Demonstrate. *(Does anyone know how to julienne a vegetable? Come show me!)*

- Perform. *(Sight-read this piece of music.)*

- Make real-world or personal connections. *(What is the role of government in our everyday lives?)*

- Sequence/order. *(Sequence these events by date. Order these negative numbers from smallest to largest.)*

- Generate preliminary answers to essential questions from your lesson or unit. *(Can numbers lie? Does fairness always mean treating everyone the same? What makes a classic novel "classic"?)*

Consider different formats, both formal and informal.

- Traditional paper-and-pencil test

- Classroom discussion or question-and-answer session

- Survey *(How many of you can define this term? Solve this problem?)*

- Memory Box (See pp. 92–95 for a description of this technique.)

- Range Finder (See p. 27 for a description of this technique.)

- White Boards or Letter Cards (See p. 73 for a description of these techniques.)

What Comes to Mind?

What is it?

A quick and easy way to assess the background knowledge, questions, and feelings that students have about topics we're planning to teach

What are the benefits of using this tool?

Determining what students know, feel, and wonder about a topic before we begin teaching it can prepare us to teach that topic more effectively. With all that we're expected to accomplish, however, finding the time to gather this kind of information can sometimes be challenging. This tool addresses the challenge and makes the pre-assessment process more manageable by providing a fast and no-fuss way to uncover students' thoughts, feelings, and interests. It provides us with a wealth of valuable information, and it helps students activate their prior knowledge—all within a matter of minutes.

What are the basic steps?

1. Introduce the topic you're about to teach. ("For the next few days, we'll be learning about ____.")

2. Ask students what they know, feel, and wonder about that topic. Have them record their responses on the reproducible organizer (p. 30) and/or share their responses aloud.

3. Review students' responses. Use what you learn to guide and inform your instructional plans. Among other things, you might

- Address and correct factual errors or misconceptions.
- Make connections between things students already know and things you're about to teach.
- Adjust the entry point for instruction according to students' existing knowledge. If most students already know the material you were planning to teach, for example, you might choose to skip ahead.
- Incorporate students' questions into your lesson plans.
- Explore the causes of—and look for ways to change—negative feelings or perceptions. See Attitude ACE (pp. 31–33) for ideas.

How is this tool used in the classroom?

✔ To determine what students know, feel, and wonder about a topic before you begin teaching

✔ To adjust instruction according to students' interests and needs

What Comes to Mind?

What comes to mind when you think about _____?

Facts?

Feelings?

Questions?

Anything else?

Attitude ACE

What is it?

A survey-based tool that helps us understand and improve students' attitudes toward our content areas

What are the benefits of using this tool?

Because students' attitudes can have a powerful impact on learning, it's important to find out what those attitudes are, why students have them, and how we can improve them. This tool presents a customizable attitude survey for gathering this kind of information. By giving us insight into the things that engage and motivate our students, the survey prepares us to cultivate more positive attitudes. It also raises students' awareness of the attitudes they're bringing to class, so that they, too, can work on improving them.

What are the basic steps?

1. Determine what subject area you want to assess students' attitudes about (reading, math, etc.).

2. Think about the kind of information you want to gather, and design an Attitude ACE Survey that will help you gather it (see p. 32 for instructions and sample questions). Include as many questions as you see fit—and whatever blend of *A*, *C*, and *E* questions best serves your purpose.

   • Use "A" questions to uncover Attributions (why do you have this attitude?) and Aspirations.
   • Use "C" questions to learn about students' Confidence level and Challenges they've faced.
   • Use "E" questions to learn what students are good at (Expertise) and what they find Engaging.

   Note: Surveys can be used with individual students or groups of students (e.g., struggling students) instead of with the class as a whole.

3. Before administering the survey, explain its purpose. ("This survey will help me understand how you feel about this subject, how I can make it more enjoyable, and how I can help you succeed.")

4. Administer the survey and analyze students' responses. Use what you learn to inform and improve future instruction:

   • Identify and address content-specific challenges that are getting in the way of learning.
   • Increase engagement by designing lessons and assessment tasks that appeal to students' interests.
   • Boost confidence by creating assignments and assessments that capitalize on students' talents.

5. Teach students what they can do to improve their confidence and develop a more positive attitude toward your content area. Help them recognize that attitude and effort really do matter. (See the Effort Tracker tool, pp. 227–230, for ideas about how to do this.)

Creating an Attitude Ace Survey

Instructions: Think about the kind of information you're looking to gather and use a mixture of *A*, *C*, and *E* questions to help gather it. Choose from the questions below or generate your own using these as models.

A

Attribution & **A**spiration questions

- How do you feel about this subject area? Why do you have this attitude?

- Have you been successful in this subject area before? To what do you attribute your success or lack of success?

  ☐ your attitude ☐ your ability ☐ your effort level ☐ other: _____

- What kind of grade do you expect to get in this class? Why?

- What do you hope to learn, achieve, or get better at in this class?

- What do you expect from me as your teacher? What can I expect from you?

C

Confidence & **C**hallenge questions

- When it comes to this particular subject area, my confidence level

  ☐ is at an all-time low ☐ isn't very high ☐ is reasonably good ☐ goes through the roof

- My confidence/lack of confidence (*circle one*) in this subject area stems from…

- When I feel comfortable and confident in class, it's probably because…

- Classes in this particular subject area are most like

  ☐ a thrilling ride ☐ a stroll in the park ☐ climbing a mountain ☐ walking on hot coals

- I find it challenging to pay attention in this class/subject area because…

- The things that make this subject area challenging/not challenging (*circle one*) for me are…

- Some learning challenges that I've overcome in this subject (or another subject) are…

E

Expertise & **E**ngagement questions

- Three things I can contribute to this class are…

- My two greatest strengths in this subject area are…

- I am good at the following things:

  ☐ reading ☐ listening ☐ building or drawing things ☐ helping others
  ☐ analyzing information ☐ writing ☐ supporting an idea with evidence
  ☐ remembering facts ☐ thinking creatively ☐ solving problems
  ☐ asking questions ☐ following directions ☐ sharing my feelings

- I do my best work ☐ on my own ☐ with a partner ☐ in a group

- If I am paying attention in class, it's probably because…

- The kinds of lessons/activities/homework assignments that I like most are…

- If you want to get me excited about learning something, you should try…

How is this tool used in the classroom?

✔ To understand and improve students' attitudes toward specific content areas

EXAMPLE: A remedial reading teacher designed the survey below to assess her students' attitudes about reading and their perceptions of themselves as readers. To gather the information that she needed, she used some of the sample questions from p. 32 and generated some questions of her own.

ATTITUDE ACE SURVEY

Subject area: READING

1. Do you consider yourself a good reader? ☐ Yes ☐ Sort of ☐ No Explain: _____

2. What is the name of the last book that you read? _____
   Did you like the book? ☐ Yes ☐ No Why? _____

3. Given your choice, what would you prefer to read? (Check off one or more boxes.)
   ☐ newspaper ☐ magazine ☐ online article ☐ novel ☐ play ☐ short story ☐ comic book
   ☐ textbook or other informational text ☐ poem ☐ something else: _____ Why? _____

4. What kinds of texts do you avoid like the plague? (Check off one or more boxes.)
   ☐ newspapers ☐ magazines ☐ online articles ☐ novels ☐ plays ☐ short stories ☐ comic books
   ☐ textbooks or other informational texts ☐ poems ☐ something else: _____ Why? _____

5. Do you enjoy being read to? ☐ Yes ☐ No Why? _____

6. What are your strengths as a reader? Name at least TWO. _____

7. What would you like to get better at? List at least TWO things. _____

8. What kind of grade do you expect to get in this class? Why? _____

9. Do you prefer working solo? Or do you enjoy working with others? _____

10. What do you expect from me? What can I expect from you? _____

When this teacher reviewed the survey data, the following things jumped out at her:

- 90% of her students didn't perceive themselves to be good readers.
- 87% of her students felt that they wouldn't get anything above a C in the class.
- 75% of students enjoyed working in groups, and almost all students enjoyed being read to.
- Students' favorite reading materials were magazines, short stories, and online articles.

She responded to the data by taking the following steps:

- To boost students' confidence and skill level, she spent the first two months of school teaching them the tricks and techniques that good readers use to help make sense of complex texts (previewing, summarizing, note taking, etc.).
- To take advantage of students' fondness for group work, she set up peer-reading partnerships.
- To improve students' perceptions toward reading, she tried to make reading more enjoyable for them by designing assignments around their preferred reading materials (e.g., "Write a well-crafted summary paragraph about the magazine or online article of your choice").

When the teacher re-administered the survey three months later, she was pleased to find that these strategies had significantly improved students' attitudes about themselves as readers.

Best Foot Forward

What is it?

A survey-based tool that prepares us to differentiate instruction by helping us gather information about students' strengths and talents

What are the benefits of using this tool?

Differentiation expert Carol Ann Tomlinson reminds us that we can enhance the effectiveness of classroom instruction by paying attention to who our students are as individuals. And in working to create differentiated, student-centered classrooms, what could be more important to pay attention to than the things our students are good at? Teaching in a way that acknowledges and capitalizes on students' natural strengths is a sure-fire way to boost confidence and accelerate learning. This tool, which was inspired by Tomlinson's (2010) work, helps us do that by showing us what our students are good at and how we can motivate them.

What are the basic steps?

1. Initiate a conversation with students about their personal strengths and talents. ("What are you really good at doing? When are you at your best?")

2. Tell students that you're interested in learning more about their individual strengths. Explain that having this kind of information will enable you to teach in a way that helps everyone be successful.

3. Distribute and have students complete the Best Foot Forward Survey on p. 36. When using this tool with younger students, feel free to simplify the survey or administer it orally.

4. Have students share and compare responses with a partner, in small groups, or as a class. (This is a good way to help students get to know each other and build classroom unity.)

5. Use students' responses to highlight the idea that different people have different talents. Make it clear that all talents are valuable, and that all should be appreciated and respected.

6. Review students' surveys. Keep students' responses in mind when designing lessons, activities, and assessment tasks. *Think:* What can I do to appeal to or capitalize on students' talents?

How is this tool used in the classroom?

✔ To gather information about individual students' strengths and talents

✔ To differentiate instruction and assessment

The examples below illustrate some of the many ways teachers have used Best Foot Forward survey data to boost engagement, confidence, and achievement in their classrooms.

EXAMPLE 1: Using survey data to make instruction more engaging and effective for everyone

After finding out that a lot of her students learned best by "doing things" rather than sitting still and listening, a social studies teacher replaced some of her usual lectures with interactive activities, hands-on projects, and field trips to the library. Her reward for making this simple swap? Higher levels of engagement and achievement—plus fewer disruptions and discipline problems!

EXAMPLE 2: Using survey data to reach out to individual students

A third-grade teacher learned that a student ("Marti") who was having trouble forming relationships with her peers viewed "helping others" as her greatest strength. To help Marti and her classmates develop their social and interpersonal skills, this teacher began pairing students up for review and study sessions. The peer partnerships that he established proved to be beneficial for nearly all his students, but they were particularly beneficial for Marti, whose ability and willingness to help others laid the foundation for future friendships.

EXAMPLE 3: Using survey data to design differentiated assessment tasks

After teaching two lessons on the growing antibiotic-resistance problem, a science teacher let his students demonstrate their learning in ways that were consistent with their talents. He designed five different assessment tasks, each of which was linked to a subject area students had said they were good at on their surveys, and let students choose which task to complete.

CHOOSE YOUR ASSESSMENT TASK	
If you're good at this subject...	*... you might want to try this task:*
English, journalism, or debate	Write an editorial that presents and logically outlines the importance of changing the ways that we prescribe, administer, and use antibiotics.
art or music	Prepare and present an informative billboard or song for a public service campaign about the responsible use of antibiotics.
math	Create "formulas" to help doctors, patients, farmers, and product-development teams (like the ones that develop antibiotic-containing cleansers and tooth-pastes) make smarter decisions.
health or science	Research and report on the public health and safety implications of antibiotic-resistant strains of bacteria.
drama or physical education	Meet with students who share your talents to develop and act out a play that's designed to educate others about the dangers of misusing antibiotics.

Best Foot Forward Survey

1. I learn best when…

2. My greatest strength is…

3. You'll be happy to have me in your class because…

4. I'm happiest when…

5. A nice thing that a teacher, friend, or family member might say about me is…

6. The subject that I do best in is _____ . Here are some reasons why:

7. Things I'm good at outside school include…

8. Things I'm good at in school include…

9. If I'm paying attention or working really hard, it's probably because…

10. I do my best work when lessons, activities, and assignments are…

From Topics to "Top Picks"

What is it?

Inspired by Tomlinson's (2001) Interest Questionnaire, this tool prepares us to design more engaging lessons by providing information about students' interests. (Students examine the topics from an upcoming unit and identify their "top picks.")

What are the benefits of using this tool?

Everyone knows that students learn better when they're interested in what they're studying. The bad news is that with all the other demands teachers face, student interest often gets overlooked, despite its power to improve learning. The good news is that assessing students' interests relative to the content you're teaching isn't a difficult process. All it takes is a simple ranking system ("Rank these topics from most to least interesting") and some time for students to identify their top picks. Once you've gathered this information, you can use it to design instruction that both appeals to and expands students' existing interests.

What are the basic steps?

1. Make a list of the topics you plan to cover during an upcoming unit. Invite students to rank the topics from most to least interesting.

2. Review the results of this student-interest survey. Use what you learn to inform and enhance classroom instruction. Specifically,
   - Look for ways to accommodate students' interests when designing lesson plans and assessment tasks. See p. 39 (upper box) for suggestions.
   - Encourage students to broaden their interest horizons by trying to make less interesting topics more appealing. See p. 39 (lower box) for suggestions.

3. Repeat the survey at the end of the unit so that you and your students can see how (or if) their interests have changed.

How is this tool used in the classroom?

✔ To assess students' interests and use those interests to inform instructional decisions

EXAMPLE 1: The social studies teacher who designed the interest survey below made an effort to carry the interest concept throughout her unit. She aimed to *engage* student interest by generating creative names for her unit topics (see Part 1 of the survey) and by setting up visually appealing learning centers where students could go to learn about each topic. She also tried to *broaden* students' interests by using a fun format (scavenger hunt) to make the topic voted least interesting (Gold Rush) seem more exciting.

EXAMPLE 2: At the start of a gymnastics unit, a physical education teacher asked her students to rank the various events (balance beam, floor, etc.) from most to least interesting. As the unit progressed, she encouraged them to reevaluate their interests and devote the bulk of their practice time to their top three choices. Students were told that their end-of-unit grades would be largely determined by their performance in those same three events.

EXAMPLE 3: A first-grade teacher used the Shared Interest Groups variation described on p. 39 to deepen her students' grasp of critical story elements (Common Core RL.1.3). After introducing a particular story element (e.g., setting), she'd put different books on tables around the room, have students examine the books, and ask them to sit at the table with the book that looked most interesting. The students at each table would then read their selected books and discuss whatever story element they had been learning about at the time. ("The setting in our group's book is…")

STUDENT INTEREST SURVEY

Name: Date:

We're headed west…

Next week, we'll start learning about America's westward expansion. Before we begin, I am interested in finding out what you already know about this topic *and* what you're interested in learning. Please help me by completing this three-part survey.

PART 1: The topics that we'll cover in this unit are listed below. Please rank them from most to least interesting (1=most interesting, 10= least interesting).

If there are any topics that you wish we'd cover, go ahead and add them to the list!

___ *O Pioneers! Who Were You? And How Did You Live?*
___ *The Rush Is On: Looking for Gold in California*
___ *Famous Trails and Travelers*
___ *The Country Moves West: Will Slavery Follow?*
___ *Traveling West (Wagons and Ponies and Trains…Oh, My!)*
___ *Exploring New Lands with Adventurous Explorers*
___ *Trappers, Trailblazers, Gunslingers, and Outlaws*
___ *The Trail of Tears and the Fate of the Native Americans*
___ *From Sea to Shining Sea: Our Country Is Growing!*
___ *Law and Order in the Wild West*
___ *Other:* _____

PART 2: Do you already know anything about our country's westward expansion? If so, please tell me about it on the back.

PART 3: Reevaluate your responses at the end of the unit to see how much you've learned and whether your interests have changed.

Teacher Talk

→ The idea *isn't* to teach the topics students are interested in and skip the rest; the idea is to use students' interests to make instruction more engaging and effective. The teacher who created the survey in Example 1, for example, covered all ten survey topics in class; she simply used students' interests to decide where to begin, which topics to emphasize, and which topics to try and make more interesting.

→ To make this tool do double duty, design your survey to assess students' background knowledge as well as their interests; use the survey in Example 1 (see Part 2) as a model.

Six Ways to Accommodate Students' Interests

✓ Build choice into activities and assessment tasks so that students can work on things that interest them. ("Which of the dance styles we studied do you like best? Choreograph an original piece in that style.")

✓ Create enrichment centers where students can go to learn more about topics that interest them.

✓ Allocate more instructional time to topics that students select as their "top picks."

✓ Begin your unit with whatever topic students deem most interesting. ("Since most of you picked 'gunslingers and outlaws' as your top choice, we'll start there.")

✓ Develop—or invite students to develop—projects related to their interests.

✓ Organize students into Shared Interest Groups so that they can discuss, explore, or report on topics of interest with like-minded classmates. (The Shared Interest Groups variation is explained in more detail below; it's also illustrated in Example 3.)

Six Ways to Broaden Students' Interests

✓ Create interesting and provocative names for the topics you plan to teach. Use the survey in Example 1 as a model.

✓ Connect your content to students' interests, hobbies, and personal experiences.

✓ Present less interesting topics in more engaging and interactive ways (e.g., use a hands-on activity instead of a sit-still-and-listen lecture).

✓ Give students the option to acquire content knowledge that *doesn't* interest them in a way that does. ("Review the list of learning targets for the arteries/veins portion of our circulatory system unit. Then decide how you want to learn the relevant material. You can read your textbook, browse the Internet, dissect a frog, or watch a video.")

✓ Let students demonstrate their learning in a way that appeals to them. ("Summarize what you learned by building a model, creating a podcast, or writing a descriptive paragraph.")

✓ Pair up students with different interests. Challenge them to change each other's opinions.

Variation: Shared Interest Groups

The purpose of establishing Shared Interest Groups (Silver, Strong, & Perini, 2007) is to let students explore material that interests them with classmates who share their interests. To establish the groups, present students with a choice of books to read, topics to investigate, activities to complete, or problems to solve. Let them sample the different options (e.g., skim the first page of each book or read a one-sentence summary of each topic), choose the option that interests them, and work on their selected task with students who made the same choice. Whenever possible, have students discuss their choices as a class before breaking off into groups. ("Why does this interest me? Why did I pick this as opposed to that?") These kinds of discussions can give you insight into students' likes and dislikes. They can also serve to expand students' interests. ("Hmmm…that topic sounds more interesting than I thought. Maybe I should switch groups.")

One way to use this variation is to have students select their favorite topic from a student-interest survey and research that topic with like-minded classmates. These "expert groups" can then be called on during the course of the unit to provide insight into the topics they've pursued.

Hand of Knowledge

What is it?

A tool that provides insight into students' interests, talents, and learning preferences by having them complete a hand-shaped organizer with six getting-to-know-you questions

What are the benefits of using this tool?

The current emphasis on standards and accountability has us so focused on assessing *what* our students know that we're spending less and less time assessing *who* they are as individuals. The problem with prioritizing standards over students is that we can actually teach our students a lot more effectively when we're aware of their interests, talents, challenges, and aspirations. This tool makes it easy to gather this kind of information by getting students to think and talk about who they are, how they learn, and what's important to them.

What are the basic steps?

1. Download copies of the Hand of Knowledge Organizer (www.ThoughtfulClassroom.com/Tools) or have students trace one of their hands on a piece of paper. (The organizer will offer students more room for writing.)

2. Post the following questions on the board or read them aloud:

Pinky finger $\longrightarrow$ What do you do for fun in your free time?

Ring finger $\longrightarrow$ What is something that you're really good at?

Middle finger $\longrightarrow$ Think about something interesting that you learned outside of school. What is it? Why is it interesting? How did you learn it?

Index finger $\longrightarrow$ What word or phrase best describes you as a learner?

Thumb $\longrightarrow$ When school feels hard or boring, what makes it feel that way? Be specific.

Palm $\longrightarrow$ What is a dream that you have for your future?

3. Have students record their responses (words and/or pictures) on the appropriate parts of their "hands."

4. Help students get to know their classmates by having them share and compare hands with a partner or by posting their hands around the room. Tell them in advance if their hands will be on display.

5. Review students' hands to gather information about interests, talents, intelligences, and learning preferences/challenges.

6. Think about how you can use this information to make future learning experiences more productive and enjoyable for students (specific individuals as well as the entire class). Here are a few ideas:

- Design (or let students design) lessons, activities, and assignments around their interests.
- Provide opportunities for students to demonstrate and use their individual talents.
- Explain how the things that students are learning are relevant to their dreams for the future.

How is this tool used in the classroom?

✔ To learn about students' interests, talents, learning challenges, and dreams

EXAMPLE 1: A mathematics teacher whose students were less than enthusiastic about calculating percentages abandoned her usual percentage worksheets and instead created themed problem sets around her students' interests and hobbies. To get a group of her sports-obsessed students excited, for example, she challenged them to calculate the free-throw averages, on-base percentages, and pass-completion statistics for their favorite athletes.

Since one of these students had used the word "slow" to describe himself as a learner (see Hand of Knowledge at the right), she also worked with him to develop his confidence and basic skills. Among other things, she often reminded him that learning the material was what mattered—not learning it quickly.

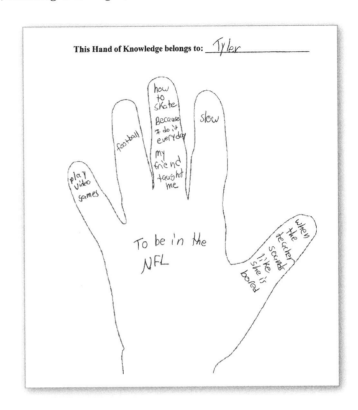

This Hand of Knowledge belongs to: Tyler

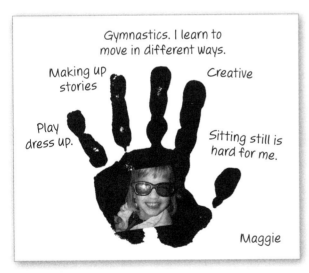

Gymnastics. I learn to move in different ways.

Making up stories

Creative

Play dress up.

Sitting still is hard for me.

Maggie

EXAMPLE 2: A kindergarten teacher made this tool more fun and personal for students by recording their responses on handprints and having them decorate their prints with photos that captured their personalities. One student's print, and the photo that her grandmother helped her select, is shown at the left.

Based on this student's index- and ring-finger responses, her teacher tried to engage her in activities that let her express her creativity as often as possible. The result? Getting Maggie to sit still became less of a problem!

EXAMPLE 3: At first, Kaitlyn's teacher wasn't sure the information on her Hand of Knowledge (not shown) was all that useful. After thinking about it for a few minutes, however, he realized that Kaitlyn's fondness for tailgating, talking to friends, and people watching were suggestive of a strong interpersonal and social intelligence—and that he might be able to engage Kaitlyn's interest and help her thrive by involving her in activities (e.g., cooperative learning activities, discussions, debates) that would let her capitalize on her social, interpersonal, and oral communication skills.

How Will I Prepare Students to Produce High-Quality Work?

Quality is everyone's responsibility.

—W. Edwards Deming, quality management expert

We had to write our first lab report. And it was like, Hello! We never really learned what a good lab report was supposed to have in it. I mean I guess we sort of knew from middle school. But this was high school science, and I just wasn't clear about what I was supposed to do. The teacher just assumed we would be able to do it on our own. And that's how I got my first F in school.

—Claire B., frustrated high school student

In an important article on the power of formative assessment, D. Royce Sadler (1989) lays out the "indispensable conditions" that lead to improvement in student work. Chief among these conditions is "that the student comes to hold a concept of quality roughly similar to that held by the teacher" (p. 121). In other words, an appreciation for quality—what it looks and sounds like—needs to be taught directly to students. This chapter is about how to begin the process of teaching students to recognize and create quality work. In it, we present five tools that help teachers introduce tasks early in the learning process, ensure that students know what these tasks will demand of them, and specify the criteria for distinguishing average work from exemplary work:

1. **7-Step Directions** prepares students to complete assigned tasks more successfully by spelling out the directions using a clear and simple format.

2. **Checklists** uses a simple to-do list format to help students understand and fulfill the requirements for assigned tasks/procedures.

3. **Guiding & Grading Rubrics** helps students understand what quality work entails; the tool is used to guide and grade their work on assigned tasks.

4. **Questions, Comments, Concerns (QCC)** promotes clarity on assigned tasks by having students raise questions and concerns before they begin working.

5. **Student-Generated Assessment Criteria** helps students identify the criteria that define excellence by having them look at samples of high-quality work.

7-Step Directions

What is it?

A seven-question framework that helps students complete their assignments more successfully by clarifying instructions, expectations, and what-to-do-when-stuck strategies before they start working

What are the benefits of using this tool?

When students fail to complete their assignments (or complete them properly), we often assume that a lack of effort, ability, or readiness is to blame. In many cases, however, students fail for an entirely different reason—they fail because they're unclear about what they've been asked to do or how to do it. This tool prevents these kinds of failures from happening and increases time-on-task by clarifying instructions up front. It also prepares students to be more self-sufficient and successful on future assignments by making them aware of the kinds of questions they should ask themselves before beginning *any* assigned task.

What are the basic steps?

1. Ask yourself the following seven questions before giving students a homework or classwork assignment:

    a) WHAT is the assigned task?

    b) WHO should perform the task? Some students? All students? Pairs of students? Teams?

    c) WHEN should students start the task? And how long do they have to complete it?

    d) HOW should students go about completing the task? What steps are involved?

    e) What should students do if they need HELP? What strategies should they try?

    f) What should students do AFTER they complete the task?

    g) What CRITERIA will you use to evaluate students' work?

2. Record your answers on a 7-Step Directions template (p. 46) or write the questions and answers on the board.

3. Review your answers with students before they begin working on the assigned task. Use the "see it & say it" technique to do this:

    See it: Let students see the questions and answers. Depending on what you did in Step 2, this will entail distributing copies of your completed template or calling students' attention to the board.

    Say it: Go through the questions one at a time. Have students say what the assignment entails by asking them to read the answers aloud or explain the answers in their own words. Address any questions that students have before moving on.

4. Teach students to seek out the answers to the 7-Step Directions questions before they begin working on *any* assigned task. Explain that having these answers can help them complete their tasks more successfully.

How is this tool used in the classroom?

✔ To help students complete their work more successfully by clarifying expectations up front

EXAMPLE: A sixth-grade mathematics teacher regularly uses the 7-Step Directions framework to introduce her students' homework assignments. (She finds that it helps them get started on the right foot.) The template that she completed for one of these assignments (addressing Common Core Standard 6.EE.A.3) is shown here:

WHAT	Work on tonight's homework assignment: problems 1–10 on p. 45 of your text.
WHO	People who have finished their classwork
WHEN	Start working as soon as you finish your classwork. Stop working two minutes before the bell rings so that you have time to pack up your things.
HOW	Work on your own or with a partner. Before you begin, review what we've learned about equivalence and applying the properties of operations to generate equivalent expressions. Check your class notes as well as your text.
HELP	Ask three before me.*
AFTER	Reflect on the assignment. Were the problems hard? Easy? Medium? Why do you think so? Record your thoughts and feelings in your Learning Log and be prepared to share them in class tomorrow.
CRITERIA	Problem sets will be evaluated for completeness and accuracy. All work should be shown.

*The "ask three before me" concept is explained in Teacher Talk, below.

🗨 Teacher Talk

→ Teachers who use this tool on a regular basis often leave the seven prompts on the board so that they can simply fill in the answers when introducing each new assignment.

→ If students need help completing an assigned task, you may want to refer them to the "ask three before me" rule. This rule, which states that they should ask three people (e.g., classmates, parents, school librarian) for help before asking you, teaches students to become more self-sufficient. It also promotes collaboration and builds interpersonal skills by encouraging students to seek help from others.

7-Step Directions

WHAT	
WHO	
WHEN	
HOW	
HELP	
AFTER	
CRITERIA	

Checklists

What is it?

A tool that guides and improves students' work on assigned tasks by spelling out steps to follow and components to include

What are the benefits of using this tool?

In our everyday lives, many of us count on checklists to help us complete essential tasks. And in the classroom, students can count on them to do the same. Checklists improve students' performance on assigned tasks by reminding them what they need to do or include in order to complete those tasks successfully. When used repeatedly, checklists help students internalize the requirements for specific kinds of tasks so that they can ultimately complete those tasks without needing the help of a checklist.

What are the basic steps?

1. Identify an assessment task that you want students to complete. It can involve creating a product, demonstrating a procedure, or delivering a performance.

2. Create a checklist that will help students complete the task successfully (use specific and student-friendly language). Depending on the task, your checklist might include

   • Steps to carry out ("Count how many atoms of each type are on each side of the equation")

   • Directions to follow ("Read three different accounts of the event" or "Reduce all fractions")

   • Elements to include ("Include a bibliography" or "Include five words from our Word Wall")

   Note: The items on your checklist *should* remind students what to do or what to include in their work. They *should not* require students to make subjective judgments about the quality of their work—like whether their work is interesting, creative, or easy to understand.

3. Review the checklist with students before they begin working on the assigned task.

4. Encourage students to keep the checklist handy as they work. Have them check off the items that they complete, either as they complete them or at the end.

   Optional: Have students submit their checklists along with their completed assignments.

5. Help students understand that fulfilling the requirements on the checklist is necessary but not sufficient to do well on the assigned task. (Completing a checklist guarantees that required steps and components have been completed. It does *not* guarantee that they have been done well!)

6. Review students' assignments and give them feedback about their work. Identify checklist items that were completed, but not as well as they could be, and discuss strategies for improvement. ("You gave examples to support your thesis as the checklist said you should—and that's a good start. The next step is to make those examples even stronger. Let's talk about how to do that.")

How is this tool used in the classroom?

✔ To guide and improve students' work on assigned tasks

✔ To teach students a procedure and help them execute it correctly

✔ To help students understand and internalize the requirements for specific kinds of tasks

EXAMPLE 1: An automotive technology teacher created the checklist below to guide his students through the process of replacing a vehicle's battery. Students referred to the checklist as he explained and demonstrated the battery-change procedure. They then completed the procedure on their own using the checklist as a guide.

BATTERY-CHANGE PROCEDURE CHECKLIST

To replace a vehicle's battery, follow these steps:

☐ Turn off the engine.

☐ Pop the hood.

☐ Remove the negative cable from the battery terminal.

☐ Remove the positive cable from the battery terminal.

☐ Remove the battery hold-down clamps.

EXAMPLE 2: A third-grade teacher made this checklist to teach and help her students remember the essential components of a book review. Students used this checklist throughout the year to guide their work and check their book reviews for the required elements before submitting them.

CHECKLIST FOR WRITING A BOOK REVIEW

☐ I mentioned the book's title, author, and genre in my opening paragraph.

☐ I provided a brief summary of the basic plot.

☐ I introduced and described the main characters.

☐ I explained what I liked and disliked using specific examples from the book.

☐ I concluded by saying whether I would recommend the book to a friend and why.

☐ I spell-checked and proofread my work.

☐ I fixed any errors that I found while proofreading.

EXAMPLE 3: A fifth-grade teacher designed this oral-presentation checklist to develop and assess students' command of specific Common Core Speaking and Listening Standards (SL.5.4–5). Notice that she added an extra column so that she and her students could comment on their performance.

When I am giving an oral presentation...	Comments (mine and my teacher's)
☐ I make a conscious effort to speak slowly, loudly, and clearly.	*I was nervous and forgot. I think I rushed. You're right. You did*
☑ I use visual displays like charts/graphs to try and clarify my points.	*The bar graphs made your data easier to understand.*
☑ I support my statements and positions with specific evidence and examples.	*Good examples of how changes in supply and demand affected prices!*
☑ I stop at various times to address people's comments/questions.	*Excellent job responding to your classmates' questions!*

EXAMPLE 4: A math teacher developed the checklist below to help his students assess and improve their performance on constructed response items. In creating this checklist, he drew both on the Common Core Standards for Mathematical Practice (particularly Standards 1 and 6) and on his personal experience as an educator (i.e., what types of errors were his students prone to making?).

TWELVE-POINT CHECKLIST FOR CONSTRUCTED RESPONSE ITEMS

☐ I read the problem and the directions.

☐ I underlined what the problem was asking me to do.

☐ I determined what was known/unknown and drew a diagram if appropriate.

☐ I thought about possible problem-solving strategies before I started working.

☐ I showed my work.

☐ I wrote neatly so the person grading my work would be able to read it.

☐ I checked that I answered all parts of the question.

☐ I underlined or circled my final response(s).

☐ I labeled any drawings and graphs.

☐ I explained any abbreviations and symbols.

☐ I proofread my work and revised it if needed.

☐ I checked my solution to make sure that it was reasonable.

 Teacher Talk

→ Use student-friendly language and complete sentences when crafting your checklists. Whenever possible, begin your sentences with "I," "My," "Did I," or "Did you."

→ Make checklist items as specific as possible to help students understand what good work entails (e.g., "I explained what I did and didn't like using specific examples from the book" instead of "I shared my opinion about the book").

→ If students will be completing the same type of task multiple times throughout the year (e.g., preparing a lab report, writing an argument essay, solving a word problem, giving a slide-show presentation), create a checklist for that type of task and use it every time. Having students use the same checklist over and over again can help them internalize the required elements so that ultimately, they're able to complete that type of task without needing the checklist.

Note: You may want to turn these "multiple-use checklists" into posters and hang them around your classroom so that students can refer to them throughout the year. Another option is to make printed copies of the checklists for students to keep in their notebooks.

→ Once students are familiar with the checklist concept, invite them to help you develop checklists for various tasks and procedures. Involving students in generating the criteria for successful work can help them internalize those criteria.

→ Some teachers use online tools to create (and help their students create) task-specific checklists. See this website for an example: http://pblchecklist.4teachers.org/index.shtml.

Guiding & Grading Rubrics

What is it?

A tool that describes what work looks like at different levels of quality; it is used both to guide and grade students' performance on an assigned task

What are the benefits of using this tool?

We often use rubrics to look at students' work, figure out where it lies on a scale, and give students a grade. But when fully integrated into the instructional process, rubrics can shift the focus from evaluation to learning. Presenting a rubric at the beginning of a unit helps students understand what high-quality work looks like and how to produce it. Students refer to the rubric throughout the process, measuring their work against the descriptions and seeking ways to move it up the levels. Finally, the rubric greatly enhances the feedback process by giving us and our students an objective scale for assessing their work and discussing ways to make it better.

What are the basic steps?

1. Create a rubric that can be used to guide and grade students' work on an upcoming task. Follow the steps below, use the examples on pp. 51–52 as models, and see p. 54 for a list of tips.

   - Decide what dimensions to focus on when assessing students' work (e.g., content knowledge, creativity, craftsmanship). See The C-List (p. 182) or the Content-Process-Product tool (pp. 185–187) for ideas.

   - Describe three or four levels of performance for each dimension (e.g., explain what *creativity* looks like at the expert, proficient, and novice levels). Use simple but specific language.

   - Decide whether to weight some criteria more than others when evaluating students' work (e.g., "I'll count *content knowledge* twice as much as *creativity*").

2. Review the rubric with students before they begin working. Explain that its purpose is to clarify expectations, give them concrete targets to aim for, and help them assess their work along the way.

3. Remind students to refer to the rubric on a regular basis to see how their work stacks up and how they can improve it. (What does expert-level work look like? What does *my* work look like? What can I do to close the gap?)

4. Use the rubric to grade students' completed assignments, provide students with feedback about their work, and explore strategies for improvement (e.g., "Let's look at the word-choice section of the rubric to see if it tells us how you could convey the events in your narrative more precisely").

How is this tool used in the classroom?

✔ To teach students what high-quality work looks like

✔ To help students assess and improve their performance on assigned tasks

✔ To evaluate and give students specific feedback about their work

EXAMPLE 1: To develop the kinds of thinking skills that the Common Core State Standards call for, a math teacher assigns complex problem-solving tasks on a regular basis. He gives his students the same exact rubric for every assignment (below), both to save himself some time and to help them internalize the attributes of high-quality work. He also requires his students to revise and resubmit novice-level work.

DIMENSIONS TO BE ASSESSED

		Problem-solving strategy	Problem-solving process	Solution quality
LEVELS OF PERFORMANCE	**MASTER** *5 points*	You selected an appropriate strategy for tackling the problem.	Your strategy, steps, and reasoning process are clearly explained.	Your solution is correct!
	APPRENTICE *4 points*	You chose an appropriate overall strategy, but got off track due to a conceptual error, misunderstanding, or incorrect assumption.	You showed your work, but your explanation is unclear and/or incomplete.	Your solution is incorrect due to a careless or simple calculation error.
	NOVICE *Revise and resubmit.*	See me to discuss strategies for tackling this problem. Then give the problem another try and resubmit your work.	You need to show your work/explain what you did. Try again and resubmit your work.	Your solution needs to be completed or corrected. Try again and resubmit your work.

EXAMPLE 2: A seventh-grade teacher invited his students to help him generate a rubric for the kinds of argument pieces that are a focal point of the Common Core Standards (Writing Anchor Standard 1). The rubric they came up with and the method they used to create it are presented in the Student-Generated Assessment Criteria tool (p. 58, see "Three-Level Approach").

EXAMPLE 3: At the end of a unit on reptiles and amphibians, a fifth-grade teacher assigned her students the following assessment task: "Write a well-crafted piece explaining how reptiles and amphibians are both similar and different." Her goal in giving students this task was twofold: to test their grasp of the relevant content material and to test their explanatory writing skills (Common Core Writing Anchor Standard 2).

This teacher chose to consider three different dimensions when evaluating students' assignments—*content* knowledge, thinking *processes*, and *product* quality—and she designed her rubric accordingly (see p. 52). She used this rubric to clarify expectations, grade students' final drafts, and give students feedback about their work.

Content-Process-Product Rubric: Reptile/Amphibian Comparative Writing Task

CONTENT KNOWLEDGE	EXCELLENT	ALMOST THERE	KEEP WORKING
A thorough understanding of the critical characteristics of reptiles and amphibians	You clearly and completely summarized the critical attributes of reptiles and amphibians.	You mentioned a lot of key reptile and amphibian characteristics, but some are missing or unclear.	You need to describe the critical characteristics of reptiles and amphibians.

THINKING PROCESSES	EXCELLENT	ALMOST THERE	KEEP WORKING
• *Comparison* • *Explanation* **A well-illustrated explanation of key similarities/differences** (Common Core W.5.2b)	You used specific examples to illustrate the critical similarities and differences between reptiles and amphibians.	Use more (or more specific) examples to demonstrate the key similarities/differences between reptiles and amphibians.	You need to describe the key similarities and/or differences between reptiles and amphibians. Support your points with specific examples.

WRITTEN PRODUCT	EXCELLENT	ALMOST THERE	KEEP WORKING
Content and clarity of introduction (Common Core W.5.2a)	You opened with a clear introduction of the topic you were writing about.	You opened by explaining what you were writing about. Now see if you can explain it more clearly.	Begin your piece with an explanation of what you are writing about.
Organization (Common Core W.5.2a)	You grouped related information together in a logical way.	Some related information is grouped together. Try to be more consistent.	Group related information together. For example, start with the similarities.
Logic and flow (Common Core W.5.2c)	You linked the ideas within each section and between sections using appropriate transitional words.	Link more of your ideas together with transitional words. This will make your piece smoother and easier to follow.	Try to connect your ideas together using transitional words like *also, for example, another, especially,* and *in contrast.*
Content of conclusion (Common Core W.5.2e)	Your conclusion sums up the main point and the specific information you presented.	Your conclusion relates to the information you presented, but doesn't pull everything together.	Add a conclusion that relates to and summarizes what you explained in your piece.

Variation 1: Dimmer Switches

For a more playful take on the traditional rubric, use "dimmer switches" like the ones below. Note that the criteria on dimmer switches, like the criteria on a standard rubric, should be specific, student friendly, and thoroughly discussed with students before they begin working.

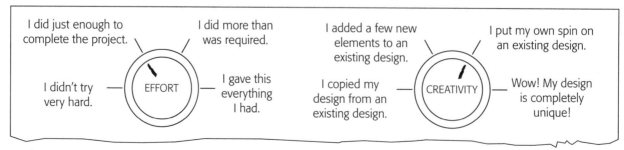

Variation 2: Rating Scales

Like a rubric, a rating scale can be used to guide and grade students' work on an assigned task. To create a rating scale, identify the key dimensions of a quality performance and describe what each dimension would look like *at the highest level of quality only* (i.e., the top level of a rubric). When evaluating students' work, indicate what level of performance students achieved for each dimension and then explain your ratings. (Why, for example, is a student's use of transitional words "almost there" as opposed to "right on target"?) Offer concrete suggestions for moving to the next level, either verbally or in writing.

Note: Because rating scales don't spell out the specific elements that distinguish one level of performance from another, they provide less guidance than rubrics about how to produce quality work or grade students' assignments. They do, however, offer a simple and less overwhelming format for teaching students what quality work looks like and for engaging them in conversations about levels of quality and strategies for improvement. Three different rating-scale formats are shown below.

NUMERICAL FORMAT

The example below shows what the reptile/amphibian rubric on p. 52 would look like as a rating scale. Another example of a numerical rating scale can be found on p. 180 of The C-List tool (Example 1).

> **DIMENSION:** Content knowledge
> **LEVEL 3 WORK** will clearly and completely summarize the critical attributes of reptiles and amphibians.
> **SCORE:** 1 2 3
> **EXPLANATION & SUGGESTIONS FOR IMPROVEMENT:**
>
> **DIMENSION:** Thinking processes
> **LEVEL 3 WORK** will use specific examples to illustrate the key similarities/differences between reptiles and amphibians.
> **SCORE:** 1 2 3
> **EXPLANATION & SUGGESTIONS FOR IMPROVEMENT:**

BULL'S-EYE FORMAT

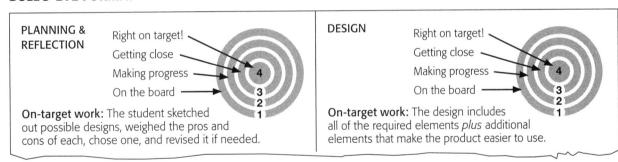

PLANNING & REFLECTION	
Right on target!	
Getting close	
Making progress	4
On the board	3 2 1

On-target work: The student sketched out possible designs, weighed the pros and cons of each, chose one, and revised it if needed.

DESIGN	
Right on target!	
Getting close	
Making progress	4
On the board	3 2 1

On-target work: The design includes all of the required elements *plus* additional elements that make the product easier to use.

FLOWCHART FORMAT

> **DIMENSION:** Use of digital media and visual displays of data (Common Core SL.CCR.5)
>
> **MISSION:** Create a top-notch presentation by using visuals, sound clips, and/or animation to enhance your audience's understanding of the critical data, concepts, and conclusions you're presenting.
>
> 1. Getting Started   2. Making Progress   3. Almost There   4. Mission Accomplished!

Tips for Developing Good RUBRICS

Remember your audience.

A rubric isn't for academics or content-specialists. It's for students! Make sure yours is student friendly by asking yourself questions like these: Is it too much to process? Can I simplify it? Have I described the levels using simple language that will make sense to students? Confirm that students understand the information on your rubric by discussing it with them, giving them concrete examples, and/or challenging them to restate the characteristics of quality in their own words (younger students can use pictures).

Underscore what's important; unload extraneous criteria.

When deciding what to include on your rubric, focus on the criteria that are essential for a quality performance. In the case of a slide-show presentation, this might include *accuracy of content knowledge*, *readability of text/images*, and *logical organization of slides*. (Something like *use of multiple fonts*, on the other hand, shouldn't appear on your rubric since using multiple fonts isn't essential to giving a good presentation.) The goal is to include all the elements that define quality work while avoiding arbitrary or irrelevant criteria.

Borrow ideas from others.

Developing rubrics doesn't need to be a solo endeavor. Talk to colleagues about the tasks they assign and the rubrics they use. Trade notes, borrow ideas, and adapt each other's rubrics to suit your purposes.

Another option: Invite students to help you define the attributes of quality work (see the Student-Generated Assessment Criteria tool, pp. 57–59, for ways to do this). When done properly, involving students in the process of generating assessment criteria can help them "internalize the criteria and bring them to bear on their own work" (Stiggins et al., 2006, p. 209).

Reuse if possible.

To save time and help students internalize the qualities of top-notch work, design rubrics for recurring types of tasks (e.g., writing an argument essay, preparing a lab report, solving a word problem) and reuse them throughout the year. (The "repeat rubric" concept is illustrated in Example 1 on p. 51.)

Inspire growth.

Rubrics should be used to help students become better thinkers, learners, and problem solvers. To inspire growth, replace descriptions that emphasize what's wrong (e.g., *contains numerous grammar, punctuation, and spelling errors*) with ones that map out a path for improvement (e.g., *proofread more carefully to root out avoidable grammar, punctuation, and spelling errors*); use the "keep working" column in Example 3 (p. 52) as a model.

Another option: Encourage students to revise and resubmit novice-level work (or anything less than expert-level work) as shown in Example 1.

Clarify expectations.

Replace "fluffy" descriptions that are too vague to be helpful with descriptions that are specific and clear. (It's one thing to ask for a *meaningful* conclusion; it's quite another to ask for one that *follows from and summarizes the information in the preceding paragraphs*.) Whenever possible, help students understand what each level of performance entails by providing examples for them to look at (e.g., Level 1, 2, and 3 concluding statements from a previous year's class).

Stop and review.

Whenever possible, test-drive your rubric using samples of student work (e.g., samples from a previous year's class, a different class period, a colleague's students, or a previous assignment of the same type) and make sure you feel good about the scores that you come up with. If your rubric is causing you to give low scores to samples of work that you feel are strong—or high scores to samples of work that aren't that great—take time to revise it. Change your criteria, your "level descriptions," or your weighting system/point values.

👁 Teacher Talk

→ Since the notion of a rubric can be abstract and hard to grasp, especially for younger students, look for ways to make the rubric concept more concrete. A first-grade teacher we know introduced the concept of differing levels of quality by laying out four spoons: a flimsy plastic spoon, a durable plastic spoon, an everyday flatware spoon from her kitchen, and a sterling silver spoon from her fine china cabinet. After having students discuss the qualities that distinguished one spoon from the next, she used this four-spoons activity to introduce the rubric concept. For the remainder of the year, she included pictures of the four spoons on every rubric to remind her students of the difference between "flimsy plastic work" and "sterling silver work."

→ Teach students what quality work looks like and help them better understand the criteria on a rubric by showing them samples of work that represent the different levels (e.g., essays with excellent, average, and below-average concluding sentences). Choose representative samples from a previous year's class or different class period (remove identifying information to protect students' privacy)—or create your own samples from scratch as shown in the example below.

Samples of work at five different levels of quality:

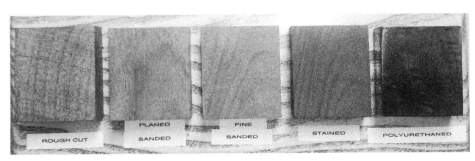

SOURCE: David Hamilton, Career and Technical Education Program, GST-BOCES Coopers Education Center, Painted Post, NY

A career and technical education teacher initially made this series of five blocks to illustrate the different levels of quality in a finished woodworking product, but we often use the blocks ourselves (he made us our own set) to illustrate the levels-of-quality concept in a more general way. Because each block in the series is smoother and more polished than the one before it, the set as a whole helps students see that creating a "finished" final product involves a series of steps—and that they can move their work from rough to polished one step at a time.

→ To save time, you may want to take advantage of the many rubrics and rubric-designing tools that are available online (see http://rubistar.4teachers.org for one example). But be selective! Since the quality of available rubrics can vary significantly, it's important to assess and improve them as needed before using them with your students (use the tips on p. 54 to help you).

Another option: Borrow scoring rubrics from state assessment tests (rewrite them in student-friendly language before giving them to students). Besides saving time, using these rubrics in your classroom can help students develop the kinds of skills they'll need to succeed on these tests.

Questions, Comments, Concerns (QCC)

What is it?

A technique that helps students start their assignments on the right foot by encouraging them to ask questions, share comments, and raise concerns before they begin working

What are the benefits of using this tool?

Middle school teacher Laura Bollinger (Durand, MI) found that too many of her students were taking a "start-now-and-finish-quickly" approach to their assignments. Instead of actively identifying areas of concern and confusion, they would jump right in—and that lack of preparation would show up in their work (personal communication, May 5, 2011). In response, Laura developed a technique that she called QCC (questions, comments, concerns). QCC gives students a quick and easy way to get clarity on their assignments before they begin working. It also teaches them to curtail their impulsivity and ask questions to address gaps in understanding—habits of mind that have been linked to successful individuals across disciplines (Costa & Kallick, 2008).

What are the basic steps?

1. Introduce a project or assignment to the class.

2. Ask students if they have any QCCs (questions, comments, or concerns).

3. Address all questions, comments, and concerns before students begin working.

How is this tool used in the classroom?

✔ To help students produce higher-quality work by clarifying expectations up front
✔ To have students assess and improve their understanding of assigned tasks
✔ To teach students to take more responsibility for their own learning

Student-Generated Assessment Criteria

What is it?

A tool that prepares students to produce high-quality work by showing them examples of what it looks like and helping them identify its essential attributes

What are the benefits of using this tool?

Establishing the criteria by which students' work will be evaluated has traditionally been the teacher's prerogative. Shifting some of this responsibility to students can be extremely worthwhile since students have an easier time understanding and applying assessment criteria that they themselves generate. This tool initiates such a shift by giving students samples of exemplary work and helping them identify the elements that define quality. Under the guidance of their teacher, they then convert these "quality elements" into a list of assessment criteria that helps them focus, evaluate, and improve their work on an upcoming task.

What are the basic steps?

1. Present an assessment task that requires students to create a product or performance.

2. Help students identify the characteristics of high-quality work *before* they tackle the assigned task. To do this, choose and use one of the following approaches (divide students into three- to five-member teams before they begin working):

   - *High-Performance Approach:* Select or create three different samples of exemplary work. Help students compare the samples and identify the common characteristics. (What are the essential attributes of high-quality work?)

   - *Three-Level Approach:* Select or create samples of excellent, average, and below-average work. Help students compare the samples and identify the critical elements that distinguish one level of quality from the next.

3. Invite students to discuss their findings as a class. Help them refine, synthesize, and transform their ideas into a list of mutually acceptable assessment criteria for the assigned task. Ensure that the final list includes all the critical dimensions of a quality product/performance.

4. Explain that *students* should use this list of criteria to guide, assess, and improve their work on the assigned task. Then explain how *you* will use the list to evaluate their completed assignments.

5. Make it clear that this strategy of analyzing and learning from high-quality work is one that students can and should use independently—not just when you tell them to.

How is this tool used in the classroom?

✔ To help students identify and internalize the characteristics of high-quality work

✔ To involve students in defining the criteria by which their work will be evaluated

✔ To give students criteria for guiding, assessing, and improving their work

HIGH-PERFORMANCE APPROACH: "What does good work look like?"

To help his students identify the characteristics of a top-notch narrative (working toward Common Core Standard W.2.3), a second-grade teacher read them three high-quality examples from his previous year's class and asked them to think about what the examples had in common. He recorded their thoughts on the board, helped them refine their list of ideas, and printed up copies for them to keep. The next day, students used the list of criteria they had generated (below) to help them write their own narratives. Before submitting their drafts, students worked with a writing buddy to check that they had met all the criteria and to revise their work as needed (Common Core W.2.5).

What do we notice at the BEGINNING?

The first sentence is interesting and makes you want to read more.

The first sentence tells you what event or experience the writer is going to be writing about.

Example: "I bet you would never guess what happened to me on the playground."

What do we notice in the MIDDLE?

The writer uses "order words" to help you understand the order in which things happened.

Examples: first, next, after that, finally

The writer describes actions, thoughts, and feelings. The writer uses strong verbs and adjectives to help you picture what's happening.

Examples: "I rode my shiny yellow bike." "She yelled in a loud voice." "I felt sad like I was going to cry."

Note: This same list of criteria was used to provide students with specific feedback about their completed drafts during teacher/student writing conferences.

THREE-LEVEL APPROACH: "What's the difference?"

After comparing excellent, average, and below-average argument essays from a previous year's class, a group of seventh graders identified the characteristics that distinguished one level of quality from the next. They then used this information to create the rubric below. After confirming that their "criteria for excellence" were consistent with the Common Core Writing Standards (W.7.1), their teacher encouraged them to use this rubric throughout the year to help craft the kinds of coherent and logically argued pieces that the standards call for.

	EXCELLENT SAMPLES	AVERAGE SAMPLES	BELOW-AVERAGE SAMPLES
POSITION	Writer's position is clearly stated and easy to find.	Writer's position is a little bit hard to follow or hard to find.	Writer doesn't take a position or position isn't clearly explained.
EVIDENCE	Position is supported with logical and relevant evidence.	Needs more (or more convincing) evidence to support the position.	Evidence is missing, unconvincing, or irrelevant.
ORGANIZATION	Reasons/evidence are presented in a logical order.	Reasons/evidence would make better sense in a different order.	Components (position, evidence, conclusion) are absent/out of order.

Teacher Talk

→ The samples of work that you give students to analyze in Step 2 can be created by you, by experts, or by other students. (To help students understand the characteristics of a top-notch story, for example, you could write three of your own, grab three from a library, or select three good examples from a previous year's class.) To protect students' privacy, use samples of work from previous years' classes or other class periods—and remove students' names/other identifying information before distributing copies of their work (ask for permission as well).

Tip: If you spend this year filling a notebook or folder with samples of work at different levels of quality, you'll have an extensive collection of samples to draw on in subsequent years.

→ With the Three-Level Approach, students are typically told which sample of work represents which level of performance. To make the task more challenging, give students the responsibility of figuring out which sample of work is which; then have them explain their reasoning.

→ Teachers who use the High-Performance Approach often have students describe the *differences* between the three samples as well as the similarities. Why? Because calling students' attention to these differences is a good way to teach them that there's more than one "right way" to complete a given assignment.

→ Having students examine samples of high-quality work *after* they've completed an assignment can be useful as well. A teacher we know scans students' graded tests, selects three high-quality responses for each test question, and distributes copies of those responses to students along with their graded tests. Her goal is twofold: to show students what high-quality responses look like and to teach them that there are multiple ways to answer a question well.

→ Be sure to guide students through the criteria-generating process. The goal is to *help* them identify the criteria that define quality—not to leave the criteria-generating process entirely in their hands.

Note: Without this kind of guidance, students can easily come to the wrong conclusions about the critical attributes of a top-notch performance. They might, for example, mistakenly conclude that having decorative borders on slides is important simply because the slides in three high-quality presentations all have decorative borders. (In this case, it would be important to help students understand that decorative borders aren't in any way linked to quality; one way to do this would be to show them examples of top-notch slides that *don't* have decorative borders.)

How Will I Check for Understanding *While* Presenting New Information?

Your audience gives you everything you need. They tell you.

—"Funny Girl" Fanny Brice

When we refer to formative assessments, we are referring to the informed judgments that the teacher strategically gathers and uses within the classroom to move a student from point A to point B. Such assessments require skilled teachers who continuously take note of and respond to where their students are.

—Pérsida Himmele and William Himmele, *Total Participation Techniques*

Every day, in almost every classroom, teachers present new learning to students. Some students will "get it" almost immediately. Others will struggle just to get the basic gist. Most will likely fall somewhere between these two bookends of understanding.

This wide range of student understanding requires teachers to continuously take note of how well the class and individual students are responding to instruction. Teachers can't wait until the end of the lesson to gather this kind of feedback; they need to gauge student learning in real time so they can adjust instruction accordingly and immediately. In this chapter, we present five tools that teachers can use to get on-the-spot feedback about what students know and understand:

1. **Because** gives teachers a read on depth of understanding by requiring students to back up their responses with reasons, evidence, and examples.

2. **Calling All Students** provides teachers with a collection of techniques for getting all students to respond to the questions they pose during class.

3. **Questioning in Style** shows teachers how they can use four different styles of questions to test different facets of content knowledge.

4. **Speedy Feedback** lets teachers gather real-time feedback about students' grasp of the material from the entire class at once.

5. **Stop, Slow, Go!** empowers students to give on-the-spot feedback about the pace and effectiveness of classroom instruction.

Because

What is it?

A checking-for-understanding technique that requires students to give a "because" for every claim they make and answer they give ("Curious George is a good name for this character *because...*"; "That strategy won't work *because...*"; "Macbeth is a tragic hero *because...*")

What are the benefits of using this tool?

We knew the Because technique was a winner the minute we saw it being used by teachers we work with in Durand Area Schools (Durand, MI).* By asking their students to explain, justify, and elaborate on the things they were saying in class, these teachers were getting immediate feedback about students' understanding of the content being taught. They were also promoting the kind of logical and evidence-based thinking that's a cornerstone of the Common Core State Standards.

What are the basic steps?

1. Tell students that you want them to start giving you a "because" for every answer they give and claim they make. ("I think Jimi Hendrix is the greatest guitar player of all time *because...*")

2. Remind students to do this by writing the word *because* in an easily visible location (e.g., on the board or on a piece of poster paper). If students forget to give you a *because*, prompt them to do so by pointing at the word. For example:

> *Teacher:* Is the solution on the board correct?
>
> *Student:* No. [Teacher points at the word *because* to remind the student to continue talking.]
>
> *Student:* Because you forgot to follow the order of operations.

3. Use students' responses to gauge their understanding of the material and their ability to support a claim with evidence, reasons, and examples. Respond accordingly.

---

*The Because technique was initially developed by Cathy Mitchell, a teacher at Robert Kerr Elementary School in Durand, MI.

How is this tool used in the classroom?

✔ To check for depth of understanding

✔ To get students in the habit of supporting their claims with reasons, evidence, and examples

The examples that follow illustrate some of the many different ways this tool can be used in the classroom. Notice that the tool can be used to target specific Common Core Standards as shown in Examples 1, 2, 4, and 6—and that it works just as well with written assignments (see Examples 1, 4, and 5) as it does with classroom lessons and discussions.

EXAMPLE 1: Ask students to identify and explain flaws in logic or procedures

A high school math teacher posts an incorrectly solved problem on the board at the start of every class period and challenges his students to explain what's wrong. ("This solution is incorrect *because…*")

Note: Besides testing students' grasp of key concepts and procedures, using the tool in this way develops students' ability to identify and explain flaws in logic and reasoning—a goal of Standard 3 from the Common Core Standards for Mathematical Practice.

EXAMPLE 2: Ask students to share and justify their opinions during a discussion

A first-grade teacher uses this tool to have students share and justify their opinions about books they've read. Sometimes she does it via classroom discussions (see sample dialog below); at other times, she addresses Common Core Writing Standard W.1.1 by having students present and support their opinions in writing.

Teacher:	What did you think of *Alexander and the Terrible, Horrible, No Good, Very Bad Day*?
Student:	I liked it.
Teacher:	*Because?*
Student:	*Because* it reminded me of me.
Teacher:	*Because?*
Student:	*Because* I once had a bad day like that.
Teacher:	Anything else?
Student:	I also liked the book *because* the pictures were funny.

EXAMPLE 3: Check for understanding during a lecture

A high school biology teacher used the tool to check for understanding during a lecture.

Teacher:	Does everyone agree with John that DNA and RNA are more similar than different?
Student 1:	I agree *because* they both have sugar-phosphate backbones. And *because* they both carry genetic information.
Student 2:	Another reason to agree is *because* three of the four nitrogenous bases in DNA and RNA are the same.
Student 3:	I disagree *because* they have different sugars (deoxyribose vs. ribose), bases (uracil vs. thymine), and functions.

EXAMPLE 4: Check for understanding at the end of an instructional episode

A second-grade teacher designed the worksheet below to test her students' understanding of critical shape attributes and to address Standard 7 from the Common Core Standards for Mathematical Practice ("look for and make use of structure").

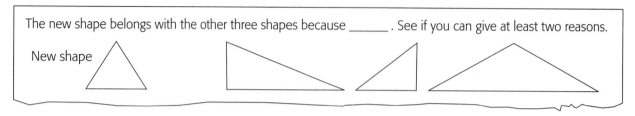

The new shape belongs with the other three shapes because _____ . See if you can give at least two reasons.

New shape

EXAMPLE 5: Check for understanding on a test

A computer science teacher often includes "because" questions on his end-of-unit tests. One of these questions and a student's response is shown here:

Question 6: Why might someone argue that Linux is better than the more commonly used operating systems that we've discussed? Give at least four reasons.

Because Linux is free to obtain.

Because Linux has fewer security issues (viruses, spyware, adware).

Because open-source software is a major advantage. You can use and modify the source code.

Because there's a large community of users constantly adding and improving programs.

EXAMPLE 6: Test students' reading comprehension

A team of elementary teachers uses the Because tool to test students' understanding of literary and informational texts. After reading (or having students read) a designated text, these teachers pose different kinds of checking-for-understanding questions and have students support their responses with specific examples from the text. They vary the kinds of questions that they ask to test different dimensions of comprehension and address different Common Core Reading Standards (see below for two examples; the specific standards being addressed in each case are noted in parentheses).

Teacher: We just read two fables from different cultures. How are these fables similar? (RL.2.9)

Student 1: They are similar *because* they both have animals as their main characters.

Student 2: They are similar *because* the animal you don't expect to win ends up winning.

Student 3: They are similar *because* they teach you the same lesson.

Teacher: Does the author of this article present a convincing argument that coral reefs are in trouble? (RI.4.7, RI.4.8)

Student 1: Yes, *because* the graph shows that reefs are disappearing at an alarming rate—twice as fast as rainforests!

Student 2: Yes, *because* the article shows pictures of what the reefs look like now vs. what they looked like before.

Calling All Students

What is it?

A collection of techniques for getting *all* students—not just the usual hand-raisers—to respond to the checking-for-understanding questions that we pose in our classrooms

What are the benefits of using this tool?

Imagine you've just posed a question to see how well students have understood what you've taught. Which students are raising their hands to respond? If you're like most teachers, you can probably rattle off your hand-raisers by name—and you probably call on them quite often to keep things moving in your classroom. But if we expect to get a true reading on student understanding, we need to call on *all* our students, not just the ones who are eager to contribute. This tool helps by describing a variety of techniques for increasing student involvement during classroom questioning sessions. By using these techniques, we can get a more complete picture of student comprehension and create a classroom environment where every student's voice is heard.

What are the basic steps?

1. Check for understanding while you're teaching by posing a variety of content-related questions.

2. Pause for at least three seconds after posing a question so that students have time to think. Count to three in your head, and don't call on anyone before time is up!

3. When it's time to call on someone, use one or more of the Response Techniques described on p. 66. After a student responds, wait another few seconds before replying.

4. Vary the Response Techniques that you use, both within a single lesson and throughout the year.

How is this tool used in the classroom?

✔ To check for understanding as instruction is happening

✔ To engage all students in the process of answering classroom questions

🌀 Teacher Talk

→ Resist the temptation to call on anyone or respond before time is up (Steps 2 and 3). Providing these few seconds of "wait time" may feel uncomfortable at first, but the payoff is worth it. Among other things, wait time can increase the length, quality, and logic of students' responses—and boost participation, attentiveness, and confidence (Rowe, 1986).

→ If you're looking to diversify your usual questioning repertoire, check out the Questioning in Style tool (pp. 67–71).

Response Techniques

Give Me a Hand

Call on students who raise their hands.

Random Calling

Instead of calling on students who raise their hands, call on students at random.

One option: Write each student's name on an index card or popsicle stick and randomly pull cards/sticks to determine who will answer each question. To make things more fun and interesting for students, add your own name into the mix. If your card or stick is pulled, you have to respond instead of them.

Student Calling

Whoever answers a question gets to call on a classmate to answer the next question.

Whip

Call on a group of students rather than calling on a single student (e.g., students wearing yellow or students in the front row). Have each student in the group share an idea and/or add to the previous student's response.

Note: To keep things moving, some teachers limit each student's response to a single idea. Others use a "buzz" sound to signal that one student should stop and the next should start.

Numbered Heads Together (Kagan, 1989/1990)

Before starting your lesson, organize students into teams of four and assign each team member a number from one to four. Whenever you ask a question during your lesson, give students time to develop a response as a team. Then call out a number between one and four, ask the students with that number to stand up, and select one of the "standing students" to share his response with the class. If needed, invite one or more students with the same number to elaborate on the previous student's response.

Surveying

To get a response from everyone at the same time, survey the class using one of the Speedy Feedback Methods described on p. 73:

- Whiteboards
- Letter Cards/Clickers
- Hand Signals
- Word Cards

Questioning in Style

What is it?

A questioning technique that uses four different styles of questions to deepen and test students' thinking about critical content—and keep different styles of learners engaged

What are the benefits of using this tool?

Asking students questions and evaluating their responses can be an effective strategy for monitoring comprehension. Because no one style of question can give us a complete picture of what students know and understand, it's important to vary the kinds of questions that we pose in our classrooms. This tool helps us broaden our questioning repertoires by identifying four different styles of questions that we should be asking regularly.

What are the basic steps?

1. Familiarize yourself with the four different styles of questions described below.

   MASTERY questions ask students to *remember* (facts, formulas, definitions, procedures).

   UNDERSTANDING questions ask students to *reason* (analyze, explain, justify with evidence).

   SELF-EXPRESSIVE questions ask students to *create* (similes, predictions, solutions, alternatives).

   INTERPERSONAL questions ask students to *relate* (connect with the content on a personal level).

2. Familiarize students with the four different styles of questions. Explain that each type of question will require them to use a different but equally valuable style of thinking.

3. Generate all four styles of questions about a topic or text that you plan to teach (use the Question Stem Menu on p. 69 as a reference). Use the planning form on p. 70 to record your questions.

4. Pose some or all of these questions during an upcoming lesson. Adjust instruction based on the responses that you receive.

   Note: It's critical to get *all* students (not just the usual hand-raisers) involved in answering your questions. Use the Response Techniques described on p. 66 to help you do this.

5. Survey students at the end of the lesson to determine which styles of questions (remembering reasoning, creating, relating) they're most and least comfortable answering. Help them develop the skills they'll need to answer all four styles of questions successfully.

   Optional: Use the Introduction to Questions in Style handout (www.ThoughtfulClassroom.com/Tools) to help familiarize students with the different styles of questions and how to respond to them.

How is this tool used in the classroom?

✔ To assess student learning in real time and adjust instruction accordingly

✔ To develop and test students' ability to think in different styles

✔ To differentiate instruction and engage different styles of learners

Teachers in all grade levels and content areas use this tool to build different styles of questions into their lessons. Two sets of questions are shown below, and an additional set is available for download at www.ThoughtfulClassroom.com/Tools. (The words that tip you off to each question's style have been italicized for your reference.)

EXAMPLE 1: A first-grade teacher poses different styles of questions during story time to keep her students engaged, check their understanding of what she's read, and target Common Core Reading Standards (in this case, RL.K.6, RL.1.1–3, RL.1.7). The questions that she developed for William Steig's *Sylvester and the Magic Pebble* are shown below.

MASTERY QUESTIONS	INTERPERSONAL QUESTIONS
• William Steig is the author and illustrator of this book. *What* does an author do? *What* does an illustrator do? • Can you *retell* what happened so far in your own words? • *Who* are the main characters in this story?	• *How would you feel* if you were turned into a rock? • *If you were Sylvester*, would you use the pebble again? • How do you think Sylvester's parents are *feeling* in this picture? How can you tell?
UNDERSTANDING QUESTIONS	**SELF-EXPRESSIVE QUESTIONS**
• Is this story more happy or more sad? *Give a reason why* you think so. • Do Sylvester's parents love him? *Explain* how you can tell. Can you *find a specific example* from the book?	• What do you *predict* Sylvester will wish for? • *Can you think of another* (better) wish that Sylvester could have made to escape from the lion?

EXAMPLE 2: Before every lecture, a world history teacher maps out different styles of questions that he can use to check for understanding while teaching. One of his question maps is shown here:

MASTERY QUESTIONS	INTERPERSONAL QUESTIONS
• What is a city-state? *Define* the term and give some examples. • Can you *locate* Sparta on a map? How about Athens? • *Describe* key geographical features of Athens and Sparta.	• Would *you* rather have lived in Athens or Sparta? Would *you feel* the same if you were in *someone else's shoes* (e.g., if you were female, poor, or a slave)? *Share your feelings*. • What do *you* admire about each city-state? Describe an accomplishment, value/belief, institution, etc. • Do *you* see any value in learning about these city-states?
UNDERSTANDING QUESTIONS	**SELF-EXPRESSIVE QUESTIONS**
• *Agree or disagree*: Geography plays a critical role in shaping civilizations. *Give examples* from this or other units. • Does Athens deserve its reputation as the superior city-state? What *evidence* points to yes? What argues no? • How did Athens and Sparta *compare* with regard to views on government, education, the arts, women's rights, etc.?	• *If* one of Athens or Sparta's key geographical features had been different, *how might* the city-state have been different? Pick any feature you want and *speculate*. • Would Sparta have been just as successful *if* it had been a democracy instead of an oligarchy? • Can you *create an original* nickname, motto, or symbol for either city-state that captures the essence of that state?

Question Stem Menu: Four Different Styles of Questions

MASTERY QUESTIONS
ask students to *remember facts and procedures:*

✓ **Recall facts and formulas**

✓ **Observe and describe**

✓ **Locate, organize, or sequence**

✓ **Perform procedures/calculations with accuracy**

✓ **Define, restate, or summarize**

Sample question stems:
- Who? What? When? Where?
- What do you know or remember about __?
- Can you list the key points/facts/details from __?
- What did you see, hear, smell, taste, do?
- What are the characteristics or properties of __?
- Can you put these __ in order based on __?
- What happened first? Second? Third?
- Can you show me how to __?
- Can you describe the formula/procedure for __?
- Can you define, retell, or restate __?
- Can you locate or give an example of __?
- Can you calculate __?

INTERPERSONAL QUESTIONS
ask students to *relate on a personal level:*

✓ **Share their feelings, reactions, and opinions**

✓ **Draw connections to their own lives**

✓ **Assist or advise other people**

✓ **Put themselves in someone else's shoes**

✓ **Consider personal preferences and values**

Sample question stems:
- How did you feel about __? React to __?
- Where do you stand on __?
- What do you think of __'s choice?
- What was most/least __ (interesting, difficult, etc.)?
- How is __ relevant to your own life? To society?
- Have you experienced something like __ before?
- How could you explain __ to someone else?
- How would you advise this person or character?
- How might this look from the perspective of __?
- If you were this person or character, how would you feel? What would you do?
- Which of these __ is most important to you?

UNDERSTANDING QUESTIONS
ask students to *reason, analyze, and explain:*

✓ **Compare and contrast**

✓ **Explain, reason, or understand why**

✓ **Give reasons, evidence, and examples**

✓ **Analyze, interpret, evaluate, or conclude**

✓ **Classify or categorize**

Sample question stems:
- What are the key similarities and/or differences?
- Are __ and __ more similar or different? Why?
- What are the causes and/or effects of __?
- Why __? What is the reason for __? Explain.
- How would you support, prove, or disprove __?
- Do you agree or disagree with __? Why?
- Does __ make sense? Explain your reasoning.
- Do you see any flaws or inconsistencies in __?
- What do you think __ means? Why?
- What can you conclude or infer from __?
- What are the central ideas or themes?
- What connections or patterns do you see?
- What larger category/concept does __ belong to?

SELF-EXPRESSIVE QUESTIONS
ask students to *create and explore possibilities:*

✓ **Speculate (what if?), hypothesize, or predict**

✓ **Generate and explore alternatives**

✓ **Create or design something original**

✓ **Represent concepts visually/symbolically**

✓ **Develop and explore similes**

Sample question stems:
- What if __? What might happen if __?
- How might __?
- Can you make a prediction about __?
- How many ways can you __?
- Can you think of another __ (explanation, solution, ending, strategy, hypothesis)?
- What other perspectives should we consider?
- Can you create or invent an original __?
- Can you put these __ together in a unique way?
- Can you devise a plan/procedure to __?
- What comes to mind when you think of __?
- How can you represent __ visually or symbolically?
- How is __ like a __?

Lesson or unit topic: _____

Questioning in Style Planning Form

MASTERY QUESTIONS
ask students to *remember facts and procedures*:

- ✓ Recall facts and formulas
- ✓ Observe and describe
- ✓ Locate, organize, or sequence
- ✓ Perform procedures/calculations with accuracy
- ✓ Define, restate, or summarize

My questions:

INTERPERSONAL QUESTIONS
ask students to *relate on a personal level*:

- ✓ Share their feelings, reactions, and opinions
- ✓ Draw connections to their own lives
- ✓ Assist or advise other people
- ✓ Put themselves in someone else's shoes
- ✓ Consider personal preferences and values

My questions:

UNDERSTANDING QUESTIONS
ask students to *reason, analyze, and explain*:

- ✓ Compare and contrast
- ✓ Explain, reason, or understand why
- ✓ Give reasons, evidence, and examples
- ✓ Analyze, interpret, evaluate, or conclude
- ✓ Classify or categorize

My questions:

SELF-EXPRESSIVE QUESTIONS
ask students to *create and explore possibilities*:

- ✓ Speculate (what if?), hypothesize, or predict
- ✓ Generate and explore alternatives
- ✓ Create or design something original
- ✓ Represent concepts visually/symbolically
- ✓ Develop and explore similes

My questions:

🌀 Teacher Talk

→ Before using this tool for the first time, assess the "stylishness" of your *existing* questioning repertoire by recording how many of each style of question you ask during a given class period. Notice any patterns? If you favor certain styles over others, aim for a more balanced approach.

→ Aim to incorporate all four styles of questions into written assignments and tests as well as classroom lectures and activities. One way to do this is to create a Comprehension Menu (see pp. 85–87 for details). Another is to create A Test Worth Taking (see pp. 219–222).

→ Prepare students to be successful by modeling the kinds of thinking and responses that different question types require (e.g., show them how to respond successfully to a comparison question).

→ The Questioning in Style framework can be used to develop a variety of Common Core thinking skills (e.g., retelling, comparing, supporting a position with evidence), to target all six categories in the cognitive domain of Bloom's Taxonomy, and to generate the kinds of "deep explanation questions" that studies show can improve academic performance (Pashler et al., 2007). Posing different styles of questions is also a great way to engage the interests and talents of different styles of learners.

→ Style-based questions can be used to do more than check for understanding while teaching. They can be used for a number of different purposes (e.g., to hook students' interest, help students access their prior knowledge, encourage reflection)—and at all stages of the instructional process. The ultimate goal is to pose different styles of questions throughout your lessons/units.

A Unit Blueprint Organizer like the one below can help you achieve this goal.* Use it to map out specific questions that you can ask during each phase of an upcoming unit, and then pose those questions at the appropriate points in the unit. Here is how a math teacher did this for a unit on long division addressing Common Core Standard 6.NS.B.2:

PHASE OF INSTRUCTION	QUESTIONS THAT I WILL ASK DURING THIS PHASE	STYLE
Preparing students for new learning: Establish purpose, spark interest, activate prior knowledge.	*How can you make a complex problem easier to solve?*	*Understanding*
Presenting new learning: Present and help students engage with/acquire the content.	*Watch as I solve these two problems on the board. What are the steps in long division? Describe them.*	*Mastery*
Deepening and reinforcing learning: Help students review, practice, and deepen their learning.	*What happens if you change or add a digit to the divisor or dividend? Experiment. Notice any patterns?*	*Self-Expressive*
Applying and demonstrating learning: Challenge students to demonstrate and apply their learning.	*Two of the long-division problems on the board are incorrect. Can you locate and explain the errors?*	*Understanding*
Reflecting on and celebrating learning: Help students reflect on and celebrate their learning.	*How did you feel about long division at the start of the unit? How do you feel now?*	*Interpersonal*

*To download a blank organizer, visit www.ThoughtfulClassroom.com/Tools. For more on The Thoughtful Classroom's Blueprint Model for lesson and unit design, see *Classroom Curriculum Design: How Strategic Units Improve Instruction and Engage Students in Meaningful Learning* (Silver & Perini, 2010). For more on using different styles of questions throughout the instructional process, see *Questioning Styles and Strategies: How to Use Questions to Engage and Motivate Different Styles of Learners* (Silver Strong & Associates, 2007).

Speedy Feedback

What is it?

A tool that prepares us to teach more effectively by giving us on-the-spot feedback about students' grasp of the material

What are the benefits of using this tool?

If students are struggling, it's better to find out sooner rather than later. With Speedy Feedback, you don't have to wait for end-of-unit test scores to find out how students are doing—you can get this feedback *while* you're teaching, and you can get it from the entire class at once! By alerting you at the first sign of trouble, Speedy Feedback allows you to clarify misconceptions before they take root in students' minds and adjust instruction before students become hopelessly lost. The tool also prepares students to become more proactive and successful learners by getting them in the habit of assessing their understanding of the material as instruction is happening.

What are the basic steps?

1. Familiarize yourself with the four different Speedy Feedback Methods described on p. 73: Whiteboards, Letter Cards/Clickers, Hand Signals, and Word Cards.

2. Decide which method you'll use to assess students' grasp of the material. Explain the method to students and provide them with whiteboards, cards, or electronic clickers if needed.

3. Explain that your goal in gathering feedback is to improve instruction—not to grade or judge.

4. Begin teaching. Stop at various points to ask questions that will help you check your students' understanding of the material.

5. Give students at least three seconds to think after posing a question. Then have them share their answers using whatever feedback method you selected (whiteboards, clickers, etc.).

Optional: Invite students who have different answers to explain their reasoning (don't say who is correct). Encourage everyone to listen and rethink their original answers. Then do a revote.

6. Examine students' responses and adjust instruction accordingly. *Think:* Should I back up and reteach? Give more examples? Ask students who "get it" to help those who don't? Move forward?

7. Take advantage of the fact that Speedy Feedback offers information about every single student in the class:

- Identify individual students who are really struggling and offer them extra assistance. Doing this can help close the gap between low and high achievers.
- Identify students who are excelling and find ways to challenge them. Doing this can keep these students from getting bored and losing motivation.

How is this tool used in the classroom?

✔ To assess students' grasp of the material in real time and adjust instruction accordingly

✔ To have students monitor their understanding of the material as instruction is happening

---

Speedy Feedback Methods

Whiteboards

Before starting a lesson, give each student a whiteboard or pad of paper and a marking pen. Stop at various points in your presentation to ask content-related questions or give students problems to solve. Have students record their responses in large print, show their work if appropriate, and hold up their boards/pads for you to see.

Sample questions: If you have three toys and a friend gives you two more, how many toys will you have?

What word helps us remember the space notes in the treble clef?

If a ball falls freely from rest, how far will it fall in the first two seconds?

Letter Cards/Clickers

Before beginning a lesson, give each student a set of eight index cards labeled *A, B, C, D, True, False, Yes,* and *No.* (If you have access to electronic clickers, use them instead.) Stop at various times throughout your presentation to ask questions (multiple-choice, yes/no, true/false) about the material you've presented. Have students hold up the card that reflects their response or enter a response on their clickers.

Sample questions: Yes or no: Is the solution shown on the board the correct solution to this problem?

True or false: If you translate this sentence into Latin, the underlined words should be *pueri.*

Was that a demonstration of Newton's (a) First, (b) Second, or (c) Third Law of Motion?

Hand Signals

Similar to Letter Cards except that students respond using simple hand signals rather than index cards (e.g., thumbs up/thumbs down instead of yes/no or true/false—or one, two, three, or four fingers up instead of *A, B, C, D*)

Word Cards

Similar to Letter Cards except that students' cards have content-related vocabulary terms printed on them

Example 1: A first-grade teacher used Word Cards as follows to test her students' ability to distinguish long from short vowel sounds (Common Core RF.1.2a): "Do you hear a long sound or a short sound when I say the word 'meet'? Hold up your long card or your short card to show me."

Example 2: Following a unit on animal classification, a teacher read the names of various animals aloud (mouse, frog, snake…) and had students hold up the appropriate "category card"—mammal card, reptile card, amphibian card, etc.

Example 3: An English teacher used Word Cards to help his students review and clarify their understanding of six terms from the previous week's vocabulary list (vivacious, brawny, resourceful, lethargic, altruistic, reserved). After having students write the vocabulary words on index cards—one word per card—he described characters from popular movies and asked students to hold up the word that best described each character. For example:

- No matter how many times James Bond got captured, he always managed to figure out how to escape. He was an extremely ____ guy. (answer = *resourceful*)

- Hugh Jackman worked out for months to develop the muscular, chiseled body that he needed to play Wolverine. By the time cameras rolled, Jackman was one ____ guy. (answer = *brawny*)

Stop, Slow, Go!

What is it?

A tool that provides real-time feedback about the pace and effectiveness of classroom lessons

What are the benefits of using this tool?

Determining how well students are following along during a classroom presentation is important, but it's not always easy. After all, you can't necessarily tell how well students are getting the material just by looking at them—and they're often reluctant to admit when they're confused. The Stop, Slow, Go! tool solves this problem by having students use colored index cards to provide on-the-spot feedback about the pace of instruction (*red* = stop, I'm lost; *yellow* = slow down; *green* = go ahead, I've got this!). The tool also prepares students to be more proactive and successful learners by teaching them to monitor their understanding and speak up when they're confused.

What are the basic steps?

1. Prior to beginning a lesson, give each student three index cards: one red, one yellow, one green.

2. Explain the purpose of the cards (to tell you how well students are following along so that you can adjust instruction accordingly). Then explain the meaning of each color. Use a traffic light analogy to help students remember the color-coding system:

Red card	$\longrightarrow$	STOP and reteach. I'm lost.
Yellow card	$\longrightarrow$	SLOW down. I'm not 100% clear about this.
Green card	$\longrightarrow$	GO forward! I'm understanding things perfectly.

3. Begin your lesson. Stop every few minutes to gather feedback about the pace of instruction and students' grasp of the material. ("How well are you following along? Hold up the appropriate card.")

4. Respond to the feedback that students provide. Adjust the pace of instruction as needed, use probing questions to identify sources of confusion, and review or reteach material that's unclear.

5. Take note of students who are really struggling (red cards up when others have green) so that you can work with them at a later time. Identify high-achieving students as well (green cards up when others have red) so you can think about ways to challenge them.

6. Explain that students should *always* monitor their understanding of new material and speak up or take action if they're confused—not just when they're using this tool, and not just in your class, but all the time.

How is this tool used in the classroom?

✔ To gather real-time feedback about the pace of instruction and students' grasp of the material

✔ To get students in the habit of assessing and monitoring their understanding of the content

EXAMPLE 1: A mathematics teacher used Stop, Slow, Go! cards to help deliver a more effective lecture on integer exponents and their related properties (Common Core 8.EE.A.1). She stopped at regular intervals to check her pace of instruction. ("Too fast, too slow, or just right?") She also checked for understanding by giving students practice problems (e.g., $3^2 \times 3^{-5} = \underline{}$) and asking them to "signal" their level of success. Whenever red and yellow cards outnumbered the green, she stopped to answer questions and clarify points of confusion. To keep her green students engaged, she invited them to help their red and yellow classmates.

EXAMPLE 2: After completing a unit on weather, a third-grade teacher was inspired to replace students' traditional Stop, Slow, Go! cards with weather-themed cards (clear skies, hazy, severe fog). Students used these cards during an end-of-unit review session to give her feedback about which topics to review in depth (severe fog) and which ones to breeze through (clear skies). Students continued to use their "weather cards" long after the weather unit was over since they preferred them to the red, yellow, and green cards they had been using before.

 Teacher Talk

➔ Instead of stopping at various points to ask students how well they're following along, get a constant stream of feedback by having students fold an index card into thirds, tape the edges together to create a triangular prism (make each face a different color: red, yellow, green), and rotate their prisms on their desks throughout a lesson to reflect their comfort level (e.g., red-face forward if they're lost).

➔ Look for other ways to use the tool's color-coding system. If students are working at their seats (alone or in groups), for example, have them place a colored card on their desks to signal that they do (red) or don't (green) need help.

➔ Feel free to change things up. Instead of red, yellow, and green "traffic light cards," for example, create "weather cards" (see Example 2), "cartoon-face cards" (smiles, puzzled looks, frowns), or "windshield cards" like the ones below, which were inspired by the Glass/Bugs/Mud technique (Narvaez & Brimijoin, 2010). If you prefer, you can forgo the index cards entirely and use hand signals instead (e.g., thumbs up, thumbs down, thumbs to the side).

CLEAR

A BIT BUGGY

TOTALLY MUDDY

➔ Talk to students about the importance of admitting when they're confused. If they understand that you're using Stop, Slow, Go! cards to help you teach them more effectively rather than to judge or grade them, they'll be more willing to do this.

How Will I Check for Understanding *After* Presenting New Information?

I know that you believe you understand what you think I said, but I'm not sure you realize that what you heard is not what I meant.

—Robert McCloskey, US State Department spokesman

Instruction should not be a Ouija-boardlike game in which teachers guess about what to do next. Educating kids is far too important for that sort of approach. Rather, instructing students should be a carefully conceived enterprise in which decisions about what to do next are predicated on the best available information. And the best available information about what to do next almost always flows from a determination about what students currently know and can do.

—W. James Popham, *Transformative Assessment*

Teachers need to check for understanding at all stages of the learning process. If the previous chapter was about assessing student understanding in real time and adjusting instruction accordingly, then this chapter is about doing deeper checks for understanding *after* students have acquired new information (also for formative purposes). Assessing learning more deeply when an instructional episode or lesson comes to an end is essential because real-time assessments serve only as snapshots, and only so much information about student learning can be obtained from a snapshot. To get a better, more nuanced read on what students know, understand, and are able to do, teachers need assessment techniques that ask students to reflect on what they've learned and begin to shape that learning into meaningful forms, such as summaries and explanations.

In this chapter, we present eleven tools that are ideal for gathering quality information about student learning after an instructional episode has come to its natural conclusion and then using that information to inform instruction:

1. **3-2-1** assesses students' capacity to summarize and personalize their learning experiences by asking them to identify three things they've learned, two questions they have, and one big idea.

2. **Assess & ASSIST** offers teachers six simple techniques for addressing gaps in understanding that they uncover during the assessment process.

3. **Association Triangles** tests students' ability to make and explain connections between key terms or concepts.

4. **Clear or Cloudy?** gives students a fun and simple format for indicating what is clear to them and what is cloudy.

5. **Comprehension Menus** uses four distinct styles of questions to test different dimensions of comprehension.

6. **Defining Knowledge** gives teachers a variety of ways to test students' grasp of key terms and concepts.

7. **Explaining Solutions** helps teachers develop and assess students' problem-solving skills and ability to explain their thinking in writing.

8. **Memory Box** asks students to review what they've learned about a specific topic and then fill a box with everything they can remember about the topic.

9. **Most Valuable Point (MVP)** tells teachers whether students have gotten the big idea by asking students to identify and elaborate on the most important point from a lesson or text.

10. **Question Quarry** gives students a safe and anonymous forum for asking questions about what they've learned, thereby helping teachers identify and address areas of confusion.

11. **Reading for Meaning** teaches and assesses critical reading skills, especially the ability to support a position with textual evidence.

3-2-1

What is it?

A tool that tells us what students are getting out of their learning experiences by having them record *three* things they learned, *two* questions they have, and *one* main idea

What are the benefits of using this tool?

Checking for understanding and adjusting instruction accordingly are two of the most important things we can do as educators. Because it's not necessary or feasible to do in-depth checks all the time, it's important to have quick-check tools like 3-2-1 in our repertoires. In a matter of minutes, 3-2-1 gives us specific feedback about what students have learned, what they have questions about, and whether they've grasped the big picture. It benefits students as well since the process of recording facts, questions, and big ideas helps them review and synthesize what they've learned.

What are the basic steps?

1. Present information to students via lecture, video, reading assignment, etc.

2. Help students review and synthesize what they learned by having them record the following:

THREE key facts $\longrightarrow$ "Three important things that I learned are…"

TWO questions $\longrightarrow$ "Two questions that I have are…"

ONE main idea $\longrightarrow$ "The main idea of today's lesson seemed to be…"

3. Review students' responses. Use what you learn to gauge the effectiveness of your lesson. (Did students remember the key facts? Get the big picture? What kinds of questions do they have?)

4. Revisit any material that students missed, misunderstood, or asked questions about.

🌓 Teacher Talk

➔ Adjust the 3-2-1 stems as needed to fit your content and goals; use Example 3 as a model.

➔ Use students' questions to identify areas of interest as well as areas of confusion. Address interest-driven questions during future lessons (a good strategy for boosting engagement) or encourage students to pursue these questions on their own.

➔ When using this tool with very young students, you can have them complete the 3-2-1 stems as a class (students speak their ideas aloud, you help refine and record them). If students aren't ready to identify main ideas on their own, use questions and prompts to help them.

How is this tool used in the classroom?

✔ To get immediate feedback about the effectiveness of classroom lessons

✔ To assess students' understanding of key facts and main ideas

✔ To have students review, synthesize, and demonstrate what they've learned

EXAMPLE 1: A world history teacher used 3-2-1 at the start of class to see how well her students had understood and remembered the key points from the previous day's lesson on early cave art.

Three facts that I learned during today's lesson:

Thousands of years ago, artists painted on caves, not paper.
Cave paintings can show us what life was like in the past.
Cave paintings are both realistic and symbolic.

Two questions that I have:

Why did people make these paintings? ←
What did the artists use for paint?

Great question, Paul! We don't actually know the answer, but we can discuss some possibilities in class.

The *single* most important point of today's lesson seemed to be:

You can learn a lot about people by examining their art.

EXAMPLE 2: A kindergarten teacher used 3-2-1 to check in on student learning during a science unit on observation and pattern-finding. After helping students complete the 3-2-1 stems as a class (they spoke their ideas aloud), she helped them design experiments to investigate their two questions.

---

3 things we observed:	• You can see the sun in the daytime. At night, you can see the moon. • The sun looks like a circle. • The sun moves around during the day.
2 questions we have:	• If we watched the moon, would it move around too? • Can you ever see the moon in the daytime?
1 main idea:	• You can learn a lot about something by watching it carefully.

EXAMPLE 3: A US history teacher often uses 3-2-1 to keep students engaged during the last few minutes of class when they'd otherwise be packing up and tuning out. The writing stems that she used to help her students review and demonstrate what they had learned by watching a video about Abraham Lincoln are shown below. (Note the creative way that she modified the traditional 3-2-1 writing stems to fit her subject material and goals. Her "2" stem, for example, was designed to help identify topics for future discussion.)

The **3** most important events in Abraham Lincoln's life were…

2 aspects of Lincoln's life or presidency that I'd like to learn more about are…

If I were Lincoln, the **1** thing that I'd want people to remember me for would be…

EXAMPLE 4: The big-picture purpose of a science and technology teacher's lesson was to have students recognize that advances in technology can have positive *and* negative effects on people and society. After reviewing the "one main idea" portion of his students' 3-2-1 assignments, however, this teacher realized that most of his students had missed this idea entirely. (Their main ideas focused solely on the *positive* aspects of technological advances.) For this reason, he revisited the material from his lesson the following day, but used a different approach to try and get his message across.

Assess & ASSIST

What is it?

A tool that presents six simple techniques for addressing gaps in understanding (one technique for each letter in the ASSIST acronym)

What are the benefits of using this tool?

In "The Rest of the Story," Thomas Guskey (2007/2008) notes that "formative assessments alone do little to improve student learning or teaching quality. What really counts is what happens *after* the assessments… [and] unfortunately, many educators today overlook this vital aspect of formative assessment" (p. 28). Assess & ASSIST helps us addresses this all-important "rest of the story" by outlining simple techniques for giving students the help they need when assessments reveal gaps in understanding.

What are the basic steps?

1. Assess students' grasp of the material using any method you want: quiz, homework, etc.

2. Review students' work. Use one or more of the approaches below to ASSIST students who need help.

   Alternative instructional approaches and/or materials: Reteach the content using a different method and/or materials than you did the first time around (e.g., use a hands-on activity instead of a lecture or let students read firsthand accounts of a journey instead of reading about it in a textbook).

   Stations and centers: Set up stations where students can go to learn more about the given topic or practice the relevant skills. When possible, include hands-on activities and multimedia resources.

   Self-correction: Have students examine their graded assignments and take steps to improve their performance (e.g., review and practice the types of problems they got wrong; use a rubric, checklist, or written feedback to take their work to the next level; or revisit content they missed).

   Independent work: Accommodate students with different needs and abilities by creating customized packets of materials (reading materials, assignments, activities) that they can use on their own.

   Strategy instruction: Model specific strategies that students can use to improve their performance (e.g., note-taking strategies, study strategies, strategies for writing a strong topic sentence).

   Tutoring (teacher-student or peer-peer): Work with students one-on-one or in small groups. Invite students who have already mastered the material to coach and support students who haven't.

3. Reassess students' grasp of the material to determine whether the ASSISTance you've provided has had a positive impact. If it hasn't, select and try a different approach.

How is this tool used in the classroom?

✔ To check for understanding and respond accordingly

Association Triangles

What is it?

A tool that assesses big-picture understanding by challenging students to explain the connections between important terms or concepts

What are the benefits of using this tool?

Checking if students can explain how key concepts and terms relate to one another is an important part of checking for understanding. We know this, yet we often test students' knowledge of isolated facts, terms, and ideas instead of asking students to make these bigger-picture connections. This tool puts the focus back on the big picture by challenging students to explain the relationships between three things they've learned about. Asking students to make these kinds of connections serves both to develop and test their depth of understanding.

What are the basic steps?

1. Select three important terms from a lesson, unit, or reading assignment. Note that "terms" can be anything from concepts to events to real or fictional characters (pictures are also fine).

   Other options: Give students a list of terms to choose from (have them pick three) or invite them to choose their own terms from a given topic or text.

2. Instruct students to draw a triangle on a piece of paper and record one term on each of its points.

3. Ask students to explain how adjacent terms on the triangle relate to one another. Have students record their explanations along the side of the triangle that connects the two terms.

4. Challenge students to think about how *all three* terms are connected. (Do they share a common theme? Fit into a bigger picture?) Have them record their ideas in the middle of the triangle.

5. Invite students to share and refine their ideas with a partner and/or as a class. Use students' responses, as well as their completed triangles, to gauge their understanding of key relationships and their sense of the big picture. Help them fill in any gaps.

🎯 Teacher Talk

→ To have students draw connections between two terms instead of three, use Vocabulary Bridges rather than Association Triangles. (Draw a picture of a bridge, put one term on either side, and have students explain the connection across the length of the bridge.) For four terms, use the Four-Corners variation. (List each term on the point of a square and have students connect the points.)

→ This tool can be used to target various Common Core State Standards. To target Reading Anchor Standard 5, for example, put individual lines/stanzas/scenes from an assigned text on the points and ask students to explain how these textual elements relate to each other and to the text as a whole. For other ideas, see Examples 1 and 2.

How is this tool used in the classroom?

✔ To check (and have students check) their understanding of key concepts and ideas

The examples below show how Association Triangles can be used in different grade levels and content areas. Additional examples are available at www.ThoughtfulClassroom.com/Tools.

EXAMPLE 1: A math triangle

A fourth-grade teacher designed this triangle to develop and test his students' ability to reason with shapes and their attributes (Common Core 4.G.A.2, building on 3.G.A.1).

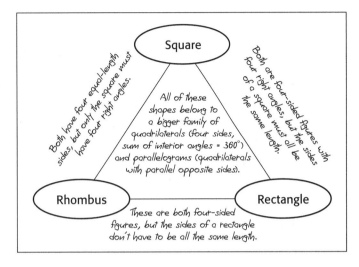

EXAMPLE 2: A literature triangle

A third-grade teacher used this triangle to see how well his students had understood the plot and central message of a fable (Common Core RL.3.2).

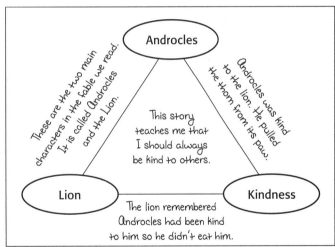

EXAMPLE 3: A history triangle

A history teacher had her students complete Association Triangles like this one for homework throughout a unit on the American Revolution. Her goal was to reinforce and test students' understanding of key people, events, documents, and themes.

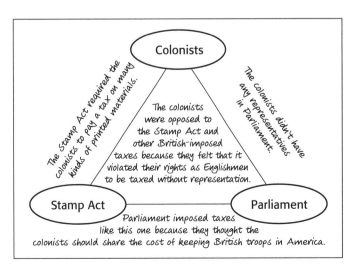

Clear or Cloudy?

What is it?

A checking-for-understanding tool that tells us what students are *clear* about and what's still *cloudy* (adapted from Tomlinson, 2010)

What are the benefits of using this tool?

In order to teach our students effectively, we need them to identify and tell us about the things that are confusing them. This tool encourages them to do exactly that by putting a fun and friendly spin on the usual self-assessment process. Instead of simply telling us what they do and don't get, students "report" their level of understanding using weather terminology. (What is clear to me? What is cloudy or hazy?) Linking an abstract process like self-assessment to something concrete and familiar like the weather not only ups the fun factor, it also makes the process more understandable for students.

What are the basic steps?

1. Teach students new material using any format you want (lecture, reading assignment, lab, etc.).

2. Ask students to assess their understanding of what they learned. Have them create individual "weather reports" (oral or written) by describing what's clear to them and what's cloudy.

3. Review students' weather reports. Think about things you could do to make the cloudy areas more clear. Challenge students to do the same.

Optional: List the cloudy points on the board so you remember to address them while teaching.

How is this tool used in the classroom?

✔ To gather information about students' understanding of recently taught material

This tool can be used at any point in an instructional sequence. Use it *at the start of class* to determine an entry-point for instruction. (How well did students understand the previous day's material? Where should I begin today's lesson? What if anything do I need to review?) Use it *during class* to check for understanding and adjust instruction accordingly. And use it *before an end-of-unit test* to determine what you and your students need to review.

EXAMPLE: Here is a second grader's report from the middle of a measurement unit addressing Common Core Standards 2.MD.A.1 and 2.MD.A.3:

What do you understand clearly?	**What's still a bit cloudy?**
How to measure things with a ruler	How to estimate the length of something

Variation: Target Progress

Use this tool with learning *targets* rather than *topics*. Have students identify areas where they've made clear progress toward the targets and cloudy areas that are standing in their way.

Comprehension Menus

What is it?

A checking-for-understanding tool that weaves four different styles of comprehension questions into a single, easy-to-use framework

What are the benefits of using this tool?

Comprehension Menus provide a simple but effective way to check the depth and breadth of students' content knowledge. Unlike some assessment tools, which only test a single dimension of comprehension, Comprehension Menus test four. They do this by asking students four distinct styles of questions about critical topics and texts: remembering questions, reasoning questions, creating questions, and relating questions.

What are the basic steps?

1. Familiarize yourself with the four styles of questions that appear on a Comprehension Menu:

    MASTERY questions ask students to *remember* (facts, formulas, definitions, procedures).

    UNDERSTANDING questions ask students to *reason* (analyze, explain, justify with evidence).

    SELF-EXPRESSIVE questions ask students to *create* (similes, predictions, solutions, alternatives).

    INTERPERSONAL questions ask students to *relate* (connect with the content on a personal level).

2. Generate at least one question in each style about a topic, text, or skill you plan to teach. Use the Question Stem Menu on p. 69 to help you.

3. Create a Comprehension Menu by recording your questions in four-box format (use the examples on pp. 86–87 as models).

    Optional: Introduce each question with a descriptive word/phrase that reflects its style as shown in the examples. This will help students understand and focus on the type of thinking each question is asking them to do.

4. Have students respond to all the questions on the menu, either during class or for homework.

    Tip: When using this tool with very young students, you can read the questions aloud and have students respond orally or using simple words/pictures. A sample primary-grade menu is available for download at www.ThoughtfulClassroom.com/Tools.

5. Review students' responses to identify any misconceptions or gaps in understanding, and address these gaps during future lessons. If you want, you can have students revise their initial responses.

6. Survey students to see which styles of questions they felt good about and which were challenging.

7. Take note of the types of questions that caused students problems. Teach students skills and strategies that can help them answer these types of questions more successfully in the future (e.g., strategies for responding to comparison questions).

How is this tool used in the classroom?

✔ To assess students' comprehension of critical topics and texts

✔ To engage and assess different styles of thinking and differentiate assessment by learning style

Comprehension Menus can be used in all content areas/grade levels to test students' understanding of different types of texts (picture books, plays, articles, etc.). They can also be used with non-text-based materials like lectures and activities. The examples that follow, and the additional examples that are available for download (www.ThoughtfulClassroom.com/Tools), illustrate this versatility.

Note: Introductory words that reflect each question's style have been added in italics to illustrate the optional portion of Step 3.

EXAMPLE 1: A Comprehension Menu for a *book*: Chapter 1 of *My Brother Sam Is Dead*

MASTERY QUESTIONS	INTERPERSONAL QUESTIONS
State the facts: What are Sam and his father arguing about? What is Sam's position? What is his father's?	*Connect personally:* What are some things the author did to get you personally interested in the story or the characters?
UNDERSTANDING QUESTIONS	**SELF-EXPRESSIVE QUESTIONS**
Take a position: Who makes the better case: Sam or his father? Explain using evidence from the text.	*Explore this simile:* How is an argument like a puzzle?

EXAMPLE 2: A Comprehension Menu for a *textbook chapter* on plate tectonics

MASTERY QUESTIONS	INTERPERSONAL QUESTIONS
Locate and define: Identify the critical vocabulary terms that were introduced in this chapter. What do they mean? Define them in your own words.	*Connect personally:* Why should people care about plate tectonics? How is the motion of the earth's plates relevant to you and people around the world?
UNDERSTANDING QUESTIONS	**SELF-EXPRESSIVE QUESTIONS**
Make a case: If a classmate didn't believe in the existence of continental drift, what evidence could you present to convince him or her?	*Make a prediction:* What will a world map look like five million years from now if the earth's plates continue to move?

EXAMPLE 3: A Comprehension Menu for a high school mathematics *lecture* on arithmetic and geometric sequences (working toward Common Core Standard HSF-BF.A.2)

MASTERY QUESTIONS	INTERPERSONAL QUESTIONS
Define and give examples: How would you define an arithmetic sequence? A geometric sequence? Give two examples of each type and one example of a sequence that is neither arithmetic nor geometric.	*Reflect personally:* With regard to sequences, has your learning process been more arithmetic or geometric? Why do you feel that way?
UNDERSTANDING QUESTIONS	**SELF-EXPRESSIVE QUESTIONS**
Analyze and explain: For each question, answer *sometimes*, *always*, or *never*. Then explain your choice. • If the first two terms of an arithmetic sequence are positive, how often will the third term be positive? • If the first two terms of a geometric sequence are negative, how often will the third term be negative?	*Create something original:* The familiar decimal 0.666… can be represented as the decimal sequence 0.6, 0.06, 0.006, 0.0006, … or as 0.66, 0.0066, 0.000066, … Create two other repeating decimals and represent each as a decimal sequence. (Be as creative as you can!) Show that each sequence is geometric.

SOURCE: Adapted from *Math Tools, Grades 3–12: 60+ Ways to Build Mathematical Practices, Differentiate Instruction, and Increase Student Engagement* (p. 210), by H. F. Silver, J. R. Brunsting, T. Walsh, and E. J. Thomas, 2012, Thousand Oaks, CA: Corwin Press. © 2012 by Silver Strong & Associates. Adapted with permission.

EXAMPLE 4: A Comprehension Menu for two *primary documents* (excerpts from the Gulf of Tonkin Resolution and the War Powers Act)

MASTERY QUESTIONS	INTERPERSONAL QUESTIONS
Summarize the facts: What was the impetus for each resolution? What was the goal of each resolution?	*Connect personally:* Pretend that you're a senator who voted for the Gulf of Tonkin Resolution nine years ago. What thoughts and feelings have now convinced you to vote for the War Powers Act?
UNDERSTANDING QUESTIONS	**SELF-EXPRESSIVE QUESTIONS**
Make a comparison: How are these documents similar and different? Consider content, format, language, etc.	*Speculate:* How might the way that Congress and the president approach war/international conflicts be different if the War Powers Act hadn't passed?

EXAMPLE 5: A Comprehension Menu for a *painting*

MASTERY QUESTIONS	INTERPERSONAL QUESTIONS
Observe and describe: What details do you notice in this painting?	*Share your feelings:* How does this painting make you feel?
UNDERSTANDING QUESTIONS	**SELF-EXPRESSIVE QUESTIONS**
Interpret and justify: What do you think the artist was trying to say with this painting? Why do you think so?	*Speculate:* Pick a compositional element that you think is particularly strong (symmetry, balance, etc.). Now imagine the painting without it. How might the loss of this element affect the painting?

SOURCE: Adapted from *Task Rotation: Strategies for Differentiating Activities and Assessments by Learning Style* (p. 54) by H. F. Silver, J. W. Jackson, and D. R. Moirao, 2011, Alexandria, VA: ASCD. © 2011 by Silver, Strong, and Associates. Adapted with permission.

🔴 Teacher Talk

➔ By including four different styles of questions, the Comprehension Menu framework allows all styles of learners to shine and grow (*shine* when answering questions that play to their strengths, *grow* when responding to questions that push them outside their normal comfort zones).

➔ Teach students to use this tool independently (e.g., "Check your understanding of newly learned material by asking yourself all four styles of questions after a reading assignment or lecture").

➔ Comprehension Menus work well with the different types of literary and informational texts called for by the Common Core State Standards (e.g., short stories, speeches, historical documents, articles). When generating a Comprehension Menu for a written text, it may be helpful to think about the different styles of questions in this way:

> **MASTERY QUESTIONS should ask students to "read the lines."**
>   Focus on the literal: Describe, define, summarize the facts (who, what, when, where), or find examples of __.
>
> **UNDERSTANDING QUESTIONS should ask students to "read between the lines."**
>   Go beyond the literal: What can you infer or conclude? What is the meaning of __? Why __? Explain __.
>
> **SELF-EXPRESSIVE QUESTIONS should ask students to "read beyond the lines."**
>   Explore possibilities: What if __? How might __? How is __ like a __? What do you predict will __?
>
> **INTERPERSONAL QUESTIONS should ask students to "respond to the lines."**
>   Personalize: What did you think or feel? If you were __, what would you feel or do? Can you relate to __?

Defining Knowledge

What is it?

A collection of simple but effective ways to test students' grasp of critical concepts/terms

What are the benefits of using this tool?

Imagine two students who've been asked to define "courage." One gives a dictionary definition that he's memorized. The other tells a story about her great-grandfather and how he survived for three years in a concentration camp. Who appears to have the better understanding of what courage means? The truth is, there are many ways to exhibit deep understanding of a concept—but none of them involves restating a dictionary definition. The Defining Knowledge tool provides a wealth of ways to assess students' knowledge of important terms and concepts: comparisons, analogies, icons, stories, and many more. By asking students to go beyond dictionary definitions, it not only deepens and tests their grasp of key concepts, it also develops their critical thinking skills.

What are the basic steps?

1. Select a critical term or concept that students have learned about (e.g., appeasement, plagiarism, linear equation, pointillism, friendship).

2. Deepen and test students' understanding of this concept by having them complete two or more of the tasks below. Tell students which tasks to complete or let them pick tasks that interest them.

- Define the concept in your own words.
- Create or find examples of the concept.
- List the critical attributes of the concept.
- Create a simile that shows your understanding of the concept (concept X is like ___ because ___).
- Write or find a story that exemplifies or illustrates the meaning of the concept.
- Draw a symbol, icon, or sketch that captures the essence of the concept. Explain your drawing.
- Explain how our understanding or definition of the concept has changed over time.
- Compare or contrast the concept to a similar concept.
- Explain the function or significance of the concept.
- Describe conflicting views about the meaning of the concept.
- Classify the concept. What larger class does it belong to? What other items are in that class?
- Discuss the etymology/historical origins of the term/concept.
- Create a sketch/diagram that shows how the concept relates to another concept from the unit.
- Create a cinquain (five line poem) about the concept; see Example 1 for details.
- Create a Concept Definition Map; see Example 4 for details.

Note: Tasks can be assigned for homework or classwork (one option is to set up stations where students go to complete the different kinds of tasks); they can also be used as quiz/test items.

3. Review students' work. (If you want, have students share, compare, and revise their work with a classmate first.) Address misconceptions and review or reteach the concept if needed.

How is this tool used in the classroom?

✔ To develop and test students' understanding of critical terms and concepts

EXAMPLE 1: At the end of a lesson on predators and prey, a third-grade teacher had students illustrate their understanding of the predator-prey relationship by creating and explaining a simple sketch. She also had them show what they knew about predators or prey (their choice) by writing a five-line poem called a cinquain. One student's sketch and another student's cinquain are shown here:

CINQUAIN	
Original term/concept	Predator
Two adjectives	Hungry and carnivorous
Three "ing" verbs	Tracking, capturing, eating
Four-word sentence or phrase	It hunts for prey.
Word that has same meaning as (or relates to) original term	Grrrrrrrr!

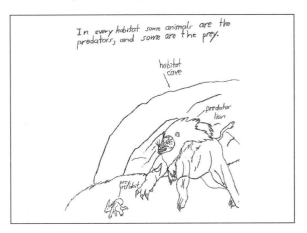

EXAMPLE 2: Middle school students demonstrated their understanding of the "colony" concept by creating a simile (below) and giving examples (not shown).

A colony is like a child because a colony depends on a country just like a child depends on a parent. Both colonies and children are younger and often rebel when they grow up.

EXAMPLE 3: Here's how a second grader explained "freedom" using words and pictures:

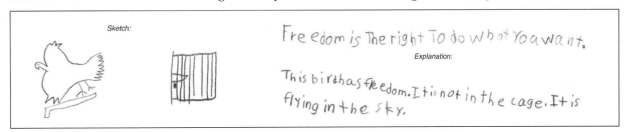

Sketch:

Freedom is The right To do what You want.

Explanation:

This bird has freedom. It is not in the cage. It is flying in the sky.

EXAMPLE 4: Concept Definition Maps (adapted from Schwartz & Raphael, 1985) combine three Defining Knowledge tasks in one. As shown in this example for alkali metals, they require students to *identify a concept's critical attributes* (right boxes), *classify it into a larger category* (top box), and *give examples and non-examples* (left-most box and circle, respectively).

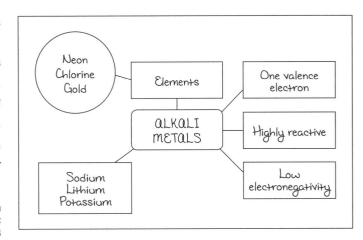

SOURCE: Other than the cinquain, the student work in Examples 1–3 is from *Word Works: Cracking Vocabulary's CODE* (pp. 38–39) by Silver Strong & Associates. © 2008 by Thoughtful Education Press. Reprinted with permission.

Explaining Solutions

What is it?

A tool that prepares us to assess and improve students' problem-solving skills by having students explain their solutions in writing (What did I do and why?)

What are the benefits of using this tool?

We often assess students' problem-solving skills by checking the accuracy of their final answers. But final answers don't tell us about the steps or strategies that students used to get them—and we can't check for understanding or give students feedback without having that kind of information. This tool lets us see what's going on in students' minds as they solve assigned problems so that behind-the-scenes thinking can be assessed and glitches rooted out. It also prepares students to handle the explain-your-thinking items that are so common on today's assessment tests by teaching them how to convert their internal thinking processes into precise and well-articulated explanations.

What are the basic steps?

1. Present students with a problem to solve. Instruct them to read the problem carefully, consider strategies for solving it, generate a solution, and show their work.

2. Ask students to write a paragraph explaining what they did to solve the problem. (What did I do first, second, third, etc.?)

Tip: Before students begin working, review transitional words and phrases that they can use to connect their ideas and highlight the logical organization of their thinking (e.g., first, next, after that, for this reason, therefore, finally, with the exception of, similarly, in conclusion).

3. Have students review their work and revise it if needed. Remind them to evaluate the soundness of their strategies and solutions as well as the clarity and precision of their explanations.

Optional: Scaffold this process by giving students specific questions to think about. For example: Does my solution make sense? Did I describe all the steps? Are they in the right order? Did I connect them using appropriate transitional words? Are there any terms/ideas that need defining?

4. Review students' explanations to gain insight into their thinking processes. Use written feedback, one-on-one conferences, or future lessons to address strengths and glitches in students' thinking.

5. Instruct students to use the tool's "ANSWERing process" on their own (e.g., on standardized tests). Use the acronym below to help them remember the steps, and give them lots of practice using it.

> **A**nalyze the problem.
>
> **N**ail down a strategy.
>
> **S**olve the problem.
>
> **W**rite out the steps.
>
> **E**valuate for logic and clarity.
>
> **R**evise as needed.

How is this tool used in the classroom?

✔ To assess (and help students assess) the soundness of their problem-solving strategies

✔ To help students communicate their problem-solving processes and solutions with precision

EXAMPLE 1: A second-grade teacher posed the following problem to her students:

> You want to make candy-filled nests for three friends. You have 14 chocolate eggs and you want to put the same number of eggs in each nest. How many eggs will each nest contain? Will there be any eggs left over? If so, how many?

She instructed her students to draw the problem, solve it, and explain their solutions in writing. One student's work is shown at the right.

A Division Problem
$14 \div 3 = 4$ R2

First I drew three nest. Next I counted 14 eggs. Then I put some eggs in each nest until there were no more eggs, but if they are not equal, then I take away 2. Then I counted the eggs and the answer was 4 and the remainder was 2. That is how I got the answer.

EXAMPLE 2: A chemistry teacher used this tool to assess his students' understanding of the concepts and procedures involved in balancing chemical equations. To do this, he had them write out a complete explanation for *one* of their homework problems. One student's work is shown below.

The problem that I picked asks me to balance this chemical equation: $C_3H_8 + O_2 \rightarrow H_2O + CO_2$

This means that I'll need to have the same number of atoms of each element on both sides.

First, I box the molecules so I don't change their formulas by mistake: $\boxed{C_3H_8} + \boxed{O_2} \rightarrow \boxed{H_2O} + \boxed{CO_2}$. Next, I count how many atoms of each element are on each side. When I do this, I get 3C, 8H, and 2O on the left and 1C, 2H, and 3O on the right. Because there are 3 times as many C on the left as right, I multiply the CO_2 on the right by 3 like this ($\boxed{C_3H_8} + \boxed{O_2} \rightarrow \boxed{H_2O} + 3\boxed{CO_2}$) to get the same number of carbon atoms on both sides (3). Next, I recount my atoms and get 3C, 8H, and 2O on the left and 3C, 2H, and 7O on the right. Since there are 8H on the left and 2 on the right, I multiply the water on the right by 4 to bring the hydrogens into balance like this: $\boxed{C_3H_8} + \boxed{O_2} \rightarrow 4\boxed{H_2O} + 3\boxed{CO_2}$. Now that my hydrogens are balanced (8 atoms per side) and my carbons (3 per side), all that's left is to balance the oxygens. Since there are 2 on the left and 10 on the right, I multiply the O_2 on the left by 5 like this $\boxed{C_3H_8} + 5\boxed{O_2} \rightarrow 4\boxed{H_2O} + 3\boxed{CO_2}$. Finally, I check my work by counting the product and reactant atoms again to see that each side of the equation has the same number of C, H, and O. I get 3 carbons, 10 oxygens, and 8 hydrogens on both sides, therefore I know that my equation is balanced!!!

Solution: $C_3H_8 + 5O_2 \rightarrow 4H_2O + 3CO_2$

Memory Box

What is it?

A review and assessment technique that has students draw a box on paper and fill it with everything they can remember about a given topic (facts, formulas, dates, etc.)

What are the benefits of using this tool?

Think "review" and you'll probably conjure up images of worksheets, recitations, and maybe a review game here and there. But what if you could redesign review sessions so they provided more information about each student's mastery of the content, took little classroom time, and didn't have the net effect of boring students to tears? Enter Memory Box, a quick and engaging review technique that helps students solidify their learning and lets teachers see what students remember and what's eluding them. Because Memory Box is so easy to implement—all students have to do is fill a box with their memories in an allotted time—it can be used for more than end-of-lesson reviews. Use it before instruction begins to assess students' prior knowledge or at any time during a learning sequence when you want to find out what students have committed to memory.

What are the basic steps?

1. Give students a few minutes to review what they've learned about a specific topic or learning target. Once the time is up, have them put their notes, textbooks, and other review materials away.

2. Ask students to draw a box on paper and fill it with everything they can remember about the given topic or target. Among other things, encourage them to
- List, define, or describe relevant terms.
- Summarize key concepts and ideas.
- Record important names, dates, and formulas.
- Draw maps, timelines, symbols, and other images.
- Use sketches and pictures to show what they know (ideal for primary-grade and ESL students).

3. Walk around the room as students work. Peek into their Memory Boxes to see what they know, and identify misconceptions and knowledge gaps that need to be addressed.

4. Use what you learn to guide future instruction. *Think:* What should I review, cover, or clarify?

🌐 Teacher Talk

→ Have students share and compare boxes with a partner to assess and deepen their knowledge.

→ Check for depth of understanding by asking students to explain how the items in their boxes relate to one another (see Example 3) or flesh out their initial ideas ("I see that you've included Magellan in your Memory Box. Do you recall what he's most famous for, when he lived, or what country he sailed for? Can you sketch his basic route?").

→ Variations and extensions on the basic Memory Box theme are described on p. 95.

How is this tool used in the classroom?

✔ To check (and have students check) for understanding at any point in the learning process

This tool is flexible enough to use at all stages of the learning process. Here are some options:

- Use it at the start of a lesson or unit to assess students' background knowledge.
- Use it at the start of a class period to determine what students remember from the day before.
- Use it after a lesson, activity, or homework assignment to see what has sunk in.
- Begin or end a test with a Memory Box question; see "Test" Your Memory, p. 95, for details.)

EXAMPLE 1: A culinary arts instructor used this tool to determine what his students had taken away from two days of lessons and demonstrations on preparing beef. One student's work is shown here:

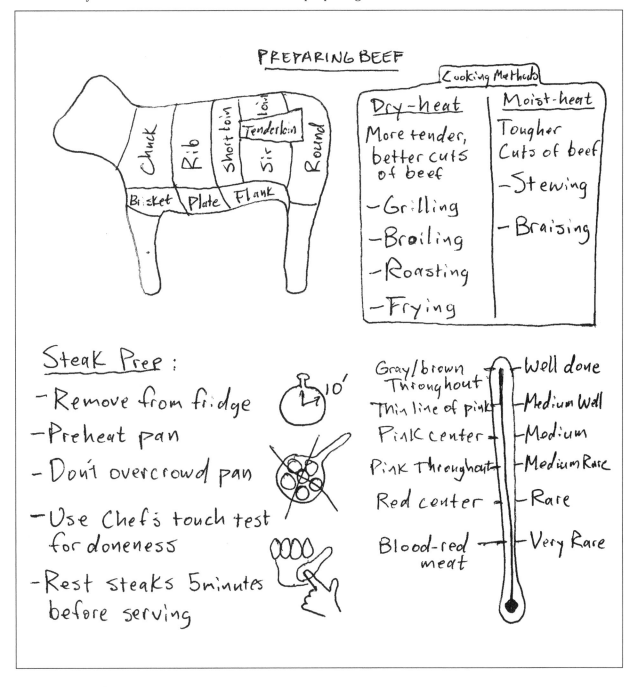

EXAMPLE 2: After listening to a book about insects, a kindergarten student created the Memory Box below with some help from her teacher.

EXAMPLE 3: A social studies teacher used Memory Box to see what students had learned from a week of lessons, readings, and activities about ancient Egypt. Besides listing relevant terms and information, students were asked to make and explain at least four connections between the items in their boxes (see arrows in sample below). They were also encouraged to add to their Memory Boxes each night for homework so they could see their knowledge increasing over time. Ultimately, many students ended up using these "expanded" Memory Boxes to study for the end-of-unit test.

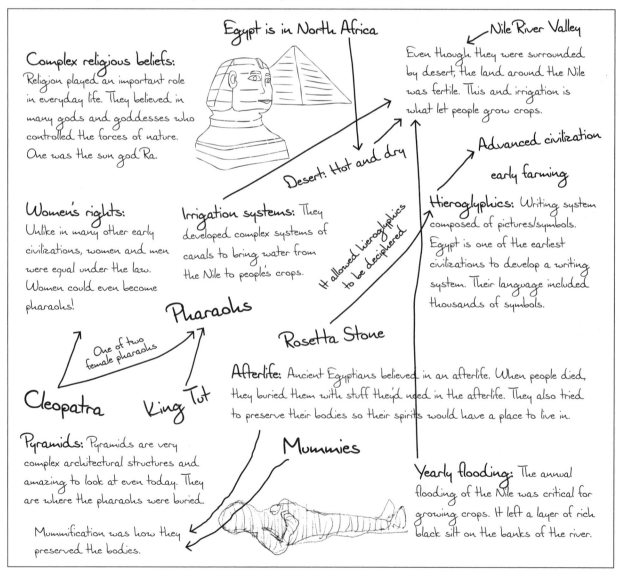

Variations and Extensions on the Basic Memory Box Theme

Class-Created Memory Box (ideal for primary-grade students)

Have students create a Memory Box as a class (they speak their ideas aloud, you draw or write them on the board).

Memory Box Showdown

Boost student engagement by adding in an element of competition. Have students compare the items in their Memory Boxes with a partner, award themselves a point for each idea that their partner doesn't have, and see who has the most points at the end.

Two-Minute Drill

To help students review (and let you check their understanding of) the content from a single lesson, use a speedier version of Memory Box called Two-Minute Drill. In a Two-Minute Drill, students get two minutes to complete each of the following "R" tasks:

- *R*eview their notes, textbooks, or other relevant materials.
- *R*ecord what they remember on paper—facts, big ideas, quotations, etc.
- *R*evise their lists with a partner (share, refine, and review ideas).
- *R*ack up points (change partners, collect a point for each item their partner doesn't have).

Memory Box Notes

Facilitate understanding by having students take Memory Box Notes rather than regular notes during a classroom presentation. Instead of frantically trying to copy down everything that you say, students listen while you speak—no note taking!—and create a Memory Box when you finish. Note that content material should be presented one chunk at a time to prevent students from getting overwhelmed. Stop after each chunk to let students create a Memory Box; help students fill in gaps/answer questions before presenting the next chunk.

Expanded Memory Boxes

Have students add to their Memory Boxes over time as illustrated in Example 3.

Memory Box MVP

To check for big-picture understanding, ask students to identify the most valuable point (MVP) in their Memory Box or create an MVP from scratch (one that summarizes/synthesizes the most important information). Then ask students to explain and justify their MVPs: "Why do you think that's the MVP?"

Memory Box Review Session

Use students' completed Memory Boxes to initiate an in-class review session. Record (or have students record) the items in their Memory Boxes on the board. Discuss these items as a class and have students add to and/or revise the information in their original Memory Boxes.

"Test" Your Memory

Have students create a Memory Box on a quiz or test.

- Begin a test with a Memory Box question to build students' confidence and help students retrieve what they know from memory. (*Fill this box with five things you know about this topic.*)
- End a test with a Memory Box question to give students a chance to demonstrate untested knowledge. (*Do you know anything else about this topic? Share three important facts or ideas in the box below.*)

Most Valuable Point (MVP)

What is it?

A tool that provides immediate feedback about students' understanding of a lesson, activity, or reading assignment by having them identify and elaborate on the most valuable point

What are the benefits of using this tool?

We know what we *want* students to get from the learning experiences that we plan for them. What they actually take away from those experiences, however, can sometimes be a mystery. This tool solves that mystery by asking students to identify the most important point from a lesson, activity, or reading assignment and then elaborate on that point in writing. It also targets a number of skills from the Common Core State Standards—skills like identifying main ideas, citing textual evidence, and writing explanatory paragraphs.

What are the basic steps?

1. Have students complete an activity that requires taking notes or listing key points. ("Take notes as you read this chapter" or "List the key ideas from yesterday's lecture.")

2. Instruct students to review their notes and identify the most valuable point (MVP).

Tip: To avoid confusion, clarify what an MVP *is* (the most important big idea or message to remember) and what it *isn't* (the name of the topic, one basic fact, etc.) before students begin.

3. Invite students to share their MVPs as a class. ("What did you pick as your MVP and why?") List students' MVPs on the board. Use questions like these to help students narrow down their list:

- Can we combine any of these ideas together to get an even bigger, more valuable point?
- How can we tell the difference between a really important point and a less important detail?
- Do any of these ideas feel more like details and less like big ideas? If so, can we eliminate them?

4. Ask students to write a paragraph about one of the MVPs on the list (choose or let them choose). Have them use the MVP as their topic sentence and provide evidence or examples to support it.

5. Use students' completed paragraphs to gauge their understanding of the relevant content and their ability to develop/support their main point. Work with students as needed to address any deficiencies in content knowledge or writing skills.

Variation: Quick-Check MVP

Use this tool to check for understanding throughout a lesson or activity instead of at the end. To do this, divide the lesson/activity into chunks, stop after each chunk to have students generate MVPs, and decide whether to move forward or back up based on their responses. *Think:* Did students get the most important points and concepts? If so, move forward. If not, back up and clarify.

How is this tool used in the classroom?

✔ To assess students' understanding of the key points from a lesson or reading assignment

✔ To develop and test explanatory or persuasive writing skills

EXAMPLE 1: A high school biology teacher used MVP at the end of a lecture to see whether his students had gotten the main point (that living things share many common characteristics) or gotten bogged down in the details. To his relief, the MVPs that students generated during class and the MVP summary paragraphs that they wrote for homework (see below for one example) confirmed that they had not only grasped the big idea, but the key details as well.

> MVP: Living things share many common characteristics.
>
> You might not guess it by looking at looking at them, but living things like polar bears, plants, and people are actually very similar on the inside. In fact, all living things share several important characteristics. At the most basic level, all living things are made up of one or more cells. And no matter what kind of organism you are, your cells actually contain the same basic ingredients—things like water, minerals, proteins, and DNA. Speaking of DNA, all living things have DNA as their...

EXAMPLE 2: Because her students weren't ready to identify main ideas on their own, a second-grade teacher had them work through the MVP process as a class. After reading them the book *Fish Do the Strangest Things*, she used guiding questions to help them generate and refine a list of important ideas. ("What are some things that you learned from this book? Which seem to be the biggest, most important ideas?") She helped students choose one of these ideas as their MVP ("Fish can do a lot of strange things") and asked them to help her support it by giving her specific examples from the book. The list of important ideas that she and her students generated, and the paragraph that they wrote as a class (MVP/topic sentence, supporting examples, conclusion), are shown below.

IMPORTANT IDEAS	PARAGRAPH = Topic sentence/MVP + 4 examples + conclusion
There are many different kinds of fish.	Fish can do a lot of strange things.
~~Some fish spit.~~ (detail, not main idea)	• Some fish can spit.
Fish are more interesting than you think.	• Other fish can fly and climb trees.
(Fish can do a lot of strange things.)	• One kind of fish can blow up like a balloon.
	• Another kind of fish lives in water, but sleeps on land.
	Fish are more interesting than you might think.

🎙 Teacher Talk

➔ The first few times that you use this tool (or when using it with very young students), you may want to complete the process as a class as shown in Example 2.

➔ If students aren't ready to identify main ideas on their own, use questions and prompts to help them—or give them a list of points to choose from and ask them to justify their selections.

Question Quarry

What is it?

A technique that helps us identify and address students' unanswered questions

What are the benefits of using this tool?

Despite our best efforts to establish welcoming classroom environments, students are often reluctant to ask questions in front of their classmates. This is a problem—both because we can't tell what students are confused about if they keep their questions to themselves, and because students can't get their questions answered if they never ask them in the first place. By giving students a place (a "Question Quarry") where they can deposit their questions anonymously, this tool frees them up to ask questions that they wouldn't otherwise feel comfortable asking. It also improves teaching and learning by helping us uncover and address areas of confusion in a timely manner.

What are the basic steps?

1. Establish a classroom environment that encourages and makes students feel comfortable about asking questions. Remind students regularly that asking questions is an important part of the learning process, and that there's no such thing as a stupid question.

2. Explain that students should never feel uncomfortable about asking questions during class, but if they ever do, they can write their questions down and place them in the Question Quarry.

3. Designate a specific location for the Question Quarry so that students know where to deposit their questions. (Should they put them in a shoebox? Tack them onto a bulletin board? Post them online using an appropriate Q & A platform?)

4. Examine the quarry on a regular basis to see what students are confused about.

   Optional: Encourage students to examine the quarry as well. Seeing that they're not the only ones with questions can provide insecure students with a much-needed confidence boost.

5. Address students' quarry questions as quickly as possible. Here are a few options:
   • Start or end a class period by picking questions out of the quarry and answering them.
   • Incorporate quarry questions (and their answers) into classroom lessons and activities.
   • Encourage students to post answers to their classmates' quarry questions.

   Tip: If a lot of quarry questions relate to the same material, you may want to go back and reteach that material instead of (or in addition to) addressing individual questions.

How is this tool used in the classroom?

   ✔ To identify and address areas of confusion in a timely manner
   ✔ To have students assess (and take steps to improve) their understanding of critical content

Reading for Meaning

What is it?

A tool that tests students' understanding of what they've read by having them examine a series of statements, decide whether they agree or disagree with each one, and cite specific evidence to support their positions

What are the benefits of using this tool?

Both common sense and the Common Core State Standards underscore the importance of preparing students to understand and interpret critical texts. This tool helps by building and testing the exact types of reading skills that the Core has identified as critical for students' success—skills like identifying main ideas, making inferences, and supporting those inferences with evidence. Plus, by teaching students to support their positions with evidence and examples, Reading for Meaning prepares them to be better writers as well as better readers.*

What are the basic steps?

1. Identify a short text or portion of a text that you want students to "read for meaning." Any kind of text is fine—poem, Internet article, primary document, fable, scene from a play, etc.

2. Generate a list of statements about the text. (Students will ultimately search the text for evidence that supports and/or refutes each statement.)
   - Statements can be true, false, or open to interpretation/designed to provoke debate.
   - Statements can be customized to fit whatever skills, standards, or objectives you're trying to address (e.g., identifying main ideas or developing interpretations). See Teacher Talk for details.

3. Tell students to preview the statements *before* they begin reading. Ask them to record evidence that supports or refutes each statement *as* (or *after*) they read.

4. Have students discuss their evidence in pairs or small groups. See if they can reach a consensus about which statements are supported vs. refuted by the text. If they can't, have them rewrite problematic statements in a way that lets them reach a consensus.

5. Invite students to share and justify their positions as a class. If necessary, help them clarify their thinking and call their attention to evidence they might have missed or misinterpreted.

6. Use students' responses to evaluate their understanding of what they've read and their ability to support a statement with evidence.

---

*For more on the Reading for Meaning technique, which is adapted from Herber's (1970) Reading and Reasoning Guides, see *Reading for Meaning: How to Build Students' Comprehension, Reasoning, and Problem-Solving Skills* (Silver, Morris, & Klein, 2010) and *The Thoughtful Education Guide to Reading for Meaning* (Silver, Reilly, & Perini, 2009).

How is this tool used in the classroom?

✔ To develop and test students' ability to understand and interpret what they've read

✔ To develop and test students' ability to support a position with evidence

EXAMPLE 1: After listening to the Native American folktale "Turtle Races with Beaver," second-grade students indicated whether they agreed or disagreed with five statements their teacher had generated. They then drew the evidence that led them to agree or disagree with each statement. The "picture evidence" that one student provided for the statement "Turtle won the race fairly" is shown here:

SOURCE: From *The Thoughtful Education Guide to Reading for Meaning* (p. 59), by H. F. Silver, E. C. Reilly, and M. J. Perini, 2009, Thousand Oaks, CA: Corwin Press. © 2009 by Thoughtful Education Press. Reprinted with permission.

EXAMPLE 2: An English teacher used this tool to test his students' understanding of a scene from Shakespeare's *Romeo and Juliet* (Act III, Scene II). A portion of one student's work is shown here:

Evidence for	Statements	Evidence against
The way she talks about Romeo is over the top. Sounds like teenage infatuation: "Take him and cut him out in little stars, / And he will make the face of heaven so fine, / That all the world will be in love with night, / And pay no worship to the garish sun."	Juliet's soliloquy (lines 1–31) reveals how young and naïve she is.	Her ability to express her love is not childish at all. The language is amazing!
When she finds out Romeo killed Tybalt, she seems conflicted: "Oh that deceit should dwell / In such a gorgeous place." Then she takes Romeo's side and reaffirms her love for him (lines 90–127).	Juliet's attitude toward Romeo changes over the course of the scene.	

SOURCE: Adapted from *Reading for Meaning: How to Build Students' Comprehension, Reasoning, and Problem-Solving Skills* (p. 14), by H. F. Silver, S. C. Morris, and V. Klein, 2010, Alexandria, VA: ASCD. © 2010 by Silver Strong & Associates. Adapted with permission.

EXAMPLE 3: Math students completed the organizer below after reading the rules governing the multistate lottery known as Powerball. They were instructed to use their knowledge of probability as well as information from the reading to support or refute each statement.

Statements	Agree or disagree?	Support your position
All you need to calculate your odds of winning is basic multiplication.		
You have a greater probability of winning the grand prize if you live in a big city than in a small town.		
The odds of winning the $4 prize should be 1 in 35, not 1 in 55.41.		

SOURCE: Adapted from *Styles and Strategies for Teaching Middle School Mathematics* (p. 52), by E. J. Thomas and J. R. Brunsting, 2010, Thousand Oaks, CA: Corwin Press. © 2010 by Thoughtful Education Press. Adapted with permission.

EXAMPLE 4: A US history teacher uses this tool to develop and test students' ability to analyze seminal documents of historical and literary significance (Common Core RI.9–10.9, also RI.11–12.6). One student's partially completed organizer for Lincoln's Gettysburg Address is shown below.

Statements	Agree or disagree? Support your position with evidence.
The primary goal of the speech was to honor the soldiers who had fought and died.	I _disagree_ since the speech seems to be more a call to action than a memorial. Lincoln charges the living with dedicating themselves to the cause for which the fallen soldiers "gave the last full measure of devotion" and the task of ensuring that "government of the people, by the people, and for the people shall not perish from the earth."
Lincoln believed that our nation was at a crossroads.	
The style of the speech (in addition to its content) contributes to its power, persuasiveness, and beauty.	
Lincoln believed that the outcome of the war had implications for the entire world, not just the United States.	
Lincoln took his listeners on a journey through time.	
Lincoln would agree that actions speak louder than words.	

EXAMPLE 5: A fifth-grade teacher used the Reading for Meaning statements shown below to test his students' data-analysis skills. After reading and analyzing a set of weather data (see inset table), students recorded the evidence/calculations that supported or refuted each statement.

Statements	Evidence/Calculations
1. Seattle receives more precipitation in a year than Boston. ☐ Agree ☐ Disagree	
2. Over the course of a year, Denver sees more snow than rain. ☐ Agree ☐ Disagree	(see table below)
3. On average, January is the coldest month. ☐ Agree ☐ Disagree	
4. If you were spending Independence Day in Boston, the temperature would not be above 81°F. ☐ Agree ☐ Disagree	

City	Avg.	JAN	FEB	MAR	APR	MAY	JUN	JUL	AUG	SEP	OCT	NOV	DEC
							Month						
Boston	Precip.	3.6	3.6	3.7	3.6	3.3	3.1	2.8	3.3	3.1	3.3	4.3	4.0
	Low	21	24	31	40	48	58	65	64	56	46	38	26
	High	35	37	45	55	66	76	81	78	72	62	52	40
Denver	Precip.	0.5	0.6	1.3	1.7	2.4	1.8	1.9	1.5	1.3	1.0	0.9	0.6
	Low	16	20	25	34	44	52	58	56	47	36	25	17
	High	44	46	52	61	70	81	88	85	76	66	52	44
Seattle	Precip.	5.4	4.0	3.5	2.3	1.7	1.5	0.8	1.1	1.9	3.3	5.8	5.9
	Low	35	37	38	41	46	51	55	55	51	45	40	35
	High	45	48	52	57	64	68	75	75	68	58	50	45

Average temperatures recorded in degrees Fahrenheit (°F)
Average precipitation amounts recorded in inches (in.)

SOURCE: From *Reading for Meaning: How to Build Students' Comprehension, Reading, and Problem-Solving Skills* (p. 15), by H. F. Silver, S. C. Morris, and V. Klein, 2010, Alexandria, VA: ASCD © 2010 by Silver Strong & Associates. Reprinted with permission.

🌗 Teacher Talk

→ Be creative! Instead of having students read and analyze a single text, have them analyze pieces of art, demonstrations, pairs of texts, or data files. See how one teacher did this in Example 5.

→ Don't assume that students know how to find evidence in a text. Explain, model, and practice this critical skill until students are comfortable with it.

→ If you're having trouble generating statements (Step 2), generate checking-for-understanding questions instead—and then turn those questions into statements. (*Question:* "Who is the wisest character in this folktale?" ⟶ *Statement:* "The wisest character in this folktale is the grandfather.")

→ Adapt the tool as needed for developing readers. Primary-grade teachers may want to read their texts aloud (or use picture books), have students search for evidence and complete the organizer as a class, or let students draw their evidence rather than writing it (see Example 1). Scaffold the evidence-gathering process for students until they're capable of doing it on their own.

→ One way to conclude a Reading for Meaning lesson is to assign a task that requires students to summarize, synthesize, or apply what they've learned (e.g., "Write a letter to the editor of your textbook describing any inaccuracies or biases in the coverage of this historical event").

→ Statements can be designed to fit whatever skills you're addressing (e.g., identifying main ideas or summarizing facts). They can also be designed around any of the Common Core Anchor Standards for Reading—and for literary as well as informational texts (see below for examples).

Anchor-Standard Concepts	Sample Statements
Determine what a text says explicitly. (R.CCR.1)	• Everyone is unkind to the ugly duckling. • All isotopes are radioactive.
Make logical inferences from a text. (R.CCR.1)	• We can tell that Pooh and Piglet have been friends for a long time. • Without taking Franklin's data, Watson and Crick wouldn't have succeeded.
Identify main ideas and themes. (R.CCR.2)	• The moral of the story is that you should be kind to everyone. • Structure and function are intricately linked.
Analyze how and why individuals, events, and ideas develop, connect, and interact. (R.CCR.3)	• After Maxim's revelation, the new Mrs. de Winter is a changed woman. • The seeds of social change for women in America were planted during WWII.
Assess how point of view or purpose shapes the content and style of a text; distinguish between what is said and what is meant or true. (R.CCR.6)	• When the narrator notes that Della and Jim "most unwisely sacrificed for each other the greatest treasures of their house," he is expressing disapproval. • The writer's personal feelings influenced his description of this event.
Integrate and evaluate content that is presented visually and quantitatively as well as in words. (R.CCR.7)	• Ferdinand is not his usual self in this picture. • According to Table 2 from this article, sun-worshippers would be happier living in Phoenix than Seattle.
Analyze how two or more texts address similar themes or topics in order to build knowledge or compare the authors' approaches. (R.CCR.9)	• Myths from different cultures have similar elements and themes. • The Cherokee people's account of their relocation differs from the account in your textbook.

How Will I Help Students Review, Practice, and Check Their Grasp of the Material?

I appear to be wiser than he, because I do not fancy I know what I do not know.

—Socrates (as recounted in Plato's *Apology*)

This research finds that, without training, most learners cannot accurately judge what they do and don't know, and typically overestimate how well they have mastered material when they are finished studying. This "illusion of knowing" is reflected in the assertion that many students make after they receive a poor grade on a test: "But I studied so hard. I thought I really knew the material cold. How could I have failed?"

—Harold Pashler et al., *Organizing Instruction and Study to Improve Student Learning*

Obviously, students need opportunities to review and practice key content and skills. But not all practice opportunities offer the same benefits. Many, in fact, fail the most fundamental test: They don't help students pinpoint what they do and don't know. And without this information, students can't take responsibility for their own improvement.

The following tools empower students to advance their learning by helping them assess where they are relative to what they're trying to achieve, and take steps to close the gaps:

1. **Convergence Mastery** gives students multiple opportunities to practice a target skill, assess their performance, and learn from their mistakes.

2. **Graduated Difficulty** challenges students to compare three increasingly difficult practice tasks, complete the task they feel most comfortable with, and establish plans for moving to the next level.

3. **Interactive Note Making** teaches students how to extract and assess their understanding of the key points from an assigned text.

4. **Mastery Review** is an in-class review technique that gives students immediate feedback about their command of key content.

5. **Spot-Check Quizzer** uses ungraded quizzes to help students zero in on what they do and don't know so that they can focus future studying.

Convergence Mastery

What is it?

A tool that helps all students converge toward mastery of a target skill by giving them multiple opportunities to practice that skill, assess their performance, and learn from their mistakes

What are the benefits of using this tool?

Some students master skills quickly, while others need more time and support to reach the same level of proficiency. Convergence Mastery (Thomas & Brunsting, 2010) ensures that all students get the support they need by using differentiated practice sessions to let them practice a target skill, get immediate feedback about their performance, and continue practicing until they achieve mastery. Perhaps best of all, the tool takes seriously the well-tested wisdom that some of the best learning comes out of making mistakes, giving students repeated chances to identify and root out the errors that plague their performance.

What are the basic steps?

1. Select a target skill that students have practiced and partially mastered.

2. Create three to five short quizzes that test students' command of the selected skill. All quizzes should be at the same level of difficulty, and all quiz questions should have clear right or wrong answers.

3. Explain the tool's steps and purpose. ("The quizzes that you're about to take will tell us if you've mastered this skill or if you need to keep practicing. If you haven't yet mastered the skill, don't worry. You'll get to keep practicing, and your classmates and I will help you!")

4. Give students a few minutes to review. Then administer one of the quizzes (make it clear that Convergence Mastery quizzes don't count toward students' grades).

5. Share the answers with students, either verbally or via an answer key, and have them check their own work.

6. Excuse the students with perfect scores from taking additional quizzes. Encourage these students to help their classmates review their mistakes and prepare for the next quiz. Assist them as needed to ensure that struggling students get the help they need.

7. Give a follow-up quiz to students who failed to get a perfect score on the previous one. Repeat Steps 5–7 until all quizzes have been administered or all students have received perfect scores.

   Note: Students who have been excused from taking follow-up quizzes can take them for extra practice, work on more challenging problems, or start their homework.

How is this tool used in the classroom?

✔ To have students practice, assess, and improve their ability to perform a specific skill

✔ To gather information about students' proficiency level

EXAMPLE 1: A first-grade teacher used Convergence Mastery to help students assess and improve their ability to use the correct end punctuation for questions and statements (Common Core L.1.2b). At the end of the activity, she set aside time to work with the few students who hadn't yet mastered the skill.

QUIZ 1	QUIZ 2	QUIZ 3
Do these sentences need a period or a question mark? Show me!	Do these sentences need a period or a question mark? Show me!	Do these sentences need a period or a question mark? Show me!
1. Do you like animals	1. Eating is fun	1. My favorite color is purple
2. I like dogs better than cats	2. What is your favorite food	2. Do you have a pet
3. Dogs like to bark	3. Do you like pizza	3. I like you
4. Did you ever pet a dog	4. I like pizza	4. Will you be my friend

EXAMPLE 2: These Convergence Mastery quizzes were generated by a Spanish teacher. Her goal was to help her students assess and improve their ability to conjugate the verb *ir* ("to go").

QUIZ 1	QUIZ 2	QUIZ 3
Translate from English to Spanish.	Translate from English to Spanish.	Translate from English to Spanish.
1. I went to the library.	1. She went home.	1. He went to the library.
2. She goes to school.	2. They are going to a party.	2. He is going to a party.
3. I will go to the store.	3. We will go to a restaurant.	3. We will go to the beach.
4. They went to the beach.	4. He went to the park.	4. I went to school.
5. We will go to the movies.	5. She will go to the store.	5. They will go on a plane.
6. She goes to camp.	6. He goes to school.	6. They went to the hospital.

EXAMPLE 3: A high school math teacher working on trigonometric identities (Common Core HSF-TF.C.9) developed five Convergence Mastery quizzes to help students test their knowledge of the sine, cosine, and tangent identities involving sums and differences. Three of the five quizzes are shown below.

QUIZ 1	QUIZ 2	QUIZ 3
Complete each trigonometric identity.	Complete each trigonometric identity.	Complete each trigonometric identity.
A. $\cos(x + y) =$	A. $\sin(x + y) =$	A. $\cos(-x) =$
B. $\cos(-x) =$	B. $\sin(-x) =$	B. $\tan(-x) =$
C. $\tan(-x) =$	C. $\cos(x - y) =$	C. $\sin(x - y) =$
D. $\sin(x - y) =$	D. $\cos(-x) =$	D. $\cos(x + y) =$
E. $\tan(x - y) =$	E. $\tan(x + y) =$	E. $\tan(x - y) =$

SOURCE: Adapted from *Styles and Strategies for Teaching High School Mathematics: 21 Techniques for Differentiating Instruction and Assessment* (p. 16), by E. J. Thomas, J. R. Brunsting, and P. L. Warrick, 2010, Thousand Oaks, CA: Corwin Press. © 2010 by Thoughtful Education Press. Adapted with permission.

🔊 Teacher Talk

➔ Encourage students to support one another by putting them into teams before the first quiz.

➔ Talk to students about the value of establishing a classroom learning community in which all members help and support each other—not just for Convergence Mastery quizzes, but always.

➔ Prepare students to help their classmates by explaining and modeling good coaching behavior.

Graduated Difficulty

What is it?

Inspired by the work of Muska Mosston (1972), this differentiating-by-readiness tool lets students choose which level to work at while practicing essential skills

What are the benefits of using this tool?

In order for students to practice critical skills in an efficient and effective way, they need to have a clear understanding of where they're going (what is the ultimate goal?) and where they are now. The problem, of course, is that "figuring out where you are" isn't necessarily as easy as it sounds. In many cases, students don't realize how well—or poorly—they've mastered a specific skill until they're asked to apply it on an end-of-unit test. Graduated Difficulty addresses this problem by having students use three increasingly difficult practice tasks to assess and improve their proficiency *before* test time. By helping students figure out what they can and can't do, these tasks prepare them (and us) to make smarter decisions about what to focus on and how to allocate review time.

What are the basic steps?

1. Identify a skill you want students to practice. Develop three different tasks that will help them practice the selected skill, each at a different level of difficulty:

   - *Level 1 tasks* should be simple enough for all students to complete.
   - *Level 2 tasks* should be challenging for most students, but doable by many.
   - *Level 3 tasks* should be challenging for all students. They should require the highest level of knowledge or proficiency that is demanded by your curriculum/standards.

2. Present all three tasks to students. Have them compare the different tasks, determine what makes one more difficult than another, and choose the task that feels right to them.

3. Prepare students to make good choices by discussing the consequences of selecting tasks that are too hard or too easy (too hard and they won't be successful, too easy and they won't improve).

   Use real-world examples to help students grasp the concept. ("What if you went skiing and stayed on the bunny hill the whole time? What if you tackled an expert slope before you were ready?")

4. Provide an answer key so that students can check their work as they go. Make it clear that they are free to change levels (up or down) at any time—that the goal is to work at whichever level will help them improve.

5. Observe students as they work to see how they're getting along. Pose questions that will help them think about their decision-making process ("How did you select that level?"), but don't tell them what level to work at. Let them choose and learn from their choices.

6. Ask students to reflect on what they learned. See Teacher Talk point 1 for a list of questions you can use to help them analyze their choices and establish plans for improvement.

How is this tool used in the classroom?

✔ To have students practice, develop, and assess their grasp of key skills

✔ To make students responsible for monitoring and managing their own learning

EXAMPLE 1: A second-grade teacher used this tool to have his students practice and improve their ability to tell time (Common Core 2.MD.C.7). His Level 1 task involved telling time to the hour, his Level 2 task involved telling time to the half hour, and his Level 3 task involved telling time to the nearest five minutes.

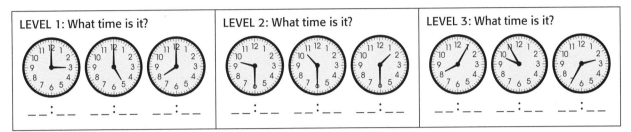

LEVEL 1: What time is it?

__ : __   __ : __   __ : __

LEVEL 2: What time is it?

__ : __   __ : __   __ : __

LEVEL 3: What time is it?

__ : __   __ : __   __ : __

EXAMPLE 2: Portions of a French teacher's tasks are shown below. Notice that students will be practicing the same skill at all three levels (conjugating verbs), but that they'll be practicing it in different ways: by selecting the correct verb to complete a sentence (Level 1), by translating sentences from English to French (Level 2), or by writing a letter in French (Level 3).

LEVEL 1:

Circle the form of the verb that agrees with the subject pronoun at the beginning of the sentence.

1. Nous (voulez, veulent, voulons) visiter Normandie.

2. Ils (veulent, voulez, veut) aller à Nice.

3. Tu (veut, veux, veulent) regarder la télévision.

LEVEL 2:

Translate the following sentences into French. Pay close attention to the subject pronoun and the form of the verb that goes with that pronoun.

1. She wants to go to Paris.

2. They (f) want to visit Alsace.

3. You (pl) want to visit Champagne.

LEVEL 3:

Imagine that you're in France. Write a letter to a friend back home that describes the places you've already seen (cities, landmarks, etc.) and the places you hope to visit before your trip is over. Include at least three sentences that use the verb *aller*, three sentences that use the verb *vouloir*, and three sentences that use a regular -er verb. Word your letter so that you can use different subject pronouns—not *je* every time!

Note: Since there can't be an answer key for a task like this, bring me your finished letter and I will check it.

EXAMPLE 3: A music teacher presents students with pieces at three different levels of difficulty, tells them that the goal is to play one of the pieces without mistakes in a week's time, and lets them choose which piece to work on.

🎯 Teacher Talk

➔ Use questions like these to guide and focus the reflection process in Step 6:

- How did you go about deciding which level to work at? What criteria did you use?
- Do you feel like you made the right choice? Would you make the same choice again? Why?
- How did it feel to be able to choose your own task? Why?
- Did you learn anything about yourself and how you make decisions?
- How can this experience prepare you to study more effectively? To achieve at a higher level?
- What would it take to move up a level? How could you acquire the necessary knowledge/skills?
- Did you learn anything that could help you improve your performance in this or a future unit?

➔ There are many ways to establish different levels of difficulty. You can have students do the same exact type of task at every level (e.g., read the time on a clock), but make each level harder than the previous one as shown in Example 1. Another option is to have students complete a different type of task at every level as shown in Example 2.

➔ Graduated Difficulty works best with tasks that have right or wrong answers, but it can be used with other kinds of tasks as well. In these cases, students should be given a specific outcome to aim for or a list of criteria to satisfy at each level. For example, if students are practicing "pulling" a baseball, they might aim to pull the ball five times in a row off a batting tee (Level 1), in a batting cage (Level 2), against a pitcher throwing fastballs (Level 3), and against a pitcher throwing a mixture of pitches (Level 4).

➔ Find ways to challenge and engage students who complete Level 3 tasks successfully. One option: Invite them to create Level 4 tasks and the answer keys to go with them—and have them exchange their tasks with other Level 4 students. Another option: Have these students coach and assist a classmate.

➔ Some teachers choose *not* to indicate which level of task is which. Why? When tasks are labeled, some students pick based on the level alone ("I'm going to pick Level 3") rather than comparing the tasks and making an informed decision about which task is right for them. Leaving the tasks unlabeled forces students to examine the tasks more deeply (what makes one different from the next?), think about what they know, and decide which task is most appropriate.

➔ Teach students that effective studying/practicing involves deciding *how long* to practice as well as *what* to practice. In the context of Graduated Difficulty, this means deciding whether they need to complete an entire task before choosing to move up or down—or whether they can make that decision sooner. ("Since I got the first three questions wrong, I won't waste any more time at this level; I will move down.") Beyond the scope of this tool, this means making thoughtful decisions about how much time to practice or study specific things. ("Do I need to spend more time reviewing these vocabulary terms? Or do I know them well enough to move on to something else?")

➔ The fact that students learn at different speeds can pose challenges for classroom teachers. This tool acknowledges and addresses some of these challenges by providing options for students at different readiness levels. Letting students choose a practice task that's at the right level of difficulty for them enables everyone to work at a personally productive pace and experience confidence-building success. Encouraging students to make thoughtful decisions about their learning has the added benefit of fostering independence and self-regulation.

Interactive Note Making

What is it?

A note-making and study tool that helps students extract and check their understanding of key ideas from an assigned text; the steps are adapted from Robinson's (1946) SQ3R reading strategy

What are the benefits of using this tool?

The Common Core State Standards remind us that teaching students how to read and understand informational texts is critical for their future success. This tool helps students get more out of assigned texts by using pre-reading questions to focus their attention on what's important, and by having them search for the answers to those questions as they read. It improves the quality of the notes that students take by helping them extract and record key ideas, and it teaches students how to use their notes as a review and study tool.

What are the basic steps?

1. Teach students to create an Interactive Note Making organizer by dividing a sheet of paper into four columns and labeling the columns *Questions*, *Main Ideas*, *Supporting Details*, and *Monitor*.

2. Have students preview an assigned text by examining section headings, opening and summary paragraphs, topic sentences, bold-faced terms, images, and/or end-of-chapter review questions.

   Note: This tool is typically used with textbook chapters or sections, but any informational text with section headings will work.

3. Have students convert each section heading or subheading into a question(s) and record these questions in the Questions column. If students are new to the tool, introduce them to the six question-starter words (*who, what, when, where, why, how*) and model the conversion process for them. For example:

SECTION HEADING	POSSIBLE QUESTIONS (students can record one or more)
The War of 1812 Begins $\longrightarrow$	*Why* did the War of 1812 begin? *Who* started the War of 1812?
Covalent vs. Noncovalent Bonds $\longrightarrow$	*How* are covalent bonds different from noncovalent bonds?

4. Tell students to keep the questions in mind as they read the text slowly, carefully, and one section at a time. Have them record the answers (main ideas and details) on their organizers. Encourage them to use their own words rather than copying from the text.

5. When students finish, instruct them to check their understanding and retention of the material. ("Fold your organizers so that only the questions are visible. Try to answer without peeking.")

6. Tell students to indicate what they know (✓), need to review (★), or have questions about (?) in the Monitor column and allocate their study time accordingly.

7. Instruct students to repeat the review-and-check process from Steps 5–6 several times (a day later, a week later, while studying for a test, etc.) and adjust their study plans accordingly.

How is this tool used in the classroom?

✔ To help students identify the main ideas and key details from an assigned text

✔ To have students review and check their understanding of what they've read

✔ To promote active reading and develop students' note-making skills

EXAMPLE: A health teacher used Interactive Note Making to have students extract, review, and test their understanding of the key points from a textbook chapter on the circulatory system. One student's organizer is shown below.

QUESTIONS	MAIN IDEAS	SUPPORTING DETAILS	MONITOR
What is the function of blood?	Brings food and oxygen to cells and carries away wastes. It also carries hormones, proteins, and infection fighters to where they're needed.		★
What are the components of blood?	Red blood cells, white blood cells, platelets, and plasma		✓
What is plasma?	Cells travel through the blood in a yellowish fluid called plasma.	Plasma is approx. 90% water.	★
What is the function of white blood cells?	White blood cells (WBCs) help the body fight infection and disease.	White blood cells can destroy infected cells and make antibodies.	? What's an antibody?

🔆 Teacher Talk

➜ When using this tool for the first time, or when using it with younger students, model the note-making process on the board and/or have students complete an organizer as a class. Scaffold and practice specific steps as needed.

➜ Remind students to leave space between each question (Step 3) so they'll have room to take notes. Encourage them to revise and/or add to their list of questions as they read.

➜ Have students record their questions in the Monitor column (Step 6). Encourage them to ask these questions during class or research the answers on their own.

➜ The process of generating questions, reading, and taking notes can be done section-by-section (i.e., convert a section heading into a question, read the section, take notes on the section) or as it's described in the Steps (i.e., generate all questions, read all sections, take notes on all sections).

➜ Once students have mastered the skill of converting section headings into questions, challenge them to transform other text features (e.g., pictures, bold-faced terms, tables) into questions as well.

➜ To have students take notes from a lecture instead of a text, list the key points in advance, have students convert each point into a question, and record the answers during the lecture.

➜ Encourage students to generate multiple questions for particularly dense sections of text. The student whose work is shown in the example above did this by creating questions about each individual component of blood that was mentioned in a single section of his textbook.

Mastery Review

What is it?

An in-class review tool that prepares students to study more effectively by giving them immediate feedback about their mastery of key facts and skills

What are the benefits of using this tool?

Mastery Review is an engaging and effective review technique that provides a welcome alternative to the often-used Q & A session. Unlike a traditional Q & A session, a Mastery Review allows *all* students—not just the ones who ask and answer questions—to actively review and test their knowledge of critical content. It also gives students immediate feedback about their performance so they leave class with a better understanding of what they do and don't know. Getting this kind of feedback prepares them to study more efficiently by helping them make smarter decisions about how to allocate their time.

What are the basic steps?

Note: If you want students to review *factual information*, follow Steps 1–7 below. To have students practice *skills*, *procedures*, or *solving problems*, use the alternative steps on p. 112 instead.

1. Write a one- to three-paragraph "story" about your content using the examples on p. 112 as models. Your story should cover the key points you want students to review and include gaps or questions where students will need to fill in a blank. Number each blank as illustrated in the examples.

Optional: Create a word bank of terms for students to choose from when filling in the blanks.

2. Have students prepare an answer sheet by telling them how many blanks they'll need to fill in and having them number a piece of paper accordingly.

3. Read your story aloud. Read slowly enough for students to follow along, and pause whenever it's time to fill in a blank. Be sure that everyone records an answer before moving to Step 4.

4. Write the correct answer on the board. Give students time to check and correct their work.

5. Continue the "read, respond, check, and correct" process until the entire story has been read.

6. Give students copies of the story. Have them fill in the blanks with the answers they recorded during the review session. Encourage them to use their completed stories as study guides.

7. Instruct students to indicate which material they already know and which needs further review. Have them use this information to focus their study time and develop targeted study plans (e.g., I'll review the definition of a biome, I'll ask my teacher to re-explain the concept of purchasing power, I'll make Spanish-English flashcards for the vocabulary words I missed).

How is this tool used in the classroom?

✔ To have all students actively review and test their knowledge of critical content material

✔ To help students distinguish between things they already know and things they need to study

EXAMPLE 1: Here is the Mastery Review story that a third-grade teacher used to check (and help his students check) how much of what he had taught them about Christopher Columbus had sunk in:

> On an August evening in the year ___ (1), Christopher Columbus departed from Spain with three ships—the ___ (2), the ___ (3), and the ___ (4). It had taken him many years, but he had finally convinced King ___ (5) and Queen ___ (6) of ___ (7) to finance his journey, and he was extremely excited to be on his way at last.

EXAMPLE 2: A fourth-grade teacher created the Mastery Review story below to determine (and help his students determine) which concepts to review in preparation for an upcoming test on angles addressing Common Core Standards 4.MD.C.5–7.

> WORD BANK: protractor, acute, obtuse, complementary, right angle, line segments, < 90°, > 90°, 90°, 180°, 60°, 30°, 45°, vertex, rays, supplementary, points, measure, lines
>
> An angle is formed by two ___ (1) that share a common endpoint. What term do we use to refer to this common endpoint? ___ (2) And what tool do we use to measure an angle? ___ (3) If you take out your protractors and use them to measure angle AOB in the drawing at the right, you'll find that it is exactly ___ (4). Angle AOB would be considered a(n) ___ (5) angle because it's less than 90°. Because angle AOB and angle BOC add up to ___ (6), they would be considered ___ (7) angles. A pair of angles that added up to 180°, in contrast, would be…

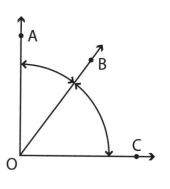

Alternative Steps (Use for reviewing skills and procedures)

A. Create a problem or task that will test students' grasp of a specific skill or procedure. Among other things, you could have students translate a paragraph, solve a word problem, or correct spelling or grammar errors within a series of sentences.

B. Write the problem or task on the board. Have students work through it at their seats while you work it through on the board.

C. Encourage students to look up at the board if they get stuck.

D. Give students time to check and correct their work.

E. Repeat Steps A–D several times, increasing the level of difficulty whenever appropriate based on students' success rate and comfort level.

Spot-Check Quizzer

What is it?

A quiz-based tool that helps students determine what they know well and what they need to study

What are the benefits of using this tool?

In order to allocate their study time efficiently, students must be able to distinguish between material they've already mastered and material that needs further review. This tool helps them make that distinction by asking them to analyze their performance on short, ungraded quizzes. Quizzing students on previously taught material not only teaches them what they need to study—it can actually improve their retention of that material (Butler & Roediger, 2007; Pashler et al., 2007).

What are the basic steps?

1. Administer a short ungraded quiz on material you've already covered.
   - *Don't* announce the quiz in advance and *don't* have students review their notes before taking it.
   - *Do* explain that the quiz is ungraded and that its purpose is to help students, not evaluate them. ("This quiz is for your benefit, not mine. It will help you understand what you do and don't already know so you can make smarter decisions about what to study.")

2. Share the answers with students, either verbally or via an answer key.

3. Instruct students to identify and revisit material that caused them problems on the quiz. Offer assistance as needed and suggest specific resources that can help them. (Are there parts of their text or lecture notes that they should review? Problem sets that they could do for extra practice?)

How is this tool used in the classroom?

✔ To help students check their grasp of key content and allocate their study time accordingly

🎯 Teacher Talk

→ Teach students how to spot-check quiz themselves. (To spot-check their understanding of a textbook chapter, for example, they could try to summarize the key points or answer the end-of-chapter questions.) Encourage students to do these spot checks on a regular basis (e.g., after every lecture or reading assignment), and remind them to use what they learn to focus their study time.

→ If you're pressed for time, borrow quiz questions instead of creating them from scratch. Use your colleagues, your textbook publisher (search the teacher's manual, the website, the textbook itself), and the Internet (search for existing quizzes as well as quiz-generating and grading tools) as resources.

→ To gather feedback about student learning and take a more active role in addressing knowledge gaps, examine students' quizzes to see which questions caused problems and review the corresponding material with individual students or the class as a whole.

How Will I Help Students Improve Their Work Through Feedback and Self-Assessment?

A coach is someone who can give correction without causing resentment.

—John Wooden

When anyone is trying to learn, feedback about the effort has three elements: recognition of the desired goal, evidence about present position, and some understanding of a way to close the gap between the two. All three must be understood to some degree by anyone before he or she can take action to improve learning.

—Paul Black and Dylan Wiliam, "Inside the Black Box: Raising Standards Through Classroom Assessment"

This chapter is about the improvement process, the *how* by which students raise the quality of their work. Clearly, one way to help students improve is to provide feedback. In fact, John Hattie (1999) reported feedback to be "the most powerful single moderator that enhances achievement" (p. 9). But not all feedback is created equal. By synthesizing the work of a number of experts on feedback (Brookhart, 2008; Chappuis, 2009; Hattie & Timperley, 2007; Schute, 2008), we can identify some clear guidelines for providing good, usable feedback to students. For example, we know that good feedback must focus on the work or performance, not the student. We know that good feedback is specific and directs the student's attention to the intended learning. And we know that good feedback highlights strengths in the student's work while offering strategies and suggestions for improvement.

The following tools were designed to help teachers give this kind of high-quality feedback to students:

1. **Glow & Grow** is a simple feedback technique that focuses students' attention on what they've done well and how they can make their work better.

2. **Points Worth Praising** helps students recognize the quality elements in their own work and boosts their confidence through positive, constructive feedback.

3. **The "Ps" to Better Work** presents four types of feedback for helping students improve their work.

4. **STAIRS to Successful Feedback** outlines six principles for providing students with effective feedback.

5. **What & Why Feedback** helps students understand what they've done well, what needs work, and why.

Teacher feedback is not the only way to help students get better at what they're doing. We now recognize that students play a vital role in empowering each other to improve. In addition to the teacher-feedback tools above, this chapter also includes three tools aimed at helping students review and respond constructively to each other's work:

6. **Knee-to-Knee Conference** is a peer-review tool that teaches students how to listen deeply and give each other useful feedback about their work.

7. **PEERS** spells out five ground rules for improving the productivity of peer-feedback sessions.

8. **Writer's Club** gives students a forum for sharing, discussing, and improving their writing.

The third way teachers can help students improve is by teaching them the skills of self-assessment. After all, students who can monitor and evaluate their own performance produce better work, tend to be more motivated to learn, and typically achieve at higher levels in the classroom (Schunk & Zimmerman, 1998). Thus, the third group of tools in this chapter helps students pay closer attention to their performance and seek out ways to improve their work:

9. **I Think, You Think** invites students to assess their work, compare their assessment with that of their teacher, and use what they learn to improve their work.

10. **Stop, Read, Revise** builds students' ability to read their work critically and make quality revisions.

Glow & Grow

What is it?

A feedback tool that boosts confidence and achievement by telling students what they've done well (what *glows*) and what they can improve (where their work can *grow*)

What are the benefits of using this tool?

In order for feedback to be effective, it should

- Identify specific things that have been done well.
- Identify particular areas where work can be improved.
- Be easy for students to understand and apply to their work.

Glow & Grow makes it easy for teachers to meet these criteria when providing feedback to their students. The *glow* feedback helps to build students' confidence and understanding of what quality looks like; the *grow* feedback teaches students how to take a direct role in improving their work; and the tool's simple, student-friendly format ensures that the feedback isn't overwhelming.

What are the basic steps?

1. Design an assessment task for students to complete.

2. Identify the criteria that successful work will need to satisfy. Communicate these criteria to students before they begin working on the task.

3. Review students' completed work. Provide clear and specific feedback about what has been done well (what glows) and what could be improved (where students' work has room to grow).

4. Ask yourself the following questions as you generate your feedback:
   - Does your feedback address the criteria for successful work? Does it let students know which criteria they've satisfied and which have yet to be met?
   - Is your *grow* feedback manageable? Does it focus on the most critical items to address rather than point out everything that needs to be fixed?
   - Will your feedback make sense to students? Did you use age-appropriate and student-friendly language? Did you use examples or suggestions to help clarify your meaning?

5. Before returning students' work, teach students about the two different kinds of feedback they'll be receiving: positive (glow) and constructive (grow). See Teacher Talk for suggestions.

6. Set aside time for students to review and process your feedback. Have them use it to revise and improve their work. Be available to offer assistance and clarification if needed.

How is this tool used in the classroom?

✔ To provide feedback that helps students improve their work

Teachers use the Glow & Grow format to provide students with encouraging and constructive feedback about their work (homework assignments, problem sets, projects, etc.).

EXAMPLE 1: A first-grade teacher asked students to identify their favorite toy and give three reasons why it was their favorite. She discussed her Glow & Grow feedback with students during one-on-one conferences and had them use it to revise and improve their work.

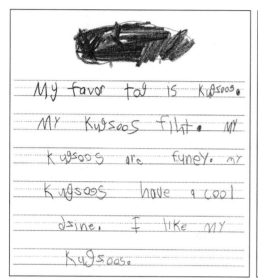

Three ways your work GLOWS:

☀ Your sentences start with capital letters and end with periods.

☀ You remembered to give three reasons why you like your toy.

☀ You stuck to the topic. Everything is about your favorite toy.

Two ways your work can GROW:

🌱 Four of your sentences start with the word "my."
   Can you start some of them with a different word?

🌱 Your letter "z" is backwards.
   Can you find and fix your mistakes?

EXAMPLE 2: A portion of a chemistry student's homework assignment and the *grow* feedback that accompanied it are shown here:

1. Find the pH of a 100 mM HCl solution.

$pH = -\log [H_3O^+]$ $100\ mM = 0.1\ M$

$pH = -\log (0.1)$

$pH = 10$

GROW: Always check your answers to see if they make sense. Does it make sense that an acidic solution would have a pH of 10?

EXAMPLE 3: An AP European History teacher prepares her students for the document-based essay question (DBQ) portion of the AP Exam by giving them practice questions. She reviews the criteria for top-notch work before they begin, and she uses these same criteria to focus her Glow & Grow feedback. The feedback that she attached to the first draft of one student's essay is shown below.

Here's where your work GLOWS:	Here's where your work can GROW:
1. You present a clear thesis that addresses the question without simply restating it.	1. Remember to address both parts of the writing prompt. (Most of your piece is about the first part.)
2. You supported your thesis with appropriate evidence from the documents that were provided. Your interpretation of the data table in document #5 was right on target.	2. Your points will be stronger and clearer if you discuss documents that have a similar focus/point together (e.g., the ones that present a negative view of immigration).
3. Your analysis of document #2 takes into account the fact that its author might not be completely unbiased.	3. Can you use information beyond that found in the documents to support your case further? If yes, do it!

🌑 Teacher Talk

➜ Before using this tool for the first time, familiarize students with the two different kinds of feedback that they'll receive: positive (glow) and constructive (grow). Here are some suggestions for doing this:

  • Present students with a list of glow statements and a list of grow statements. Have them compare the lists and explain the differences between the two types of statements (e.g., "Glow statements identify and describe specific things that have been done well, while grow statements describe specific ways that the work can be corrected or improved").

  • Give students a mixed list of statements (some glow, some grow). Ask them to identify which statements are which and explain why.

  • Invite students to analyze samples of work using a list of quality criteria that you provide. Have them use the criteria to explain where the work glows and where it can grow.

  • Discuss the way that each type of feedback works to improve the quality of student work.

➜ Since student work often glows in unanticipated ways, keep an open mind when looking for things to praise (i.e., don't limit yourself to the criteria that you identified in Step 2).

➜ Encourage students to use the Glow & Grow framework as well. Give them opportunities to review each other's work and have them provide Glow & Grow feedback to their classmates.

➜ If you're looking for a change of pace, try the "three stars and a wish" variation instead. Record three things that were done well and one thing you wish students would work on.

Points Worth Praising

What is it?

A tool that helps us provide positive feedback to our students by outlining a list of points worth praising

What are the benefits of using this tool?

When we give students feedback about their work, we often focus on things that need to be improved rather than on things that have been done well. By shifting our focus from "points that need fixing" to "points worth praising," we not only prevent students from becoming discouraged, we also teach them what they've done well so they can continue doing it on future assignments.

What are the basic steps?

1. Review an assignment that students have completed.

2. Identify points worth praising by looking for the following:

- Evidence that a specific learning goal or target has been met
- Evidence that the piece fulfills specific criteria for success (e.g., criteria on a rubric or checklist)
- Evidence that all the required elements are present or that the appropriate steps were followed
- Evidence of progress (Is there an aspect of this piece that shows improvement?)
- Evidence that students have mastered critical vocabulary terms, content, or procedures
- Evidence that students have responded to prior feedback
- Evidence that students have used appropriate strategies/thinking processes to complete the task (e.g., outlining and organizing their thoughts before writing an essay, checking and correcting their work before submitting a problem set, or using a rubric to assess and improve their work)

3. Share these "positive points" with students, either verbally or in writing. Be as specific as possible so students are clear about what they've done well.

4. Encourage students to take note of things they did well and make a conscious effort to continue doing them (e.g., "I'll continue to repeat my experiments multiple times to validate my results").

How is this tool used in the classroom?

✔ To make students aware of what they've done well so that they can continue doing it

🌐 Teacher Talk

➔ Praise should address specific aspects of students' work, not the students themselves.

➔ The Points Worth Praising framework can be used to have students assess the strengths in their own work as well. To use the tool in this way, give students the list of points worth praising from Step 2 (shorten or simplify it as needed), explain the list in terms they can understand, and instruct them to "mark and describe the positives" in their assignments before submitting them.

The "Ps" to Better Work

What is it?

A technique that uses four different types of feedback to help students improve the quality of their work: praise, prompts, probing questions, and proposed improvements

What are the benefits of using this tool?

When we think about feedback, we typically think of two types: positive feedback and corrective feedback. But there's more to feedback than that. This tool describes four different types of feedback that we can use in our classrooms: praise, prompts, probing questions, and proposed improvements. Taken together, these four "Ps" teach students what quality work looks like and how they can produce it.

What are the basic steps?

1. Review an assignment that students have completed.

2. *Praise* specific things that were done well. For a list of suggestions, see the Points Worth Praising tool (p. 120, Step 2).

3. Use prompts, probing questions, and proposals to promote improvement.

- Use *prompts* to remind students of things they've been taught to do, but forgot to do.
- Use *probing questions* to encourage students to examine, extend, or explain their work.
- *Propose* specific strategies or suggestions for improvement.

4. Frame your feedback in student-friendly language, and adjust its content to fit the needs and abilities of individual students. *Think:* Did I provide enough direction, details, and/or examples for *this particular student* to understand and act on my comments?

5. Give students an opportunity to use the feedback they've received by letting them revise and resubmit their original assignments.

🔊 Teacher Talk

➜ The four Ps can be delivered verbally or in writing.

➜ The goal is to empower and inspire students to fix their own work, not to fix it for them (e.g., prompt a student to capitalize the first word in every sentence rather than capitalizing it yourself). By clarifying how students can improve their work and giving them the opportunity to do it, you can help them recognize that the power to achieve at higher levels is under their control.

➜ Students can use the four-P format to give each other feedback during peer-review sessions. Prepare them to be successful by explaining and modeling each *P* before they begin.

How is this tool used in the classroom?

✔ To teach students what high-quality work looks like

✔ To empower students to improve their work

Teachers use PRAISE to acknowledge things that were done well.

- *Your opinion piece includes all the essential elements (introduction, opinion, reasons, conclusion)!*

- *I see that you proofread your work, caught your error, and corrected it. That's great!*

Teachers use PROMPTS to remind students of things they've been taught to do, but forgot to do.

- *Remember to respond to all parts of the question.*

- *Remember to tune your violin before you begin playing.*

- *Remember to block out after the shot.*

- *Remember to spell-check your work before submitting it.*

- *Remember to do the same thing to both sides of the equation.*

Teachers use PROBING QUESTIONS to help students examine, explain, or expand on their work.

- *Why might you have made this kind of mistake? How can you avoid making it again?*

- *This is an interesting idea. Can you tell me more?*

- *Does your solution make sense? Is it possible to get a negative answer to this kind of problem?*

- *Can you clarify how this sentence relates to your thesis? I am confused.*

- *Did you take friction into account?*

- *Why did you choose to use the subjunctive mood here?*

  Note: Probing questions should address the strategies/processes that students use to complete their work (e.g., "Did you draw out the problem before you started working?") as well as the work itself.

Teachers PROPOSE concrete ways for students to improve their work.

- *You used the word "nice" a lot of times. Peek in our thesaurus. See if you can find some alternatives.*

- *Retake the photograph with the subject a bit off-center. See if you get a more interesting image.*

- *Try to use as many descriptive adjectives in these three sentences as you did in the previous ones.*

- *Your results might be more compelling if you presented them graphically. Maybe try a bar graph?*

- *Adding visuals and sound clips might make your presentation more engaging.*

Teachers combine the different types of feedback as needed.

- *Probe/probe combo: Is the effect you're seeing significant? How can you check?*

- *Probe/propose combo: Can you explain why your dog is your best friend? Give some specific reasons.*

- *Probe/prompt combo: Why might you have gotten a different result than you expected? Remember to discuss some possibilities in the conclusion of your lab report.*

STAIRS to Successful Feedback

What is it?

A tool that improves the quality of the feedback that we give to our students by spelling out a series of simple guidelines; each guideline is linked to a letter in the acronym STAIRS

What are the benefits of using this tool?

The right kind of feedback can have a powerful impact on learning and achievement (Hattie & Timperley, 2007). But what *is* the right kind of feedback? This tool attempts to answer that question by summarizing its critical attributes in an easy-to-remember acronym.

What are the basic steps?

1. Review the attributes of effective feedback as summarized in the STAIRS acronym (see p. 124 for more on each attribute):

   Specific

   Task focused, not student focused

   Age appropriate

   Improvement oriented

   Regular and rapid

   Selective

2. Use the STAIRS to help you deliver more effective feedback to your students (written and verbal). Note that feedback is often more effective when it's *not* accompanied by a grade.

3. Give students an opportunity to act on the feedback they receive.

How is this tool used in the classroom?

✔ To improve the quality of the feedback that we give to our students

What is Effective Feedback?*

Effective feedback is Specific.

Replace vague comments like "good job" or "needs work" with specific ones that teach students what was done well or how to improve. ("You successfully explained a complicated topic in terms that your audience could understand" or "Your lab report needs a Materials and Methods section.")

Effective feedback is Task focused, not student focused.

Avoid comments that focus on the student ("You're so smart!"). Comment instead on the work that students have done—products they've created, strategies/thinking processes they've used, assessment criteria they have or haven't yet satisfied, learning targets they have or haven't yet met, the impact of their efforts, or the progress they've made (e.g., "The extra effort you put into analyzing the significance of your results paid off. This is much improved!").

Effective feedback is Age appropriate.

If students can't understand your feedback, they won't be able to act on it. Use student-friendly language and avoid technical jargon like "shows partial command of writing conventions."

Effective feedback is Improvement oriented.

Corrective feedback should teach students what they can do to improve their work and encourage them to do it. Instead of correcting students' work for them, give students suggestions and strategies that they can use to take their work to the next level. ("Refer to the rubric to see how you can make this conclusion stronger" or "One of your homework problems is incorrect. Can you figure out which one and fix the error?") Adjust the amount of guidance that you provide according to students' individual needs and abilities.

Effective feedback is Regular and rapid.

Give students feedback as often as possible—and sooner rather than later. Feedback is most useful when assignments are fresh in students' minds and when it's not too late for them to make changes.

Effective feedback is Selective.

Prevent corrective feedback from becoming overwhelming by forcing yourself to be selective. Instead of pointing out *everything* that needs fixing, identify a few important things for students to work on and leave the rest for another time.

*For more on these principles, see Schute (2008), Brookhart (2008), Chappuis (2009), and Hattie and Timperley (2007).

 Teacher Talk

➜ Develop a classroom culture in which feedback is seen as a good thing and is actively sought out by students. Explain that errors and imperfections are part of the learning process—that the goal is for students to grow and improve, and that feedback can help them.

➜ One simple way to introduce the feedback-can-help-you concept: Hide something in your classroom and give students a minute or two to find it. Do this exercise twice—the first time without feedback and the second time with it (e.g., "You're getting warmer" or "You're getting colder"). Use this activity to initiate a conversation about the impact of feedback on achievement.

➜ When it comes to providing feedback, don't forget the high achievers! Use feedback to help them take their already-good work to the next level.

What & Why Feedback

What is it?

A tool that prepares students to produce higher-quality work by helping them understand what they've done well, what needs work, and why

What are the benefits of using this tool?

Feedback has the potential to advance learning and achievement. But not all kinds of feedback are created equal. Just noting what's done well or what needs to be improved, for example, isn't good enough; we need to explain why the good things are good and why the things that need work need work. By giving students a *why* for every *what*, we help them understand what quality work looks like and how to produce it.

What are the basic steps?

1. Review an assignment that students have completed. Indicate *what* was done well and *what* needs work. (Was progress made? Were criteria met? Were appropriate strategies used?)

2. Give students a *why* for every *what* that you identify. The goal is to help them understand why the good things are good (so they can continue doing them) and why the parts that need work need work (so they know how to go about improving them). For example:

   What: This is the third problem set in a row where you've gotten a perfect score.
   Why: Your strategy of checking your calculations before submitting your work is paying off!

   What: This batch of pesto sauce is much more successful than your previous one!
   Why: You used an effective strategy (adding an acid) to brighten up your flavors.

   What: When you play this passage, it doesn't sound as smooth as it should.
   Why: I can hear your hand moving every time you shift between first and third position.

   What: Your concluding sentence needs some additional work.
   Why: It doesn't tie the ideas from your paragraph together.

3. Offer students specific suggestions about how they can improve their performance, but leave it to them to act on those suggestions.

4. Give students an opportunity to use the feedback you've provided, either by allowing them to revise their original assignments or by having them complete a similar assignment in the future.

How is this tool used in the classroom?

✔ To improve the quality of the feedback we provide to our students
✔ To empower and make students responsible for improving their work

Knee-to-Knee Conference

What is it?

A technique that helps students improve what they've written by letting them hear and discuss their work with a partner

What are the benefits of using this tool?

What's the advantage of hearing your own writing read to you? Well, as one second grader recently told us, "You can hear where it sounds 'scratchy' and where it doesn't make sense." We couldn't have said it better ourselves! Yet most students never get the chance to hear what they've written. This tool changes that by giving them a forum (a Knee-to-Knee Conference) where they can listen to their drafts, evaluate the quality of their thinking, and identify any "scratchy" areas that need attention. It also reinforces the idea that revision is an essential part of the writing process and that good writers take time to rethink and improve their work.

What are the basic steps?

1. Assign a writing task. Tell students to skip lines so that their work will be easier to read and edit.

2. Pair students up to read and listen to each other's drafts. Instruct them to

- Read both drafts to themselves.
- Read their partners' drafts aloud (slowly, so that their partners can really hear their writing).
- Listen to their own drafts being read and think about things they might want to change.

3. Have students review and discuss their drafts. Use questions like these to spark and focus their conversations (customize the questions to fit the writing task, then post or distribute copies):

Which parts of the piece are clear? Which are hard to follow? Do the ideas make sense? Are they in the best order? What are the piece's greatest strengths? How could it be improved?

4. Instruct students to use what they learn to revise and improve their drafts.

How is this tool used in the classroom?

✔ To help students assess and improve the quality of their writing
✔ To engage students in the process of giving and getting constructive feedback

🕭 Teacher Talk

➔ If you want, have students use "The Seven Cs" (a list of quality criteria for writing assignments, see p. 134) instead of a list of discussion questions to focus their conversations in Step 3.

➔ This tool is ideal for addressing Writing Anchor Standard 5 from the Common Core, which calls for students to develop and strengthen their writing with guidance and support from their peers.

PEERS

What is it?

A tool that improves the productivity of peer-review sessions by outlining steps for students to follow (adapted from Brookhart, 2008); each is spelled out by a different letter in the PEERS acronym

What are the benefits of using this tool?

Susan Brookhart (2008) reminds us that having students review each other's work can be extremely valuable—or it can be a complete waste of precious classroom time. This tool makes peer-review sessions more focused and productive by teaching students five simple steps for giving and responding to feedback. Because these steps are spelled out by the letters in the PEERS acronym, they're easy for students to remember and follow.

What are the basic steps?

1. Pair students up. Explain that they'll be assessing each other's work on an assigned task using a process called PEERS.

2. Explain and model each step in the PEERS process:

Preview the assessment criteria or rubric before reviewing each other's work.

Examine each other's work keeping the assessment criteria in mind.

Explain what was done well and what could be improved. Be as specific as possible.

Review the feedback you received. *Think:* How can you use it to improve your work?

Share your thoughts with your partner and discuss plans for revision.

3. Give students a list of assessment criteria or a rubric for the assigned task. Review and discuss the criteria as a class.

Optional: Convert the list of criteria into a feedback form like the ones on p. 128.

4. Have students review each other's work on the assigned task using the PEERS process (post the PEERS acronym in a prominent location so that they can easily refer to it). Tell students whether to speak their feedback to their partners or record their comments on paper.

Note: Before having students use the PEERS process on their own, you might want to have them practice as a class (i.e., go through the process step-by-step using one or more samples of work).

5. Listen in as students work to confirm that they're staying on task and using the PEERS process properly. Remind them that their feedback should address the criteria for successful work: Which criteria have their partners satisfied? Which criteria have yet to be met?

6. Give students an opportunity to use the feedback they received by allowing them to revise their work.

Optional: Have students submit a copy of the feedback and a note explaining how they used it (or why they didn't) along with their completed work.

How is this tool used in the classroom?

✔ To teach students how to give each other focused feedback

✔ To have students revise and improve their work with guidance from their peers

Many teachers convert their lists of assessment criteria into feedback forms that students can use to review each other's work (see below for two examples).

EXAMPLE 1: A first-grade teacher had his students use the feedback form below to check each other's work on simple word problems. (He read the criteria aloud; they marked the appropriate boxes.) Note that the criteria on the form were criteria he had been teaching and modeling for weeks.

MATH PROBLEM CHECKLIST	☺	☺
The key words in the question are underlined.		
The problem is drawn out using pictures.		
The correct number model is shown.		
The answer is boxed.		
The answer is correct.		

EXAMPLE 2: A middle school teacher used the Common Core Writing Standards to help him develop a list of assessment criteria for persuasive essays. He then converted this list into a feedback form that students could use to review each other's drafts throughout the year. (The feedback that one student received from a classmate is shown below.) This teacher also used the form himself to give students detailed feedback about their work (he stapled a completed form to each student's paper).

Assessment Criteria	Keep Working	Almost There	Excellent	Comments/Suggestions
POSITION: Position or claim is clearly stated.			✓	Position is clear and easy to find.
EVIDENCE: Position is supported with relevant evidence or reasons. Conflicting evidence/claims are addressed where appropriate.	✓			I am not clear how your third piece of evidence supports your position. Also, you didn't address any alternative positions.
CONCLUSION: Conclusion follows from and summarizes the argument/evidence.		✓		Don't think new evidence should be presented in a conclusion.
ORGANIZATION: Paper is structured as follows: position, evidence, conclusion. Evidence is linked together in a clear and logical sequence.		✓		Overall organization is great, but would your first two pieces of evidence make more sense if you reversed their order?
WRITING: Style is formal, yet easy to understand. Ideas flow smoothly and paper is free of errors.		✓		Your writing is clear, but there are a lot of spelling mistakes. Did you forget to spell-check?

Writer's Club

What is it?

A forum for students to share, discuss, and give each other feedback about their writing

What are the benefits of using this tool?

In the real world, writers rely on their colleagues to help them solidify their ideas and fine-tune their work. Student writers need this same exact kind of support, and a Writer's Club gives it to them. A Writer's Club offers students a safe place to read, discuss, and get feedback about what they've written. And it encourages them to strengthen their drafts with the help of their peers as recommended by the Common Core State Standards.

What are the basic steps?

1. Organize students into Writer's Clubs to discuss pieces they've written (three to five students per club).

2. Instruct students to read their pieces aloud and request feedback from their peers. The type of feedback can be determined by you or by your students; see below for options.

- *Tell students what criteria to focus on when giving each other feedback.* For example, "When listening to each other's persuasive essays, keep these questions in mind: Does the writer state his or her position? Support it with strong evidence? Address alternative positions?" (For a list of suggested criteria, see "The Seven Cs" [p. 134, Step 3].)

- *Have students tell their classmates what kind of input they're looking for.* For example, "My opening isn't as catchy as I'd like it to be. Does anyone have any suggestions?"

- *Distribute the list of discussion questions on p. 130 and tell students—or let them choose—which questions to respond to.* (Note that many have ties to Common Core Standards.) Modify the list as needed for specific types of writing tasks or for use with younger students.

3. Encourage students to listen carefully and be ready to share their thoughts. Remind them that effective feedback has the following characteristics:

- It's specific. (What exactly was done well? What exactly could be improved?)

- It's improvement oriented. (What can the writer do to improve his or her draft?)

- It's about the work, not the student. ("Your thesis was unique," not "You're a good writer.")

4. Have students synthesize the feedback they receive and use it to revise and refine their drafts.

Optional: Have club members meet again to review and discuss their revisions.

How is this tool used in the classroom?

✔ To have students revise and improve their writing with the help of their peers

✔ To help students develop critical speaking, listening, and interpersonal skills

Writer's Club Discussion Questions

Literal Questions

- What is this piece about? What are the key points?

- How would you summarize this piece?

- Does the piece address the question or task that was given? The purpose of the assignment?

- Are there any factual or grammar errors that need to be fixed? Is anything missing (words, details, components)?

Personal-Perspective Questions

- How did this piece make you feel?

- If this were your piece, what aspect of it would you be most proud of?

- Did you learn anything from listening to this piece that could help you as a writer?

- Who was this piece written for? Did the writer address the needs and/or interests of the intended audience?

  For example: Did the writer explain things in a way that would be easy for others to follow?

Rules of the Writer's Club

1. Everyone reads.
2. Writers choose one or more questions for listeners to respond to.
3. Listeners give additional feedback by choosing other questions to answer.
4. Writers listen to responses without becoming defensive.
5. Writers use what they learn to revise and improve their work.

Follow the guidelines for productive discussions at all times:
Take turns talking, ask and answer questions, listen respectfully to other people's ideas, and build on what other people have to say.

Analytical Questions

- What are the greatest strengths of this piece and why? What could be improved?

- Are the ideas presented and connected in an orderly and logical way?

- How well did the writer fulfill the requirements of this type of piece?

  → How clear and well supported is the writer's position? *(argument piece)*

  → How clearly and accurately is the topic explained? *(explanatory piece)*

  → How clearly and vividly is the event/experience described? *(narrative piece)*

- How does this piece compare to other pieces this writer has composed?

Original-Thinking Questions

- If this piece were a type of clothing, music, or weather, what would it be and why?

- What might be the impact of adding or deleting ___ from the piece?

- What are some possible ways to improve this piece?

  For example: How could the writer conclude the piece more strongly, add atmosphere to the story, or make the writing clearer and more coherent?

- Did the writer "paint a picture" with his or her words? Were you able to see what the writer was saying in your mind?

I Think, You Think

What is it?

A tool that invites students to evaluate a completed assignment, compare their assessment with ours, and use the combined feedback to make improvements

What are the benefits of using this tool?

Give a man a fish and you feed him for a day. Teach a man to fish and you feed him for a lifetime.

—Chinese proverb

Giving students feedback about their work is important, but teaching them how to evaluate and improve their own work is even more important for their long-term success. This tool helps students practice and refine their self-assessment skills by asking them to critique their work independently and then compare their critiques with ours.

What are the basic steps?

1. Talk to students about the importance of assessing their own work. Explain how the I Think, You Think process works and how it will help them develop their self-assessment skills. ("You'll assess your work, I'll assess your work, and then we'll compare and discuss our ideas.")

2. Explain and model the role that criteria play in the assessment process. ("Examine the criteria for quality work. Then assess the degree to which your work meets those criteria. Here's how…")

3. Have students evaluate a completed assignment using a specific set of assessment criteria. Criteria can be presented in the form of a list, a checklist (see pp. 47–49 for more on checklists), or a rubric.

4. Ask students to record their thoughts on paper. ("I think ___ .") Encourage them to be as specific as possible and to address strengths as well as weaknesses.

5. Evaluate students' work using the same set of criteria. Record your comments next to those of your students (yours should be labeled "You think" as illustrated in Example 1).

6. Ask students to compare their thoughts with yours and identify areas of agreement/disagreement. Discuss any discrepancies, and give them feedback about their self-assessment skills.

7. Help students use the combined feedback (yours and theirs) to establish plans for improvement. Encourage them to resubmit their revised work.

How is this tool used in the classroom?

✔ To help students develop and refine their self-assessment skills

✔ To use feedback (yours and students') as a means of helping students improve their work

EXAMPLE 1: An eighth-grade English teacher designed the following task to test his students' ability to comprehend a complex informational text (Common Core R.CCR.10) and craft an explanatory paragraph (Common Core W.CCR.2): "Read the selection that you've been given. Use what you learn to write a short piece explaining the influence of the blues on other musical genres."

Before students started working, he reminded them to consult their explanatory-writing rubrics (rubrics they had been discussing and using for weeks) when drafting and evaluating their essays. The I Think, You Think form that one student submitted with her completed draft is shown here:

Name: Angelica

Task and purpose for writing:

My purpose in writing this piece is to explain how the blues influenced other kinds of music.

I think (student)…	You think (teacher)…
• My piece addressed the task that I was given.	• I agree that you did an excellent job of responding to the task that was given and providing detailed examples to support the relationship between the blues and other types of music.
• I gave lots of examples from the reading about how the blues influenced other types of music.	
• I made my examples detailed and specific.	• Your conclusion doesn't really follow from or tie up the great examples that you gave in the body of your piece. Can you fix that?
• Since this is a piece about music, I tried to write and give examples in a creative way that would help people "hear" the music I was talking about. This wasn't part of the rubric, but I like how it turned out. Do you?	• You seem to be missing one of the key pieces of an explanatory essay–an opening statement that introduces your topic and previews the information to come. Look back at the first item on your rubric!
	• With explanatory writing, it's more important to be clear than creative. In this case, though, your attempts to help us "hear the music" actually added to the piece's clarity rather than taking away from it, so good job!

What can I do to improve this and/or future assignments?

• Add an opening sentence that introduces my topic and previews the rest of the piece. Review the "introduction" portion of my explanatory-writing rubric to make sure that I'm not missing anything else!

• Revise my concluding sentence so that it better wraps up my ideas. Check my rubric on this one as well.

• For future, remember that the main goal of an explanatory piece is to explain information clearly and accurately. Be careful to focus on that the most.

EXAMPLE 2: A kindergarten teacher used a variation of I Think, You Think to help her students improve their letter-formation skills (Common Core L.K.1a). (In this case, they were focusing on the letter *b*.) She began by showing them an example of a properly written *b* and discussing the four criteria for success:

- A perfect *b* should have two strokes.
- A perfect *b* should face the right direction (*b*, not *d*).
- A perfect *b* should be the right shape and size. Use the lines on your paper as a guide.
- A perfect *b* shouldn't have any extra bits or squiggles.

After practicing on sentence-strip cards, students paired up with a partner to get feedback about their work. They used the criteria for success to assess their partner's letters as well as their own. They then "pasted their thoughts on paper" using smiley-face stickers; see below for one example.

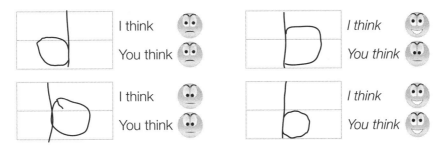

Students concluded the peer-feedback session by discussing any discrepancies in their assessments and helping each other identify their best work. They then continued practicing on their own, using their best letters as models.

🌓 Teacher Talk

→ The criteria that students use to evaluate their work in Step 3 should be given to them when the task is first assigned—not after they've completed it. The idea is to help students understand what quality work looks like and how their work will be evaluated right from the very beginning.

→ Encourage students to focus on the assessment criteria when evaluating and commenting on each other's work, but make it clear that they can comment on aspects of the work that aren't directly related to the criteria as well. (You can do this, too.)

→ As shown in Example 2, students can use the I Think, You Think process with a classmate instead of with you. One advantage of the peer-peer format is that it gives students immediate feedback about their work (students don't have to wait for you to review everyone's work and get back to them). The peer-peer format also gives students double the amount of practice evaluating work against a set of criteria.

Note: Before using the peer-peer format, be sure to teach students what effective feedback looks like and how to give it. (Feedback should be specific, descriptive rather than judgmental, and focused on the given assessment criteria.) You may also want to familiarize students with the PEERS acronym (p. 127), which spells out specific guidelines for peer-review sessions.

Stop, Read, Revise

What is it?

A process that enhances the quality of student writing by having students read and revise their work

What are the benefits of using this tool?

What students *actually* write isn't always the same as what they think they've written. When students take the time to review their writing, they often find that important words are missing or that their ideas aren't as clear as they thought. Stop, Read, Revise gets students in the habit of reading their own writing so they can root out mistakes and communicate their ideas with greater power and precision.

What are the basic steps?

1. Talk to students about the importance of reading what they write. Help them generate a list of reasons why the reading-after-writing habit is so good to develop.

2. Give students a writing task. Tell them to skip lines so they'll have room to revise their work.

3. Ask students to read their completed pieces to themselves. Tell them to check their work for "The Seven Cs" (explain the Cs beforehand; adjust them as needed for specific kinds of writing tasks):

    Completeness: Did I leave out any words, details, or big ideas?

    Coherence: Are my ideas presented in a logical and orderly way? Do they make sense?

    Clarity: Are my ideas clear and easy to understand? Is my writing clear and easy to read?

    Correctness: Are there any spelling, grammar, and/or factual errors that I need to correct?

    Composition: Do I have a topic sentence/thesis, supporting information, and conclusion?

    Congruence: Does my response address the specific question or task I was given?

    Communication skills: Would someone who's unfamiliar with this topic understand what I wrote?

4. Instruct students to revise their work as needed.

5. Invite students to reflect on and share what they learned by reading their own writing.

6. Teach students that the Stop, Read, Revise process is one that they can and should use on their own. Help them make it habitual by having them use it as often as possible.

How is this tool used in the classroom?

✔ To help students evaluate and improve the quality of their written work

🌣 Teacher Talk

→ The Seven Cs reinforce many Common Core writing and language skills—skills like adjusting writing to fit task, purpose, and audience; presenting ideas in a clear and logical way; using the conventions of Standard Written English; and improving writing via editing and revision.

How Will I Help Students Monitor Their Learning and Establish Goals and Plans for Moving Forward?

Without continual growth and progress, such words as improvement, achievement, and success have no meaning.

—Benjamin Franklin

We tend to think of students as passive participants in assessment rather than engaged users of the information that assessment can produce. What we should be asking is, how can students use assessment to take responsibility for and improve their own learning?

—Stephen Chappuis and Rick Stiggins, "Classroom Assessment for Learning"

In Chapter 1, we discussed a number of tools that help teachers establish learning goals and communicate those goals to students at the beginning of a unit or learning sequence. While both of these practices—establishing goals and sharing them with students—are essential to assessment-driven instruction, they do little on their own to increase students' responsibility for their own learning. And if we want our students to be college and career ready, then empowering them to take charge of their learning is one of the most important moves we can make. Indeed, a consistent finding across the numerous initiatives aimed at defining college and career readiness (most notably the Common Core State Standards, the Partnership for 21st Century Skills, the American Diploma Project, and research conducted by ACT and the Educational Policy Improvement Center) is that successful students are able to assess and direct their own learning.

This chapter, like the two chapters before it, is about inviting students to take a more active role in the assessment process. More specifically, it is about instilling in students the idea that learning is an ongoing process that involves monitoring progress and mapping out steps for moving forward. In this chapter, we present six tools that help students establish goals, outline plans for achieving those goals, and assess their growth over time:

1. **Goal Cards** gives students a clear format for developing personal learning goals and establishing plans for achieving those goals.

2. **GOT It!** invites students to chart and reflect on their progress as they work to achieve specific goals.

3. **In My GRASP** gets students in the habit of slowing down to think their way through challenging tasks before they begin working on them.

4. **Learning STAR** uses a simple, four-step process to build students' capacity for continuous self-assessment and improvement.

5. **Personal Best** motivates students to improve their performance and achieve "personal bests" as learners.

6. **Test Assessment** teaches students to analyze their tests, identify knowledge gaps, and establish plans for closing those gaps.

Goal Cards

What is it?

A tool that prepares students to become more self-directed and successful learners by giving them a framework (a Goal Card) that they can use to record personal learning goals, establish plans for achieving those goals, and reflect on their progress

What are the benefits of using this tool?

Not all goals need to come from the teacher. In fact, involving students in the goal-setting process is a great way to develop the kind of self-direction that the Common Core State Standards encourage. This tool invites students to identify personal learning goals, establish plans for achieving those goals, and reflect on their accomplishments. It also calls students' attention to the way that their actions (planning, effort, strategy use) can impact their success.

What are the basic steps?

1. Invite students to establish personal learning goals. Examples 1–7 highlight some of the different kinds of goals they might choose to pursue.

2. Have students record their goals and plans for achieving them on a Goal Card. Choose one of the three Goal Card formats on pp. 140–141, create your own format, or use blank index cards.

3. Meet with students one-on-one to review and discuss their plans. Once an acceptable plan has been agreed upon, sign—and have students sign—their Goal Cards.

4. Remind students to follow through with their plans, monitor/gather feedback about their progress, and adjust their plans as needed. If you want, have them check off each step in their plan as it's accomplished, as shown in Example 7.

5. Acknowledge students who worked hard and achieved their goals. Call their attention to the ways that their actions (e.g., effort, strategy use) influenced their success. For example, "This draft is much smoother than your last one. The strategy of reading your work aloud really helped you improve."

6. Use questions like these to help students reflect on the impact that effort, persistence, and strategy use can have on their success:

   - What strategies did you use to tackle your goal? What impact did they have?
   - How did it feel to achieve (or make progress toward achieving) your goal?
   - Can effort level, strategy use, and persistence influence achievement? How?
   - Do you have the power to influence your academic success?
   - Did you learn anything that could help you be more successful in the future?

How is this tool used in the classroom?

✔ To have students set goals, establish plans for achieving them, and monitor their progress

✔ To help students see that planning, effort, and strategy use can facilitate achievement

Students can establish personal learning goals at any point in the instructional process. (They can create these goals from scratch or select teacher-generated goals that they'd like to pursue with greater intensity.) The examples that follow highlight some of the many different kinds of goals that students might choose to pursue—personal-interest goals, process goals, task-related goals, etc.

EXAMPLE 1: Learn about something that interests me

After introducing an upcoming unit about ancient Egypt, a sixth-grade teacher invited his students to generate some goals of their own. ("What are you interested in learning about this topic?") One student's Goal Card is shown below.

This Goal Card belongs to *Anthony Coleman*

Goal: *To learn how structures as amazing as the pyramids were built using the tools available at the time*

Date goal established: *January 12th*   **Date goal achieved:** *January 26th*

Action plan: *I will ask the librarian if she knows of any good books about this topic. I will also look on Wikipedia and other Internet sites to see what I can find. Maybe my shop teacher would be interested in helping me with this project since it relates to tools. I will have to check about that. Once I find my information, I will make a poster to show what I learned.*

Student signature: *Anthony Coleman*   **Teacher signature:** *M. R Engel*

EXAMPLE 2: Try out a specific strategy

After weeks of learning about different reading comprehension strategies in English class, a student made a commitment to trying one of them out.

This week, my goal is to actively check for understanding while reading assigned texts. I will do this using the "stop and summarize" strategy that we learned about in class. I will try the strategy in at least two different classes to see if it helps me better understand and remember what I read.

EXAMPLE 3: Develop a specific attitude, behavior, or habit of mind

A high school homeroom teacher helps his students grow as learners by encouraging them to identify attitudes, behaviors, and habits of mind that could help them be more successful in school. Students record their thoughts on paper and show their commitment to developing the attitudes, behaviors, and habits they've identified by signing their names to their plans.

My goal is to develop the courage to participate more and ask questions when I am lost in calculus class. For starters, I am going to commit to raising my hand at least once per class. I will try a self-talk strategy ("Why do you care what other people think?" "What's the worst that could happen?" "Other people are probably lost too") to see if it helps me.

— Jennifer

EXAMPLE 4: Focus on one of the learning goals/targets from a lesson or unit

Midway through a unit on magnetic forces and fields, a physics teacher asked his students to assess their progress toward the various learning targets they had been working on in class. (Students made this assessment after reviewing completed assignments, quizzes, and teacher feedback.) He challenged them to identify the target that was proving hardest to hit, record it on a Goal Card, and map out a plan for achieving it. He offered specific suggestions for each of the targets in question (readings, activities, study strategies, etc.), but left it to students to develop a course of action.

EXAMPLE 5: Revisit a learning goal/target that was missed the first time around

At the end of a unit on graphic design principles, a teacher had students review their culminating assessment tests, identify learning goals they hadn't yet achieved, and develop plans for achieving them. The method that students used to review their tests, and the Goal Card that one student generated, can be found in the Test Assessment tool (pp. 151–154).

EXAMPLE 6: Complete a task or assignment

A second-grade teacher uses Goal Cards to help his students focus their attention and effort on specific tasks. He has students choose a goal to work on at the start of each week and reflect on their accomplishments at the end of that week. In the interim, he encourages students to share their Goal Cards with their parents to keep them abreast of the things that they're working on.

GOAL OF THE WEEK by *Christine*

What is my goal for the week? *My goal for this week is to read the two books we have to read for our animal project.*

How did I do? What did I learn? *I ran out of time and only got to read one book. I maybe should have started reading on Monday.*

EXAMPLE 7: Tackle one specific part of a larger goal or task

Fifth-grade students were training for the Presidential Physical Fitness Test in gym class. After three weeks of assessing and monitoring their progress in all five test events, students identified the event that was hardest for them, established a goal for improvement, and developed a plan for achieving that goal. One student's Goal Card is shown here:

This goal card belongs to *Arturo*　　　　　**Date:** *April 6th*　　　　　**Subject:** *Gym*

Ultimate goal: *Satisfy the requirements for all five fitness test events.*

Intermediate goal: *By the end of the month, I will be able to run a mile in under 8 minutes.*
Current time is 8 min, 6 seconds. To get the Presidential Award, I need 7 min, 57 seconds.

Action plan (✓ off each step that you accomplish)	**Completion Date:**
✓ 1　*I will ask my teacher for tips on improving my form.*	*April 7*
✓ 2　*I will run with my dad every weekend this month.*	*April 9, April 16*
✓ 3　*I will try to take 5 seconds off my time by next week.*	*April 15*
☐ 4　*I will try to cut 5 more seconds off by the end of the month.*	
☐ 5　*I will stretch after every run so that I don't pull a muscle.*	*Ongoing*

Basic Goal Card

This Goal Card belongs to _____

Start date: _____   **Achievement date:** _____

My goal is to

Here is what I will do to try and achieve my goal:

Goal Card with Action Plan

This Goal Card belongs to _____   **Date:** _____

Goal:

Action plan (✓off each step that you accomplish and record the completion date)   **Completion date**

☐ 1

☐ 2

☐ 3

☐ 4

☐ 5

☐ 6

Student signature: **Teacher signature:**

Expanded Goal Card

This Goal Card belongs to _____

Start date: _____   Achievement date: _____

The goal that I will be working to achieve is…

What do I already know that can help me achieve this goal?

What will I need to know in order to achieve this goal?

What will I need to be able to do in order to achieve this goal?

People, materials, and resources that might help me achieve this goal include…

Steps that I will take to try and achieve this goal include…

Student signature: **Teacher signature:**

GOT It!

What is it?

A tool that has students assess and chart their progress as they work to achieve specific learning goals or targets; the "GOT" in GOT It! stands for growth over time

What are the benefits of using this tool?

In order for students to become more successful and self-directed learners, they must be able to monitor and manage their own learning. This tool, which was inspired by Marzano's (2006) ideas on tracking student progress, builds students' capacity for self-regulation by teaching them to assess their starting level of achievement, develop strategies for improvement, and chart their growth over time. By enabling students to visualize their forward progress—and by celebrating improvement rather than absolute achievement—it can also improve their confidence, motivation, and commitment to learning.

What are the basic steps?

1. Identify a learning goal or target that students will be working to achieve.

   Note: A well-crafted goal/target should describe what students will need to know, understand, be able to do, or be like—and it should be framed in clear and student-friendly language.

2. Ask students to assess and record their starting (pre-instruction) level of achievement on a GOT It! Form. Customize the reproducible form on p. 145 (fill in the blanks to create an appropriate rating scale) or create your own form using the ones in Examples 1 and 2 as models.

3. Make it clear that improvement is what matters, not starting knowledge or ability.

4. Help students create a visual record of their progress over time by stopping at various points (after a quiz, lecture, assignment, etc.) to have them reassess and record their level of achievement.

5. Facilitate forward progress between each checkpoint:

   • Review students' GOT It! forms to gauge their progress and overall level of achievement. Identify steps that you can take to help all students (or specific students) improve.

   • Encourage students to take responsibility for their own success. Ask them what *they* could do to improve before the next checkpoint and help them implement their plans.

6. Help students process and learn from the overall experience by having them respond to the reflection questions/prompts at the bottom of their GOT It! forms.

How is this tool used in the classroom?

✔ To help students assess and track their progress

As shown in Examples 1 and 2, teachers often adjust the format and wording of their GOT It! forms to match the age, needs, and interests of their students—or the goals that their students are working on.

EXAMPLE 1: A first-grade teacher used the race-themed GOT It! form shown below to inspire her students to master their addition facts (Common Core 1.OA.C.6). Students charted their progress by pasting stickers on their forms.

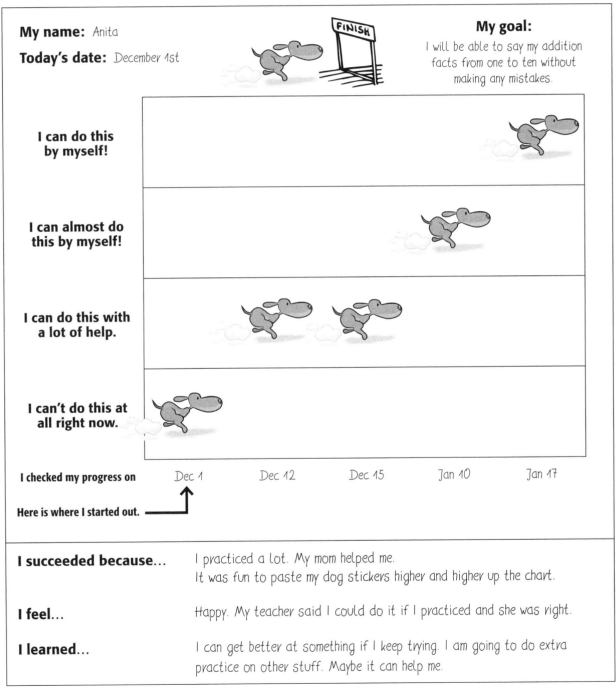

EXAMPLE 2: A teacher with a lot of sports fans in her class created this football-themed GOT It! form:

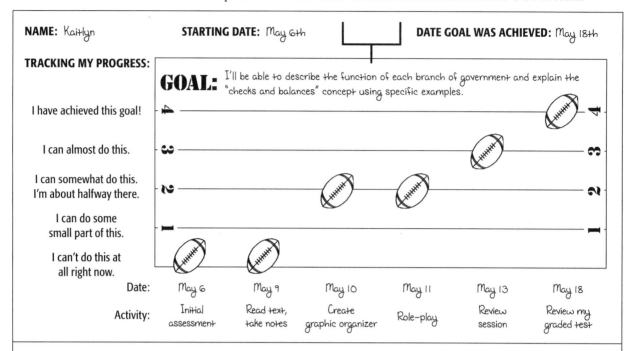

NAME: Kaitlyn   **STARTING DATE:** May 6th   **DATE GOAL WAS ACHIEVED:** May 18th

TRACKING MY PROGRESS:

GOAL: I'll be able to describe the function of each branch of government and explain the "checks and balances" concept using specific examples.

I have achieved this goal! — 4

I can almost do this. — 3

I can somewhat do this. I'm about halfway there. — 2

I can do some small part of this. — 1

I can't do this at all right now.

Date: May 6 / May 9 / May 10 / May 11 / May 13 / May 18

Activity: Initial assessment / Read text, take notes / Create graphic organizer / Role-play / Review session / Review my graded test

REFLECTION QUESTIONS:

What contributed to your success (people, resources, strategies, attitudes)?

Creating a graphic organizer helped me make sense of what I read in my textbook. The role-playing activity also helped me understand things better. Plus, it made this topic seem a lot more interesting, so I studied it more after that.

How do you feel about what you've accomplished?

I am proud because I didn't know anything about this topic in the beginning, but now I am an expert!

Did you learn anything from this experience that you could use in the future?

Since making a graphic organizer helped me more than taking regular notes, I might try that again the next time we have a reading assignment.

🞯 Teacher Talk

→ For more on crafting student-friendly learning goals/targets (Step 1), see the Student-Friendly Learning Targets tool (pp. 12–13).

→ Emphasizing the idea that improvement is what matters (not existing knowledge or ability) will help students who know very little at the start of the process feel comfortable. It will also discourage students from comparing their performance with that of their peers, thus eliminating the pressure and negative feelings that such comparisons often produce.

→ This tool is commonly used to have students track their progress with regard to teacher-established learning goals/targets, but it can also be used to have students track their progress toward goals or targets that they've established for themselves.

→ Having students assess and chart their progress teaches them to "define success in terms of their own learning as opposed to their standing relative to other students" (Marzano, 2006, p. 89)—a shift in perspective that can boost confidence and motivation.

Name: _____ Date: _____

Learning goal/target: _____

GOT It! Form

INITIAL ASSESSMENT: Check off your starting level of achievement on the scale below.

☐ **Level 5:** _____

☐ **Level 4:** _____

☐ **Level 3:** _____

☐ **Level 2:** _____

☐ **Level 1:** _____

TRACKING MY PROGRESS:

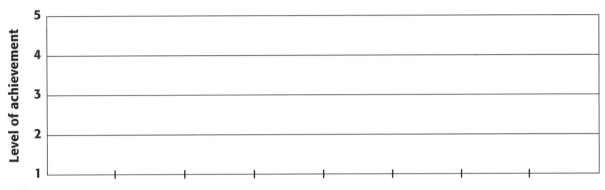

Progress checkpoints:

REFLECTION QUESTIONS:

What helped me improve (people, resources, strategies, attitudes)?

How do I feel about my accomplishments?

Did I learn anything from this experience that might help me in the future?

In My GRASP

What is it?

A five-step process that helps students analyze goals/tasks and develop concrete plans for accomplishing them; each step is linked to a letter in the acronym GRASP

What are the benefits of using this tool?

When faced with a goal or task, students often jump right in without stopping to think. This tool breaks them of that habit by getting them to think their way through a task before they begin working. By teaching students to analyze what they're trying to accomplish, identify relevant resources, map out an action plan, and address potential challenges, the tool prepares them to be more self-directed and successful learners.

What are the basic steps?

1. Tell students you'll be teaching them a process for tackling goals and tasks.

2. Distribute copies of the In My GRASP Planning Form (p. 147). Explain and model each step in the goal/task-tackling (GRASP) process.

3. Help students grow comfortable with the GRASP process by having them practice it. (Select a goal or task and have them complete the form.) Observe students as they work and offer assistance as needed.

4. Explain that students can and should use the GRASP process independently—not just when you tell them to, but whenever they're faced with challenging goals or tasks.

5. Have copies of the planning form available and remind students to use it throughout the year.

How is this tool used in the classroom?

✔ To have students analyze goals and tasks and map out plans for achieving them

✔ To help students become more self-directed learners

🔊 Teacher Talk

→ Using this tool trains students to become the kind of self-directed learners that the Common Core State Standards call for—learners who "effectively [seek] out and [use] resources to assist them, including teachers, peers, and print and digital reference materials" (NGA Center/CCSSO, 2010, p. 7).

→ When using this tool with very young students, you may want to complete the GRASP process as a class. *Sample dialog:* "If our goal is to learn how to tie our shoes, who could we turn to for help? How could we try and get better at it? If we have problems, what could we do? How will we know when we've achieved our goal?"

Name: _____   Date: _____

In My GRASP Planning Form

Identify a **Goal** that you're trying to accomplish or a task you're trying to complete.

> *What do you want to accomplish? Describe something you want to learn, make, or do.*

Identify **Resources** that could help you accomplish the goal or task.

> *What resources can you take advantage of? Consider people, places, and things—and brainstorm a list of possibilities (books, newspapers, museums, websites, podcasts, your school librarian, a specific classmate, etc.).*

Map out an **Action plan**.

> *How will you tackle your goal or task? What steps will you take? Be specific.*

Identify potential **Stumbling blocks** or challenges. Then think about how you'll address them.

What obstacles or difficulties might you face?	*How will you handle them?*

Think: What will constitute **Proof** that you've accomplished your goal or task?

> *How will you know if you've been successful? How will you show what you've learned or accomplished?*

Learning STAR

What is it?

A continuous self-assessment process that helps students achieve their goals and produce high-quality work; the steps in this process are spelled out by the letters in the acronym STAR

What are the benefits of using this tool?

Successful people assess and evaluate their efforts on a continual basis. By teaching our students to do the same, we can prepare them to be more successful, both in and beyond the classroom. This tool helps students develop their self-assessment skills by explaining the importance of continuous reflection and by outlining a concrete process for doing it. Once students become familiar with the steps in the Learning STAR process, they can use it to help them achieve their learning goals and complete their assignments.

What are the basic steps?

1. Initiate a conversation about the importance of self-assessment and goal setting. Be sure to mention the following points:

- Successful individuals constantly reflect on their performance and look for ways to improve it.
- Students can become more successful by engaging in this same type of self-reflection, and you're going to teach them how.

2. Introduce the Learning STAR process to students. Discuss and model each step so that students are clear about what the process entails.

*S*tatus check: Ask myself where I am relative to the goal or task that I'm trying to accomplish.

*T*hink: What can I do to move forward? What steps should I take? Who or what can help me?

*A*ct: Follow through with my plans for improvement. Ask for help if I need it.

*R*epeat: Go back to *S*. Repeat the STAR process until I've accomplished my goal or task.

3. Use guided practice sessions to help students master the Learning STAR process. Give them specific tasks or goals to work on. Check their progress and offer feedback along the way.

4. Explain that the Learning STAR process can be used with virtually any goal or task. Encourage students to use it as often as possible (not just when you tell them to) so that it becomes habitual.

How is this tool used in the classroom?

✔ To get students in the habit of assessing, improving, and monitoring their performance

Personal Best

What is it?

A tool that facilitates continuous improvement by having students analyze their work and establish plans for making it better

What are the benefits of using this tool?

All across the country, track athletes train hard, day in and day out. Many have no expectation of winning their races. What drives these athletes is the deep sense of satisfaction that comes from seeing their efforts pay off as their times improve. Each race becomes a chance to achieve a personal best. This tool taps into the motivational power of the personal best by encouraging students to do their best work and celebrate their achievements. Even more important, it builds the self-assessment skills students need to achieve personal bests by teaching them how to reflect on their work, identify how it has improved, and determine how it can be improved further.

What are the basic steps?

1. Select a skill that you'll be helping students develop over time (e.g., writing the letters of the alphabet, preparing a lab report, or crafting a persuasive essay).

2. Give each student a folder labeled with the name of the skill and the words "Personal Best." Tell students that they'll use these folders to store their work as they practice the selected skill.

Note: Students' folders can be traditional paper folders or computer folders/e-portfolios.

3. Begin teaching the selected skill and have students put their first sample of work into their folders. Depending on the skill, this could be anything from a problem set to a paragraph to a painting.

4. Let students know that you'll continue to teach this skill, and that they'll continue to practice it. Explain that the goal is for them to get better each time (i.e., to achieve personal bests).

5. Have students add to their folders over time—daily, weekly, or monthly depending on the skill. Remind them to date all samples of work.

6. Help students compare their current work with their previous work to see how they're improving. (Are their topic sentences stronger and better supported? Are their passes more accurate?)

7. Use the reflection worksheet on p. 150 to have students assess their progress and develop plans for improvement. (Ideally, students should store these worksheets in their folders along with their work.) Discuss or comment on students' work and worksheets as needed.

How is this tool used in the classroom?

✔ To help students evaluate their work and develop plans for improving it

✔ To have students monitor their progress and celebrate their achievements

Name: _____ Date: _____

The skill that I am working on is _____

Reflecting on My Personal Bests

Directions: Use the writing prompts below to help you reflect on your progress and make plans for improvement.

This is better than my previous work because…

One reason why the quality of my work has improved is…

Something about my work that I would like to improve further is…

Something that my teacher or a classmate thinks I should work on is…

Note: Only complete this section if you have time to discuss your work with your teacher or a classmate.

My goal for next time is to…

Test Assessment

What is it?

A tool that transforms classroom tests into learning opportunities by helping students analyze their performance and devise plans for improvement (Which content objectives did I master? Which caused me problems? What can I do to move forward?)

What are the benefits of using this tool?

When we return graded tests, the first and last thing that many students do with those tests is look at their grades. These students miss out on an important learning opportunity since a letter grade doesn't give them what they need to improve, namely detailed feedback about which aspects of the content they've mastered and which need additional work. The Test Assessment tool prepares students to achieve at higher levels by helping them analyze their graded tests, identify content objectives that need additional work, and develop targeted strategies for improvement.

What are the basic steps?

1. Record the learning goals for an upcoming unit on a Test Assessment Form (p. 154). Distribute copies at the start of the unit so that students are clear about what they're expected to learn.

2. Develop an end-of-unit test that is consistent with these goals. Make a note of which test questions are designed to test which goals (e.g., questions 3 and 5 will test students' ability to add two-digit numbers).

3. Have students assess their level of achievement with regard to each learning goal *just before* they take the test. Ask them to record these initial assessment scores on the Test Assessment Form.

4. Return students' graded tests. Tell students which test items correspond to which learning goals. Have them record this information in the Test Items column of the Test Assessment Form.

5. Give students time to review their tests. Instruct them to take the following steps for each goal:
   - Review the test items that were designed to assess their achievement of that goal.
   - Note whether they got each item correct, incorrect, or partially correct in the Score column.
   - Reassess their level of achievement. Record the new score in the Final Assessment column.

6. Ask students to identify and circle the learning goals that need further attention. Help them develop plans for achieving one (or more) of these goals, and have them record their plans on a Goal Card. (Reproducible Goal Cards are available on pp. 140–141.)

   Optional: Offer students specific suggestions for tackling each learning goal ("If you haven't yet mastered learning goal X, you might want to try one of the following options…"), but leave it to them to decide on a course of action.

7. Provide opportunities for students to show that they've improved by generating follow-up tests or tasks that assess their achievement of the targeted goals.

How is this tool used in the classroom?

✔ To have students analyze their graded tests and develop plans for improvement

EXAMPLE: A high school student completed the Test Assessment Form and Goal Card shown below at the end of a graphic design unit.

TEST ASSESSMENT FORM

Name: Will Norvell   **Date:** October 6th   **Topic:** Graphic Design Principles: Typography

Initial Assessment	Learning Goals	Test Items	Score ✓ = Correct +/- = Partly correct x = Not correct	Final Assessment
1 2 ③ 4	Know the major categories of typefaces and their distinguishing features.	1 2 4	X +/- X	① 2 3 4
1 2 3 ④	Be able to select an appropriate typeface for a given communication objective.	3 5	✓ ✓	1 2 3 ④
1 ② 3 4	Understand type measurements, including relative measurements and spacing measurements (tracking, kerning, leading, baseline shifts, alignment).	6 7 8	✓ +/- ✓	1 2 ③ 4

SELF-ASSESSMENT GUIDELINES

Use the scale below to assess your level of achievement with regard to each learning goal.

1 = I'm not even close to being able to achieve this goal.

2 = I'm about halfway there.

3 = I'm very close to being able to achieve this goal.

4 = I have achieved this goal.

GOAL CARD

Name: Will Norvell

Topic: Graphic Design Principles: Typography

Date goal established: October 6th   **Date goal achieved:**

What do I need to work on? How will I do it?

Based on my test performance, I definitely need to improve my understanding of the different kinds of typefaces. I'll make a compare and contrast organizer to see if it helps me understand and remember their key features. I'll also make some flashcards to test my ability to recognize examples of each type.

I'll also review the section of my text about kerning and check the glossary since my definition of kerning was only partly correct.

Student signature: Will Norvell   **Teacher signature:** M. McCandliss

🐾 Teacher Talk

→ This tool shows how tests can be used for formative purposes as well as summative ones (i.e., to advance student learning as well as to evaluate it).

→ To differentiate instruction according to individual students' needs, review students' forms to see who needs help with which specific learning goals. Then customize instruction accordingly.

→ The way that you reassess student achievement in Step 7 doesn't matter. What does matter is that you reassess achievement *somehow* (for example, by having students take another test, complete a problem set, or write an essay). Knowing they'll get another chance to be successful can motivate students to keep working, and seeing their efforts pay off can boost their confidence and sense of self-efficacy.

→ Encouraging students to revisit and master learning goals they've missed can have a positive impact on their attitude toward learning (Whiting, Van Burgh, & Render, 1995). Additionally, acknowledging the accomplishments of students who achieve critical learning goals *after* a unit has ended sends the important message that learning the material is what matters most—not learning it quickly.

→ If you don't have time to use this tool in its entirety, try organizing your test questions by learning goal. (Divide your test into sections and put all the questions that address a specific learning goal within the same section.) Organizing your tests this way enables students to determine which learning goals they've mastered and which need further review simply by looking at which sections of their tests they have and haven't done well on. Once students have this information in hand, they can select a learning goal(s) to revisit and establish specific plans for improvement.

Note: Grouping test questions by learning goals/topics can benefit you as well by enabling you to more quickly and easily determine which aspects of the material students have and haven't mastered.

Name: _____   Date: _____

Test topic: _____

Test Assessment Form

Initial Assessment	Learning Goals	Test Items	Score ✓ = Correct +/- = Partly correct x = Not correct	Final Assessment
1 2 3 4				1 2 3 4
1 2 3 4				1 2 3 4
1 2 3 4				1 2 3 4
1 2 3 4				1 2 3 4
1 2 3 4				1 2 3 4

SELF-ASSESSMENT GUIDELINES

Use the scale below to assess your level of achievement with regard to each learning goal.

1 = I'm not even close to being able to achieve this goal.

2 = I'm about halfway there.

3 = I'm very close to being able to achieve this goal.

4 = I have achieved this goal.

How Will I Use Writing Tasks to Help Students Synthesize and Show What They Know?

Dancing in all its forms cannot be excluded from the curriculum of all noble education; dancing with the feet, with ideas, with words, and, need I add that one must also be able to dance with the pen?

—Friedrich Nietzsche

If you detest the idea of school becoming an academic boot camp filled with six hours a day of practice multiple-choice test questions, then you should support student writing for its engagement, interest, and fun. If you worry about your child's performance in the world of high-stakes testing, then you too should support student writing, because it is the skill most directly related to improved scores in reading, social studies, science, and even mathematics.

—Douglas Reeves, *Reason to Write*

To Douglas Reeves's unassailable case for more student writing, we'd like to add another assessment-related "if": If we want to take measure of student learning with any real level of depth and thought, then we should support student writing for the wealth of assessment information that it provides. Student writing allows us to gauge how well students have learned what we have taught and the unique ways that their minds synthesize and express that learning.

The tools in this chapter help teachers take advantage of the versatility that writing brings to both the formative and summative assessment processes. Using these tools, teachers can design writing tasks to meet a variety of purposes, from assessing content mastery, to developing students' critical thinking skills, to focusing in on the writing process and how students can improve the quality of their written products. Writing tasks can be used at any point in the learning sequence—to assess prior knowledge before instruction, check for understanding during instruction, or challenge students to synthesize their learning after instruction. Students' responses can range in length from a single sentence to an extended essay, and can call for different levels of polish depending on your goals. What all these tools share is the deep commitment to writing in the classroom, to getting students' thoughts—whether new, highly developed, or somewhere in between—onto paper, where they can be assessed and refined:

1. **4-2-1 Summarize** assesses and deepens students' understanding of critical topics and texts by having students collaboratively identify, discuss, and summarize the big ideas.

2. **Constructed RESPONSE** helps students build the writing skills they need to express their knowledge and succeed on constructed-response test items.

3. **Learning Log** is a tool that uses varied and regular writing tasks to help teachers assess student learning, adjust instruction accordingly, and monitor performance over time.

4. **Reports Reinvented** helps breathe new life into the written report by offering sixteen alternative report formats.

5. **Vocabulary Storytellers** tests students' understanding of key terms by challenging students to build a story around those terms.

6. **Writing Frames** presents a collection of customizable frames for developing writing tasks to meet a wide variety of assessment purposes.

4-2-1 Summarize

What is it?

A tool that solidifies and tests students' grasp of what they've learned from readings, lectures, etc., by having them identify, discuss, and summarize the key points with their classmates

What are the benefits of using this tool?

Identifying and summarizing the key ideas/details from a text is an important skill for students to develop (Common Core Reading Anchor Standard 2). This tool uses a collaborative summarizing process to help students hone (and let us assess) this critical skill. It also gives us insight into how well students have understood what they've read and learned by having them synthesize and summarize the key points in writing.

What are the basic steps?

1. Ask students to record the *four* most important points from a reading, lecture, or other learning episode on a 4-2-1 Summarize Organizer (p. 159).

Note: Before using this tool, discuss and model strategies that students can use to identify important information within a text or presentation. ("When looking for important information, remember to check out section headings, topic sentences, and summary paragraphs.")

2. Ask students to share and compare their ideas with a partner and come to an agreement about the *two* that are most important. Explain that they can pick and choose from their original ideas, combine their original ideas, and/or add ideas that were missing from their original lists.

3. Pair up the pairs. Have each group of four reach a consensus about the *one* most important idea.

4. Invite students to share their most important ideas (and the strategies that they used to arrive at those ideas) with the class. Help them refine or refocus these main ideas if needed.

5. Choose (or let students choose) one of these main ideas to write about. Have them synthesize and summarize what they learned about this idea/topic in a written paragraph. Encourage them to use some or all of the ideas they generated during Steps 1 and 2 as supporting details.

6. Use students' paragraphs to assess their content knowledge (did they get the key points?) and/or writing skills (do they have strong topic sentences, supporting details, and conclusions?).

7. Address any deficiencies in content knowledge, writing skills, or identifying main ideas.

Variation: 4-2-1 Freewrite

Have students "freewrite" about their main ideas instead of writing formal summary paragraphs. The goal is to have them get everything they know or feel about the topic (thoughts, questions, reactions) down on paper without worrying about the quality or correctness of their writing.

How is this tool used in the classroom?

✔ To have students summarize the key ideas from a lecture, text, or other learning experience

✔ To check students' understanding of material they've read or learned about

✔ To assess students' ability to identify main ideas and support them with details/examples

EXAMPLE: Here is the organizer that a fifth grader completed after reading an article on endangered tigers. Notice that in negotiating the key ideas down from four to one, this student and his partners kept some of his original ideas (*there are fewer than 3200 tigers left on Earth*), combined some of his original ideas (*tigers are getting killed and their habitat is being destroyed*), and wrote one idea—the final main idea—from scratch (*tigers will go extinct if we don't do something about it*).

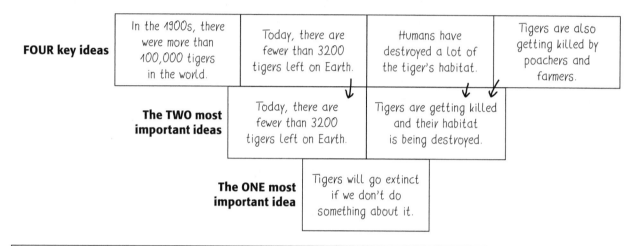

| **FOUR key ideas** | In the 1900s, there were more than 100,000 tigers in the world. | Today, there are fewer than 3200 tigers left on Earth. | Humans have destroyed a lot of the tiger's habitat. | Tigers are also getting killed by poachers and farmers. |

| **The TWO most important ideas** | Today, there are fewer than 3200 tigers left on Earth. | Tigers are getting killed and their habitat is being destroyed. |

| **The ONE most important idea** | Tigers will go extinct if we don't do something about it. |

Summary paragraph: *What did I learn by reading this article?*

Tigers are in big trouble. If we don't do something about it, they will go extinct. Last century, there were over 100,000 tigers in the world. Today, there are fewer than 3200. Tigers need lots of space and the places where they live are getting destroyed by humans. In the last ten years, about half of their habitat has been destroyed. Another problem is that tigers are getting killed by poachers. Killing the tigers is illegal, but the poachers do it anyway because they want to sell tiger skin and tiger claws and tiger teeth for money. Thinking about a world with no more tigers makes me sad. If we don't do something about this problem, kids 100 years from now might not even know what a tiger is.

🌓 Teacher Talk

➔ 4-2-1 Summarize is an ideal way to help students process the different kinds of texts that are highlighted in the Common Core State Standards. Use it with articles, speeches, essays, etc.

➔ This tool has other Common Core connections as well. It develops students' ability to identify and summarize key ideas/details from a text (Reading Anchor Standard 2), it engages students in peer-to-peer conversations about grade-appropriate topics and texts (Speaking and Listening Anchor Standard 1), it teaches students to develop and strengthen their writing via planning (Writing Anchor Standard 5), and it builds explanatory writing skills (Writing Anchor Standard 2).

Name: _____ Date: _____

Topic or text: _____

4-2-1 Summarize Organizer

FOUR key ideas

The TWO most important ideas

The ONE most important idea

Summary paragraph:

Constructed RESPONSE

What is it?

An acronym-based technique that helps students craft high-quality answers to constructed-response items; students' responses can then be used to assess their content knowledge and/or writing skills

What are the benefits of using this tool?

Constructed-response items make up a significant chunk of many standardized assessment tests. Preparing students to handle these items successfully, then, is critical for their academic success. This tool helps by outlining a step-by-step process for crafting effective responses. The steps in the process are both easy for students to remember (each corresponds to a letter in the acronym RESPONSE) and consistent with the Common Core Writing Standards.

What are the basic steps?

1. Review the definition of a constructed-response item with students.

2. Explain that you'll be teaching students a process for writing better, more focused answers to the constructed-response items that they encounter, both in your classroom and on standardized tests.

3. Explain and model the steps in the RESPONSE process (simplify as needed for younger students):

> **R**ead the question or writing prompt slowly and carefully.
>
> **E**stablish the purpose for writing. (Explain a concept? Describe a procedure? Argue a point?)
>
> **S**tart by introducing your topic or thesis. Be as clear and concise as possible.
>
> **P**rovide evidence, reasons, or examples to support your opening statement or thesis. Address conflicting evidence or arguments if appropriate.
>
> **O**rganize your supporting information. (Group related ideas, link ideas using transitions, etc.)
>
> **N**ail your ending. Write a conclusion that follows from, sums up, or reiterates your main point(s).
>
> **S**kim your draft for errors (spelling, grammar, logic), unclear terms/ideas, and "rough" writing.
>
> **E**dit and polish your original response.

4. Present students with a content-related writing prompt or question. Have them craft a response using the RESPONSE technique.

> *Tip:* Create at least one response as a class before having students use the process independently.

5. Use the responses that students generate to gauge their understanding of the relevant material and their skill as writers. Address any gaps in content knowledge or writing skills.

6. Have students use the RESPONSE process to complete future classroom writing assignments. (The more they use it, the more it will become habitual.) Clarify that students should use the process on their own as well—not just when you tell them to, but with any constructed-response item.

How is this tool used in the classroom?

✔ To help students master the process of writing high-quality constructed responses

✔ To help students express their content knowledge in writing

✔ To test students' understanding of the content they're writing about

✔ To develop and assess Common Core writing skills

EXAMPLE: Fifth-grade teacher May Stoller familiarizes her students with the RESPONSE process by modeling it and having them work through it as a class.

Read the question or writing prompt slowly and carefully.

After having her students examine a photograph of a polar bear, May presents them with the following question: *How does the polar bear appear to be adapted to life in the tundra?* She asks them to read the question carefully and instructs them to discuss three specific features in their response.

Establish the purpose for writing.

Students determine that the purpose of their final piece is to explain how polar bears are uniquely adapted to their environment.

Start by introducing your topic or thesis.

May reminds her students that they can create a topic sentence by converting the initial question into a statement. The sentence they come up with is this: *The polar bear is uniquely adapted to life in the tundra.*

Provide evidence, reasons, or examples to support your opening statement or thesis.

By listing what they know about the Arctic tundra (permanent frost, cold, few plants, etc.) and connecting this knowledge to the picture of the polar bear, May and her students identify three physical features that make the bear uniquely suited for life in its environment: thick fur, white color, big teeth and claws.

Next, they explain how these physical features benefit the bear:

- Thick fur keeps the bear warm.
- White color blends into permanent frost (camouflage). Prey have a hard time seeing the bear.
- Big teeth and claws allow the bear to kill and eat its prey.

Organize your supporting information.

Since two of the three features they identified have to do with predation (white fur and big teeth/claws), students decide to group and discuss these features together. They then think about transitional words they might use to introduce their third physical feature and draft their response accordingly.

Nail your ending. Write a conclusion that follows from, sums up, or reiterates your main point(s).

May and her students develop the following conclusion: *Although life in the tundra is very difficult, the polar bear's white color, big teeth and claws, and thick fur make it ideally suited for its environment.*

Skim your draft for errors, unclear terms/ideas, and rough-sounding writing.

After helping students draft a response as a class, May reads the draft aloud so students can listen for things that need to be fixed, explained, or made smoother. Students then skim the draft by eye to look for grammar, spelling, and other errors.

Edit and polish your original response.

With May's help, students share and discuss their thoughts about what should be fixed or improved. They work together to make the necessary revisions and review their revised draft one more time.

Learning Log

What is it?

A place for students to log their responses to various questions, writing prompts, and tasks

What are the benefits of using this tool?

The more we ask students to jot down their thoughts, feelings, and understandings, the more we discover about who they are and what they're learning. Learning Logs encourage students to do this kind of writing on a daily basis—and they prepare us to teach more effectively as a result. Students' logs can give us immediate feedback when reviewed on the spot, or bigger-picture feedback when reviewed over time (how are students growing as learners?). The comments we record on students' entries, in turn, can serve to encourage and guide future learning.

What are the basic steps?

1. Set students up with Learning Logs (anything from a marble composition book to a section in a notebook).

2. Give students a question, writing prompt, or task and have them record their responses in their logs. Note that the type of task you assign will determine the length (single words, sentences, paragraphs) and format (words, diagrams, pictures) of students' responses.

Tip: Logs work best when they're used regularly—ideally, at least once each day.

3. Review students' responses, either by walking around the room as students work or by collecting and reading their logs at a later time. Adjust instruction/respond accordingly.

4. Comment on at least one Learning Log entry per week. Record your thoughts, questions, and feedback (positive and corrective) directly in students' logs. Here are some sample comments:

- Wow! You already know a lot about dinosaurs. Let's have you share with the class.
- This idea is really interesting. Can you tell me more?
- It seems like you might be mixing these ideas up. See me and we can review them together.

5. Encourage students to review your comments.

🔊 Teacher Talk

➔ You can generate Learning Log prompts from scratch (see sample prompts on the next page) or you can borrow them from other tools. Any tool that engages students in a short writing task will work (e.g., MVP, Memory Box, 3-2-1, Writing Frames, What Comes to Mind?, or Reflection Stems). Simply use the tool as written and have students record their responses in their logs.

➔ Make it clear that Learning Logs are public (can be viewed by you, classmates, and parents). Encourage students to share their logs with others.

How is this tool used in the classroom?

✔ To assess what students know, feel, and understand about the things they're learning

✔ To get students writing on a daily basis

Learning Logs can be used for a variety of different purposes and at all stages of the instructional process (before, during, after). Among other things, they can be used to

- *Assess and help students activate prior knowledge at the start of instruction.*

    Sample prompts: What comes to mind when you think about being healthy? •• What do you know about percentages? •• Write down everything you know, think, and feel about insects.

- *Gather information about students' interests, strengths, preferences, and feelings.*

    Sample prompts: Which of these topics would you like to explore further? •• Which task appeals to you most and why? •• What are you an expert at? •• How do you feel about capital punishment?

- *Check for understanding during or after an instructional episode.*

    Sample prompts: Summarize the key points from today's lecture. •• How is a firewall like a security guard? •• What do you think will happen when we flip the switch? •• What are the distinctive elements of Hemingway's writing style? •• Draw what you know about Thanksgiving.

- *Assess (and help students assess) their progress over time.*

    Sample prompts: Look back at the last three summary paragraphs in your Learning Log. How has your work improved? •• Compare your most recent response to this question with the response that you generated at the start of the unit. How has your understanding grown?

- *Assess the pace/effectiveness of instruction and identify areas of confusion.*

    Sample prompts: On a scale of one to ten, how well did you follow today's lesson? •• What questions do you have about this material? •• How could I have made this lesson more interesting/effective?

- *Help students reflect on and learn from their classroom experiences.*

    Sample prompts: What was the most valuable thing you learned today? •• How could you make future teamwork more effective? •• How happy are you with your performance? Why?

- *Have students develop or share their understanding of classroom learning goals.*

    Sample prompts: Can you state this learning goal in your own words? •• Why is this learning goal worth achieving? •• What is the goal of this activity? What are we trying to learn?

- *Test Common Core skills and understandings.*

    Sample prompts: How are these two texts similar? (R.CCR.9) •• Use context clues to generate a tentative definition of the underlined word. (L.CCR.4) •• How do you feel about this book and why? (W.1.1) •• Why is the product of two rational numbers a rational number? (HSN-RN.B.3)

EXAMPLE: Using Learning Logs to check for understanding in real time

A history teacher stopped several times during a lecture and asked students to record the most valuable point (MVP) from the preceding segment of the lecture. He reviewed students' logs on the spot and decided whether to move forward or back up and review based on what he read.

Reports Reinvented

What is it?

A tool that describes sixteen creative alternatives to the traditional written report

What are the benefits of using this tool?

Written reports are a staple of classroom assessment because they can be used to assess everything from content knowledge to research skills to writing proficiency. But if we insist on using the same old report format over and over again, student engagement will begin to flag. This tool keeps the report concept fresh and interesting by providing sixteen different formats to choose from. Rotating through these different formats not only prevents students from becoming bored, it also targets a wide range of thinking, writing, research, and technology skills.

What are the basic steps?

1. Before asking students to prepare a report, think about the purpose of the assignment. (Do you want them to research and explain the causes/effects of an important event? Share their opinion of a book they've read? Something else?)

2. Review the sixteen different report formats described on pp. 165–169. Select one that fits your purpose and content material.

3. Decide what criteria you'll use to assess students' work. *Think:* Given the purpose of the report, what are the most important criteria to consider? What things are less important to focus on?

   Example: If the goal is to have students drum up excitement about a historical event, you might want their final reports to be visually appealing and engaging as well as factually accurate.

4. Present and explain the assignment to students. Clarify the purpose of the assignment, the type of report they'll be preparing (what does it entail?), and the criteria you'll use to evaluate their work.

How is this tool used in the classroom?

✔ To have students synthesize and show what they know in writing

✔ To develop students' research, writing, and presentation skills

🌐 Teacher Talk

→ This tool can be used to develop and assess a variety of Common Core writing, research, and language skills (especially those in standards W.CCR.1–5, 7–8, 10 and L.CCR.1–2). By having students use technology (think Internet searches, editing or presentation software, podcasts, blogs, e-books, digital cameras) to produce/present/publish/update their work, or to interact and collaborate with others, you can target other standards as well, including W.CCR.6 and SL.CCR.5.

→ Many of these report formats can be made primary-grade appropriate simply by having students read about/research topics as a class and speak or draw their findings rather than write them.

Sixteen Fun Report Formats

"By the Letters" Report

With this report, the information that students research and write about is determined by the name of the topic they're studying. (A report on the Civil War, for example, would contain information about topics beginning with the letters C, I, V, and so on—one section per letter.) Students can either be told which topics to write about or be given a list of letter-appropriate topics and allowed to choose the ones that interest them. The letter C, for instance, would give them the freedom to report on topics as diverse as the Battle of Chancellorsville, the importance of cotton to the Southern economy, the courage of President Lincoln, the casualties of war, or the Confederate Army.

"By the Numbers" Report

With this technique, a numerical framework like the one below is used to help students collect and organize information about a specific topic. Students who are learning about their home state, for example, might be asked to research and report on the following items:

10 important dates in our state's history

9 tourist attractions

8 products that our state produces

7 noteworthy cities or towns

6 important people who were born in (or live in) our state

5 interesting geographical facts or geological features

4 problems that our state is facing or has faced in the past

3 sports teams (college or professional level)

2 state senators, past or present

1 favorite place or fact

Note: To avoid any confusion, make it clear that *listing* the required items is not the same as *reporting on* them. Listing the names of nine tourist attractions without describing what those attractions are or why they're worth visiting, for example, wouldn't be acceptable.

Movie Poster Report

After examining sample movie posters and identifying common elements, students use the movie-poster format to summarize and drum up excitement about a scientific or historical event they've researched. The posters students create should feature the name of their event (e.g., the Apollo 11 moon landing), the starring players (Neil Armstrong, Buzz Aldrin...), key plot elements (the space race, people's reaction to the landing...), a "release date" (1969), and a catchy tagline ("Where no man has gone before"). Students' posters should also feature catchy and informative visuals that will give their classmates insight into their chosen events. Once their posters are complete, students can hang them around the room, present them to their classmates, or create short movies about their events.

Variation: Have students create digital posters rather than traditional paper ones using anything from drawing/presentation software to a platform like Glogster (http://edu.glogster.com/).

"A Day in the Life" Report

In this report, students use personification to communicate what they've learned or what they feel about an object, animal, or place they've been studying. Specifically, they imagine that they are the object/animal/place and describe a day in their lives. (What do they see? Do? Think? Feel? Wish for?) Among other things, students might be asked to describe a day in the life of

- a settler's cabin on the Western frontier
- a beaver building a dam
- the Silk Road
- a number line

- a famous painting at a museum
- a tropical rainforest
- the Berlin Wall
- a hydrophobic molecule

Stained Glass Window Report

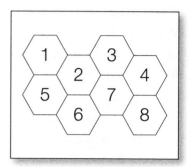

Before assigning this type of report, show students examples of stained glass windows and explain how these windows have been used to teach and tell stories throughout history. Then, challenge students to use the window format to tell a story about the topic they're reporting on. To create their reports, students should draw at least eight panels on a large piece of paper and fill each one with a picture that illustrates a key idea or event. If needed, they can explain their panels when they're done, either orally or in writing.

"My Life Is in Your Hands" Report

This alternative to the traditional biographical report asks students to do more than summarize the basic facts about someone's life; it asks them to share their thoughts, feelings, and insights about that person's life, accomplishments, and personality. To create this kind of report, students should trace their hands on a piece of paper and fill them in as instructed below.

Right hand (the "fact hand"): Put the name of the person you researched (or a copy of that person's signature) in your palm. Then record one important fact about this person on each of your fingers.

Left hand (the "feeling hand"): On your fingers, record events/accomplishments, anecdotes, or images that influenced your feelings about this person. Then choose one of the following tasks and record your response on your palm (use another piece of paper if you run out of room):

a) Explain how this individual makes you feel and why. Do you feel proud? Envious? Humbled? Curious? Confused? Ashamed? Amazed? Inspired?

b) Describe what you like most and least about this person. Explain why.

c) Pretend that *you* are the person your report is about. Explain how you feel about your life and accomplishments.

Optional: Give students an opportunity to "be" the people they researched by creating a living museum. (Students dress up like their subjects and explain who they are, why they're famous, and how they feel about their life and accomplishments.) Invite parents and students from other classes to visit the museum, or split the exhibit-time in half so that students get to visit as well as participate.

Museum-Display Report

Here, students demonstrate their understanding of a topic by creating informative and attractive museum-style display cases. They begin by making or gathering a collection of artifacts related to their topic—photographs, objects, maps, sketches, documents, etc. They then number their artifacts, display them in a box, and create descriptive placards for their displays. Placards should describe what each item is, why it was chosen, and why it is significant.

Another option: Instead of having students create physical display cases, have them create and publish virtual ones using the Museum Box website (http://museumbox.e2bn.org/). Encourage students to include a mixture of text, images, videos, and sound clips in their display cases.

Newspaper Report

After learning about the various components of a typical newspaper (feature articles, editorials, classified ads, political cartoons, book/movie reviews, comic strips, etc.), students create a mini-newspaper about a topic of importance. Students can either be told what sections to include (e.g., "two feature articles and a political cartoon") or allowed to choose for themselves. In either case, they should be encouraged to strive for accuracy, creativity, and readability when putting their papers together.

> **WANTED BY THE PRESIDENT:**
>
> Democrats and Republicans who can work together in productive ways
>
> Strategies for reducing unemployment and bringing jobs back to America
>
> An investment in American innovation and education

Poetry Report

This short report format challenges students to express what they've learned or what they feel about a given topic through poetry. Before assigning this kind of report, familiarize students with different poetic forms they might want to use (e.g., haiku, cinquain, limerick, diamante, clerihew, acrostic, free verse). To up the degree of difficulty, introduce/require them to use a specific poetic device (e.g., alliteration, metaphor, personification).

Optional: To add a digital technology component, have students present and discuss their poems via podcasts and/or blogs. Encourage them to request and respond to feedback about their work.

Flip-Book Report

The idea here is to have students research a specific set of questions about a given topic (questions can be teacher generated or student generated) and present their findings in flip-book format. When students are done, they're given time to look at and learn from their classmates' books.

Students create their flip books by following the steps below:

1. Staple blank pieces of paper together to form a booklet (# of pages = # of questions plus one).
2. Cut the pages so that each page is one inch wider than the page above it.
3. Create a cover for the report on the front page of the booklet.
4. Record the questions you researched on the overhanging one-inch margins.
5. Record the answers to those questions on the insides of the corresponding pages.

Note: When using this tool with younger students, give them pre-cut, pre-stapled pages—and let them report their findings using simple words and pictures rather than paragraphs.

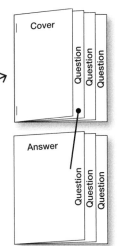

Accordion-Style Report

The basic concept is the same as that of the flip-book report (students research specific questions about a topic and present their findings using words and/or pictures). The only difference is in the presentation format. Here, students create a freestanding, accordion-shaped display like the one shown below by folding an extra-long, heavyweight sheet of paper back and forth several times or taping several pieces of heavyweight paper together (the taped areas become flexible hinges).

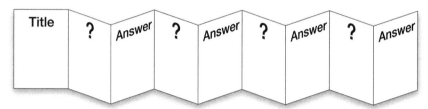

Book Review

In a book review, students describe, analyze, and share their personal opinions about a book they've read or had read to them. (What is the book about? What are its strengths and weaknesses? What feelings did it evoke? Did you enjoy it? Would you recommend it to a friend? How does it compare to similar books? Is there anything worth noting about its style, content, or message?) The goal is to give others a sense of what the book is about and help them decide whether to read it.

Note: Instead of having students create traditional written reports, you can have them speak their reviews during an in-class discussion (ideal for younger students) or deliver them via podcasts or blogs (with blogs, encourage students to read and respond to each other's reviews).

Mini-Book Report

Here, students are asked to create a miniature book about a topic they've studied. They create this mini-book by following the steps below; they then design an appropriate cover and fill the pages with relevant information about their topic (words and/or pictures).

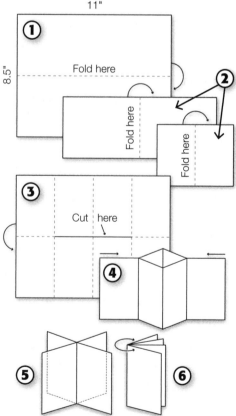

1. Fold a blank 8 ½" x 11" piece of paper in half by bringing the top edge down to meet the bottom edge (folded paper should be 4 ¼" x 11").

2. Fold the paper in half by bringing the left edge over to meet the right. Then do another left-to-right fold.

3. Unfold the paper and cut as shown (dashed lines are fold marks, solid line is cut location). Then repeat the top-to-bottom fold from Step 1.

4. Grab the left and right edges of the folded paper and gently push in (a hole should open up in the middle where the paper was cut).

5. Keep pushing until the inside edges touch and you have something that looks like this.

6. Fold the four flaps on top of each other using the existing fold line to create a mini-book with rectangular pages. The final shape of the book will look like this.

Wheaties Box Report

Since being tagged as "The Breakfast of Champions" back in the 1920s, Wheaties cereal has featured hundreds of champion athletes on its iconic orange box. To create a Wheaties box report, students paste a picture of a famous individual on the cover of a cereal box, list the "ingredients" that make this person great on the side panels, and describe the person's life and accomplishments on the back.

Simile Report

Simile reports can be autobiographical or biographical. To create them, students choose objects that represent who they are as individuals (or objects that represent the people they're studying) and explain their choices. Before putting a pen to paper, students are encouraged to think carefully and creatively about possible options. (What qualities does this object have? How many similarities can I think of? Might another object be a better choice?)

> Like a baseball mitt, I am stiff and unbending when you first meet me, but I soften up over time. I enjoy hanging out with friends, working outdoors, and being part of a team…

Jigsaw Wiki Report

This report format adds a modern technology twist to Aronson's (1978) Jigsaw cooperative learning strategy; the ultimate goal is for students to create a wiki about a topic of your choosing. Before assigning this type of report, be sure to teach students what a wiki is, what a wiki looks like (show them several examples, including Wikipedia), and how to create, add to, and edit one.*

To begin, select a topic or theme for the report. Divide students into groups and have each group research a different aspect of the selected topic/theme. (For a wiki on the Spanish Civil War, have students research causes, effects, major players, etc. For a wiki on famous women in American history, give each group a specific woman to research or let each group choose its own.)

Challenge the members of each group to become experts in their assigned subtopic and then share their expertise with their classmates by creating an engaging and informative wiki page(s). Emphasize the importance of collaboration, both within groups (group members should work together to research, organize, and edit the content on their pages) and across groups (students should read, establish appropriate links to, and add to/edit other groups' pages). Remind students that the accuracy of the information on their wiki (like any wiki) depends on its writers and editors.

Give students time to explore and learn from the completed wiki. Assign a synthesis task that requires them to demonstrate their knowledge of the topic as a whole. Encourage them to add to the wiki as their content knowledge grows over the course of the unit, semester, or year.

---

*Teacher-friendly information about wikis is widely available in print and online; see, for example, Solomon and Schrum's (2010) *Web 2.0 How-to for Educators* or http://educationalwikis.wikispaces.com/.

Vocabulary Storytellers

What is it?

A tool that tests students' command of critical vocabulary terms by challenging them to incorporate those terms into a story

What are the benefits of using this tool?

We often test students' vocabulary knowledge by asking them to define specific terms or match those terms to their corresponding definitions. The problem with these kinds of approaches is that they don't tell us whether students can actually *use* the vocabulary terms they've learned or if they've simply memorized a series of definitions. This tool, which challenges students to incorporate key terms into an original story, provides a deeper, more authentic, and more engaging way to assess vocabulary knowledge.

What are the basic steps?

1. Before beginning a lesson or unit, identify the critical vocabulary terms/concepts that students will need to know and understand.

2. Share the list of terms with students before instruction begins. Help them monitor and improve their understanding of these terms throughout the course of instruction. (If you want, you can use the Vocabulary Knowledge Rating tool, pp. 14–16, to help you with this step.)

3. At the end of the lesson or unit, ask students to demonstrate their understanding of some or all of the key terms by incorporating them into an original story (terms should be underlined).

4. Clarify the ground rules and assessment criteria before students begin working, and use specific examples (positive and negative) to help them understand what the task entails. For example:

- *Ground rules:* "Stories can take *any format* (fable, mystery, science fiction), be about any topic that interests you (friends, dinosaurs, current events), and be *as long or short as you choose.*"
- *Assessment criteria:* "The only requirements are that you underline the terms you use and that you use those terms in a way that makes it clear you understand what they mean."
- *One example:* "On its own, a sentence like 'I love planets' would *not* satisfy the requirements of the task since it doesn't make it clear that you know anything about planets."

5. Evaluate students' work using the assessment criteria you established in Step 4: Are the relevant terms underlined? Have students demonstrated a clear understanding of those terms?

6. Work with students one-on-one or as a class to improve their understanding of any misused terms.

How is this tool used in the classroom?

✔ To test students' ability to understand and use critical vocabulary terms in context

✔ To have students synthesize and demonstrate their learning through writing

EXAMPLE 1: A biology student wrote this story at the end of a unit on cell structure and function:

> Help!!!!! I'm not sure how this happened, but I've somehow been miniaturized and injected into someone's else's body! Just last week, I was sitting in biology class learning about <u>cells</u> and how they're the <u>building blocks</u> of all living things—and today, I'm getting to see some firsthand. I actually just slid inside of one, so I guess I'm one of the substances that can pass through its <u>semi-permeable</u> <u>outer membrane</u>! Now that I'm inside, I'm floating in a gelatinous material known as the <u>cytosol</u>. All around me, I see different cellular structures called <u>organelles</u>, which are performing their unique cellular functions. This would actually be kind of cool except that I'm sensing a problem with the cell's power plants, which are technically called <u>mitochondria</u>. They seem to be having trouble generating enough <u>adenosine triphosphate</u>, and that could spell trouble since <u>ATP</u> is a critical source of <u>energy</u>...

EXAMPLE 2: A kindergarten teacher tested students' ability to use shape terms to describe objects in their environment (Common Core K.G.A.1). To make the tool more age appropriate, she had students fill in the blanks in a story that she created (she read the story aloud, they shouted out answers).

> Shapes are all around us. When we enter the classroom each morning, we pass through a brown door that is a <u>rectangle</u>. We begin each day by sitting on an <u>oval</u> rug and listening to a story. We show which stories are our favorites by putting gold <u>star</u> stickers on them. After story time, we check the clock, which is a <u>circle</u>, to see if it's time for recess...

EXAMPLE 3: A high school math teacher challenged her students to demonstrate their understanding of the similarities and differences between linear and quadratic functions by writing a story. The beginning of one student's story is shown below; see www.ThoughtfulClassroom.com/Tools for the rest.

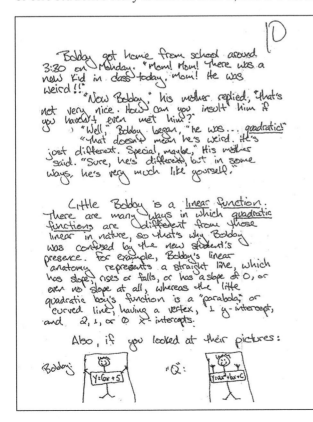

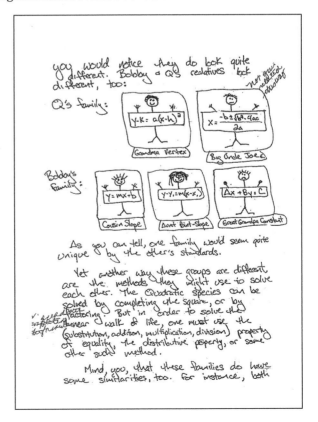

🔿 Teacher Talk

→ Feel free to modify the basic Vocabulary Storytellers format. Here are five other ways to check (and have students check) their ability to use critical vocabulary terms in context:

Option 1: Have students incorporate a select number of vocabulary terms into a different kind of written piece. Rather than a story, for instance, have them write an editorial, a book review, or a letter (e.g., "Write a letter to the president that expresses your thoughts and feelings about his State of the Union address. Include as many of this week's vocabulary terms as you can.").

Option 2: Ask students to use critical vocabulary terms in an oral presentation (e.g., a debate, classroom discussion, oral report) instead of a story. For example, "Prepare a sixty-second news report about the 2011 tsunami in Japan. Include at least six of the following ten terms in your report."

Option 3: Give students a writing prompt and instruct them to include a specific number of terms in their responses. For example, "Use five of the words from our Word Wall in your response to this prompt: 'If you were Punxsutawney Phil, how would you feel on Groundhog Day?'"

Option 4: Ask students to write a story that highlights the similarities and differences between two specific terms. A creative example using linear and quadratic functions is shown on p. 171.

Option 5: Have students write a story as a class (pick students' names out of a hat to see who writes first, second, etc.). Student 1 picks a term and writes it into the opening sentence(s); Student 2 adds to the story, including another term; and the process continues until all terms have been used.

→ This tool can be used to develop narrative writing skills (Common Core Writing Anchor Standard 3) as well as content-specific vocabulary knowledge (Common Core Language Anchor Standard 6).

Writing Frames

What is it?

A collection of customizable writing frames that can be used to assess and extend student learning

What are the benefits of using this tool?

With the Common Core State Standards' emphasis on writing, it's more important than ever to get students writing on a daily basis. This tool makes that easier to do by presenting a collection of writing frames and prompts to choose from. Teachers from all grade levels and content areas can use these frames and prompts to

- get a reading on students' understanding of key content at any time in a learning sequence;
- assess a wide range of critical thinking skills (especially by rotating through the various frames throughout the year); and
- build students' competence in producing the kinds of writing required on standardized assessment tests (e.g., comparison pieces, arguments, summaries).

What are the basic steps?

1. Identify the content knowledge/skills you want to assess. Then think about the kind of assessment you're looking to do. (Do you want to do a quick check for understanding in the middle of a lesson? Evaluate big-picture understanding at the end of a unit? Something else?)

2. Decide which of the writing frames in Figure 3 (p. 175) best meets your needs. Pick one of the corresponding writing prompts and customize it to fit your content and goals.

   Another option: Create (or have students create) a prompt for the selected frame from scratch.

3. Present the writing prompt to students and help them determine what it's asking them to do. For example, are they being asked to make a comparison? Summarize data? Argue a position?

4. Tell students how and when to respond. Should they tackle the writing prompt with a partner? On their own? During class? For homework? Is there a time limit? Do they need to polish their writing?

   Note: The length and format of students' responses will depend on the writing prompt you select.

5. Discuss the criteria for success. Make it clear that a high-quality response should demonstrate students' knowledge of the content *and* their command of the relevant thinking and writing skills.

6. Review students' responses to determine whether there are any aspects of the content material or thinking/writing skills that you should review or reteach.

How is this tool used in the classroom?

✔ To assess students' grasp of key content

✔ To develop critical thinking and writing skills

Writing frames can be used in many different ways and for different purposes:

- *They can be used to deepen and check students' grasp of critical content at any point in the instructional process* (start, middle, or end of a lesson/unit).

- *They can be used for both formative and summative purposes.* Use them to check for understanding mid-lesson and adjust instruction accordingly or to evaluate learning at the end of a unit.

- *They can be used to develop specific kinds of thinking and writing skills.* To do this, select a frame that matches a skill you're trying to develop and use that frame repeatedly. To develop students' comparative writing skills, for example, you could use the *Compare & Contrast* frame to design a series of writing tasks.

- *They can be used to differentiate assessment and boost student engagement.* To do this, simply give students a choice about how to demonstrate their learning. Options include giving them a choice of prompts to respond to, giving them a sample prompt and letting them customize it by filling in the blanks, giving them a writing frame and letting them generate their own prompts, or letting them choose a frame and prompt on their own.

- *They can be used to target Common Core State Standards.* Taken together, the thirteen frames can be used to address Writing Anchor Standard 10 (write routinely for a wide range of tasks). Taken individually, they can be used to target other standards as well. For example:

  - Try the *Interpret/Analyze* frame for Reading Anchor Standard 3 (analyze how and why individuals, events, and ideas develop and interact over the course of a text).

  - Try the *Explain* frame for Writing Anchor Standard 2 (write informative/explanatory texts to examine and convey complex ideas and information clearly and accurately).

  - Try the *Evaluate* or *Validate* frames for Reading Anchor Standard 8 (evaluate the argument and claims in a text, including the validity of the reasoning as well as the relevance and sufficiency of the evidence), Writing Anchor Standard 8 (assess the credibility and accuracy of print and digital sources), or Standard 3 from the Standards for Mathematical Practice (construct viable arguments and critique the reasoning of others).

🌐 Teacher Talk

➜ Prepare students to be successful by teaching and modeling the thinking and writing skills that each writing frame requires. ("To write a compare and contrast essay, we'd begin by…") Continue the teaching and modeling process until students are capable of crafting quality responses on their own.

➜ To see examples of math-specific writing prompts, check out *Math Tools, Grades 3–12: 60+ Ways to Build Mathematical Practices, Differentiate Instruction, and Increase Student Engagement* (Silver, Brunsting, Walsh, & Thomas, 2012, pp. 222–223).

Figure 3: Writing Frames to Choose From: Thirteen CREATIVE IDEAS

FRAMES	WRITING PROMPTS ASK STUDENTS TO...
Compare & contrast	*Compare and/or contrast two or more items using specific criteria. For example:* • Compare and contrast these two items using the following criteria… • Are __ and __ more alike or more different? Support your answer using specific examples. • Which of these items are most similar? Which are most different? Explain your reasoning.
Relate personally	*Connect with the content on a personal level. For example:* • How would you feel/what would you do if you were in __'s shoes? • How is this relevant to your life? • Have you (or someone you know) ever seen/felt/experienced __? What was it like?
Evaluate	*Assess or judge something using specific criteria. For example:* • Which idea/strategy/solution/product/model is best? What criteria did you use to make your decision? • Did this person/character make the right decision? Why? • Does this work satisfy the assessment criteria we discussed? Why or why not? Be specific.
Associate	*Generate associations or explain how given items/ideas are connected. For example:* • What comes to mind when I say __? What comes to mind when you see/hear/taste/touch/smell __? • In what way are __ and __ connected in your mind? • How is __ like a __?
Trace/ sequence	*Arrange and present information in order. For example:* • Trace the development of __ (an event, character, argument, idea, invention, etc.). • Trace the sequence of events leading up to __. • Describe the sequence of steps you used to __.
Interpret/ analyze	*Interpret or analyze information. For example:* • What can you conclude from this data? Why? • What is the meaning of this passage/parable/image/law/quotation/dream? Why do you think so? • What point or message is this artist/writer/speaker trying to convey? Why do you think so?
Validate	*Validate (or evaluate the validity of) a conclusion, statement, source, etc. For example:* • How do you know that __ is the case? Describe your evidence. • How did you check the validity/reliability of your information? Explain. • Is this a valid __ (argument, solution, conclusion, criticism, model)? Why or why not?
Explain	*Explain what, why, or how. For example:* • What do you know about __? Write an explanatory paragraph. • Why __? • How __? How could you explain __?
Identify & describe	*Describe an object, observation, individual, or event. For example:* • Identify the properties or components of __ (e.g., properties of a mineral, components of a computer). • Describe what you observed. What did you see, hear, touch, taste, or smell? • Describe who/how/what happened __. (Example: Describe what Ping chooses to do and why.)
Define	*Demonstrate their understanding of a critical term or concept. For example:* • Define the following concept or term in your own words: __. • What are the defining characteristics of a __? (Example: What are the critical attributes of a reptile?) • What makes a __ a __? (Example: What makes a sonnet a sonnet?)
Explore possibilities	*Explore alternatives, possibilities, and "what if" scenarios. For example:* • What is another way of __? What is another explanation for __? How many possible ways can you __? • What if __? What might be the consequences if __? (Example: What if the decimal point didn't exist?) • Why or how might __? (Example: How might we design a more efficient computer program?)
Argue a position	*Take a position and provide evidence to support it. For example:* • State your position on __ and provide evidence to support it. • Do you agree or disagree with __? Explain your answer using specific evidence, examples, or details. • The reason why __ is __. (Example: Babe Ruth is the greatest baseball player of all time because__.)
Summarize	*Briefly recap what they have observed, heard, or experienced. For example:* • To summarize, what I read/heard/learned was __. • The most important point or takeaway message was __. • Draw a picture that summarizes what you learned. Then explain your drawing.

How Will I Develop High-Quality Culminating Assessment Tasks and Evaluation Frameworks?

What we want is to see the child in pursuit of knowledge, and not knowledge in pursuit of the child.

—George Bernard Shaw

[Traditional tests] measure only narrow bands of skills. Broader tests can give broader ranges of scores and help students see where they have mastery and where they need to improve.

—Robert J. Sternberg, "Assessing What Matters"

The new and welcome emphasis that today's educators place on assessment *for* learning, or formative assessment, may make it seem that assessment *of* learning (a.k.a. summative assessment) is a bad guy. After all, if you scan of some of the literature on formative assessment, you'll likely see it pitted against summative assessment. You may even find someone telling you that summative assessment stops learning in its tracks. The truth is, such diatribes aren't typically aimed at summative assessment itself; rather, they're aimed at the way summative assessment is too often conducted (assign a basic recall test, hand out a grade).

The tools in this chapter work to improve the traditional end-of-unit assessment process in three distinct ways. Specifically, they encourage the creation of more challenging and authentic tests/tasks (ones that demand thinking and understanding in addition to factual recall), the use of assessments that promote learning as well as evaluate it, and the development of thoughtful assessment criteria that address content, process, and product:

1. **The C-List** presents a list of assessment criteria that teachers can use to customize the way they evaluate student performance.

2. **Content-Process-Product** outlines a simple framework for designing assessment criteria focused on three key essentials: students' understanding of the *content*, their mastery of critical thinking *processes*, and the quality of their *products*.

3. **From Puzzles to Paradoxes** presents a collection of twelve performance-task formats that require inquiry, problem-solving, and higher-order thinking.

4. **More Than Your Usual Multiple Choice** facilitates the development of multiple-choice questions that test thinking and understanding rather than just recall.

5. **Performance Task Designer** provides a planning template and a menu of options for creating authentic and engaging performance-based tasks.

6. **Second-Chance Test** turns traditional tests into learning opportunities by giving students a chance to analyze their performance and implement strategies for improvement.

7. **Show & Share** asks students to demonstrate their learning by creating posters or slide-show presentations.

A final note: It is worth mentioning that some of the tools in Chapter 3, especially **Guiding & Grading Rubrics** and **Checklists**, are also helpful for developing and communicating summative assessment criteria to students.

The C-List

What is it?

A tool that simplifies the process of creating rubrics and rating scales by providing a list of criteria (a "C-List") to choose from

What are the benefits of using this tool?

Determining the criteria by which students' work will be evaluated can be one of the most difficult steps in the assessment process. The C-List alleviates some of this difficulty by providing a list of criteria to choose from. The criteria on The C-List can be customized to fit assessment tasks from all content areas and grade levels. These criteria can also be used to differentiate assessment by mixing and matching them to fit students' unique interests and needs.

What are the basic steps?

1. Design an assessment task for an upcoming lesson or unit.

2. Decide which dimensions to focus on when assessing students' work; see The C-List (p. 182) for options. Record your selections on The C-List Evaluation Form (p. 184).

3. Record your expectations for each of the selected dimensions. (For example, what evidence of *craftsmanship* will you be looking for in students' work? What would craftsmanship look like at the highest level of quality?) Use specific and student-friendly language.

4. Decide whether to weight some dimensions more than others when grading students' work (e.g., "I will count *creativity* three times as much as *craftsmanship*"). Assign weighting factors accordingly.

5. Distribute copies of the evaluation form. Review it with students before they begin working so they understand what they're striving for. Remind them to use it along the way to guide and assess their work.

6. Use the evaluation form to assess students' work on the assigned task.
   - Score students' performance for each of the selected dimensions (1 = lowest, 4 = highest).
   - Multiply these initial scores by the appropriate weighting factors to get adjusted scores.
   - Add these adjusted scores together to get a total score.

7. Provide verbal or written feedback that will help students understand and improve their current level of performance. (Why did they get the score they did? How can they improve their work?)

How is this tool used in the classroom?

✔ To identify and communicate the criteria for quality work

EXAMPLE 1: A history teacher used the task and form below to evaluate students' knowledge of the Boston Massacre as well as their ability to analyze primary documents, evaluate and cite evidence, and craft well-supported argument essays (Common Core RH.9–10.1 and 9, WHST.9–10.1, 8, and 9).

THE TASK: In 1770, British Captain Thomas Preston and eight of his soldiers were put on trial for the murder of five Boston colonials during the Boston Massacre. Captain Preston and six of his men were ultimately acquitted, while the remaining two soldiers were found guilty of manslaughter, branded on their thumbs, and released.

Was justice served? You be the judge! Examine the documents that have been provided for your review. Then present and defend your position in writing. Remember to provide specific evidence from the documents when making your case.

I will assess my students' work for the following dimensions:

This dimension will be weighted:

☐ **Completion:** Did the student complete the assignment in a timely and responsible manner? _____

☒ **Content:** Does the student demonstrate a thorough understanding of the relevant material? _3_

☒ **Competence:** Does the student's work reflect competence in a particular skill? _2_

☐ **Craftsmanship:** Does the student's work reflect care, craftsmanship, and quality? _____

☒ **Communication:** Did the student communicate in a clear and effective manner? _1_

☐ **Creativity:** Is the student's work creative, original, and interesting? _____

☐ **Cooperation:** Did the student help others or contribute to the success of a group? _____

☐ **Character:** Did the student demonstrate positive attitudes, behaviors, or habits of mind? _____

☒ **Critical Thinking:** Does the student's work reflect complex and analytical thinking? _2_

☐ **Complex Problem Solving:** Did the student approach problems in a thoughtful/logical way? _____

DIMENSION: Content

EXPECTATIONS: Students' work should reflect a thorough understanding of the Boston Massacre – the people, the circumstances of the event (propaganda vs. reality), the events leading up to the massacre, etc.

Initial score (1 2 3 ④) X Weighting factor (3) = 12

DIMENSION: Competence in writing an argument essay

EXPECTATIONS: Students' work should reflect what they've learned about the purpose, contents, and organizational structure of an argument essay.

Initial score (1 2 3 ④) X Weighting factor (2) = 8

DIMENSION: Competence in using/citing evidence

EXPECTATIONS: Students' work should reflect an ability to integrate and cite evidence from multiple sources (paraphrase and/or provide direct quotations).

Initial score (1 2 ③ 4) X Weighting factor (2) = 6

DIMENSION: Critical Thinking

EXPECTATIONS: Students should evaluate the reliability of the information in each of the provided documents and synthesize the most reliable evidence to create a logical and well-supported position.

Initial score (1 2 3 ④) X Weighting factor (2) = 8

DIMENSION: Communication

EXPECTATIONS: Each student's position on this issue and the evidence that supports this position should be clearly stated and explained. Students' papers should be free from the kinds of grammar, spelling, and organizational problems that would get in the way of understanding the case they're presenting.

Initial score (1 ② 3 4) X Weighting factor (1) = 2

Total score | 36/40!!

EXAMPLE 2: An elementary teacher replaced the bottom portion of the standard evaluation form with a rubric as shown below. She did this because she felt it would help her students to have the specific qualities that distinguished one level of performance from another spelled out in detail (e.g., what exactly is the difference between novice-level work and apprentice-level work?).

THE TASK: *Create an eye-catching, informative, and interesting zoo exhibit that teaches people about spiders and presents convincing evidence that spiders are more helpful than harmful ("people and spiders should be friends").*

I will assess my students' work for the following dimensions:

This dimension will be weighted:

☐ **Completion:** Did the student complete the assignment in a timely and responsible manner? _____

☒ **Content:** Does the student demonstrate a thorough understanding of the relevant material? ___1___

☐ **Competence:** Does the student's work reflect competence in a particular skill? _____

☐ **Craftsmanship:** Does the student's work reflect care, craftsmanship, and quality? _____

☐ **Communication:** Did the student communicate in a clear and effective manner? _____

☒ **Creativity:** Is the student's work creative, original, and interesting? ___1___

☒ **Cooperation:** Did the student help others or contribute to the success of a group? ___1___

☐ **Character:** Did the student demonstrate positive attitudes, behaviors, or habits of mind? _____

☒ **Critical Thinking:** Does the student's work reflect complex and analytical thinking? ___2___

☐ **Complex Problem Solving:** Did the student approach problems in a thoughtful/logical way? _____

THE RUBRIC:

	Content Describe spider facts and characteristics.	**Critical Thinking** Why should people and spiders be friends? Prove your case.	**Creativity** Capture and maintain audience interest.	**Cooperation** Contribute to the team's success.
Master	The exhibit highlights all critical characteristics of spiders as a group and of some specific kinds of spiders. It also includes information about insects for comparison.	The exhibit makes a very strong case for people and spiders being friends (why are spiders important to us and our world?) and supports that position with lots of facts, examples, stories, and other items.	The exhibit is eye catching. It attracts and maintains audience interest by including a variety of interesting and unfamiliar facts, stories, and works of art.	The student had a lot to do with the group's success. The student suggested a lot of ideas and listened respectfully to other people's ideas.
Journeyman	The exhibit highlights most of the key characteristics of spiders as a group. Some information on specific spiders and insects is included.	The exhibit makes a strong case for people and spiders being friends and supports that position with facts, examples, and stories. With a few more good examples, this would be a Master exhibit.	The exhibit is eye-catching. It attracts and maintains audience interest with interesting and unfamiliar information, but could use more variety (a combination of facts, stories, art).	The student actively contributed to the group's success, both by contributing a few ideas and by listening to other people's ideas.
Apprentice	The exhibit includes information about key spider characteristics, but some is inaccurate (or very little information on insects is included).	The exhibit makes a case for people and spiders being friends, but needs more (or higher-quality) evidence and examples to support that case.	The exhibit generates some interest, but attention may stray since facts, stories, and artwork are already familiar to the audience or aren't presented in a particularly interesting way.	The student did a good job of suggesting ideas or listening to other people's ideas. The next step is to do both!
Novice	Critical information about spider characteristics and/or insects needs to be added or corrected.	An explanation of why people and spiders should be friends needs to be added and/or supported with evidence.	The exhibit needs more interesting information, eye-catching displays, and logical organization. Without these features, it's hard to hold an audience's attention.	The student needs to better help and support the team, both by suggesting ideas and listening respectfully to other people's ideas.

The C-List

I will assess my students' work for the following dimensions:

☐ **Completion:** Did the student complete the assignment in a timely and responsible manner?

☐ **Content:** Does the student demonstrate a thorough understanding of the relevant material?

☐ **Competence:** Does the student's work reflect competence in a particular skill?

☐ **Craftsmanship:** Does the student's work reflect care, craftsmanship, and quality?

☐ **Communication:** Did the student communicate in a clear and effective manner?

☐ **Creativity:** Is the student's work creative, original, and interesting?

☐ **Cooperation:** Did the student help others or contribute to the success of a group?

☐ **Character:** Did the student demonstrate positive attitudes, behaviors, or habits of mind?

☐ **Critical Thinking:** Does the student's work reflect complex and analytical thinking?

☐ **Complex Problem Solving:** Did the student approach problems in a thoughtful/logical way?

→ *Refer to the extended version of The C-List (p. 183) for a more detailed description of each "C."*

🎧 Teacher Talk

→ One of the greatest strengths of this tool is its flexibility. Among other things, it can be used to differentiate assessment, to invite students into the assessment process, and to develop rubrics as well as rating scales.

- *To differentiate assessment,* select different criteria ("Cs") for different students (e.g., to motivate a creative student, make *creativity* one of the factors you consider when assessing her work). Another option is to weight the various Cs differently for different students (e.g., to encourage a student whose work is always late to be more prompt, weight *completion* more heavily for him than for other students). Customizing the assessment criteria in this way lets you address students' unique interests, talents, and needs.

- *To involve students in the assessment process,* invite them to help you choose the Cs and/or establish the expectations for high-quality work. One option is to choose all but one of the Cs yourself and let students pick the final *C.*

- *To create rubrics rather than rating scales,* describe three to four levels of performance for each dimension that you select in Step 2. Be as specific as possible and use student-friendly language. See Example 2 for a model.

→ Several of the dimensions on The C-List are well suited to assessing Common Core State Standards. The *communication* dimension, for example, is a good fit for many Speaking and Listening Standards; the *competence* dimension can be used to assess a wide variety of Core-related skills (anything from punctuating a paragraph to graphing a linear equation); the *complex problem solving* dimension has strong ties to the Standards for Mathematical Content and Practice; and the *critical thinking* dimension covers the kinds of complex and analytical thinking skills that run throughout the standards (evaluating the validity of evidence, questioning assumptions, etc.).

The C-List (extended version)

I will assess my students' work for the following dimensions:

☐ **Completion**
- Is the student's work complete? Does it contain all the required components? Was it submitted on time?
- Did the student follow the directions for completing the task?
- Did the student establish and follow a timeline for completing the task? Monitor progress? Use time wisely?

☐ **Content**
- Does the student demonstrate a thorough and accurate knowledge of the relevant content material?

☐ **Competence**
- Does the student demonstrate competence in a particular skill (e.g., adding two-digit numbers, writing a persuasive essay, following the scientific method, taking notes)?

☐ **Craftsmanship**
- Does the student's work reflect care, craftsmanship, and quality?
- Have errors and imperfections been rooted out and addressed?
- Is the work polished and attractive? Visually appealing?

☐ **Communication**
- Did the student communicate his thoughts, feelings, or positions in a clear and effective manner?
- Did the student adapt the presentation to fit the purpose of the task and the audience's interests/needs?
- Did the student ask and answer questions?
- Did the student use digital media/visual displays of data to express and facilitate understanding of the material?
- Did the student make the presentation easy for others to follow by defining unfamiliar terms, symbols, etc.?

☐ **Creativity**
- Is the student's work creative, original, and interesting?
- Does it reflect the student's unique style, voice, or point of view?
- Did the student think flexibly, originally, or metaphorically? Consider an unusual angle or perspective?
- Did the student use different media to express his thoughts and opinions or capture audience interest?

☐ **Cooperation**
- Did the student help or collaborate with other students?
- Did the student contribute to the success of a group (solve problems, keep people on task, etc.)?
- Did the student propose and share ideas with others? Listen respectfully to other people's ideas?

☐ **Character**
- Did the student display positive attitudes/behaviors/habits of mind?* For example, did the student display persistence? A can-do attitude? Sensitivity to another person's needs?

☐ **Critical Thinking**
- Does the student's work reflect complex and analytical thinking? For example, did the student analyze and interpret data or textual information? Generate and test a hypothesis? Develop and support an argument with evidence? Respond to counterarguments? Identify similarities and differences? Analyze causes/effects? Recognize patterns and structures? Evaluate the soundness of his own (or other people's) reasoning?

☐ **Complex Problem Solving**
- Does the student approach and generate solutions to problems in a thoughtful and logical way? Can the student define the problem? Draw connections to analogous problems? Develop strategies for solving the problem? Employ appropriate tools and techniques? Develop models? Reflect on and critique the soundness of the problem-solving process and solution? Explore and weigh alternatives?

*For a list of examples, download the Habits of Mind Reference Page (www.ThoughtfulClassroom.com/Tools).

Student's name: _____ Assignment due date: _____

Lesson/unit topic: _____

The C-List Evaluation Form

Task:

I will assess my students' work for the following dimensions:

This dimension will be weighted:

☐ **Completion:** Did the student complete the assignment in a timely and responsible manner? _____

☐ **Content:** Does the student demonstrate a thorough understanding of the relevant material? _____

☐ **Competence:** Does the student's work reflect competence in a particular skill? _____

☐ **Craftsmanship:** Does the student's work reflect care, craftsmanship, and quality? _____

☐ **Communication:** Did the student communicate in a clear and effective manner? _____

☐ **Creativity:** Is the student's work creative, original, and interesting? _____

☐ **Cooperation:** Did the student help others or contribute to the success of a group? _____

☐ **Character:** Did the student demonstrate positive attitudes, behaviors, or habits of mind? _____

☐ **Critical Thinking:** Does the student's work reflect complex and analytical thinking? _____

☐ **Complex Problem Solving:** Did the student approach problems in a thoughtful/logical way? _____

☐ **Other:** _____

DIMENSION:
EXPECTATIONS:

Initial score (1 2 3 4) X Weighting factor (____) = _____

DIMENSION:
EXPECTATIONS:

Initial score (1 2 3 4) X Weighting factor (____) = _____

DIMENSION:
EXPECTATIONS:

Initial score (1 2 3 4) X Weighting factor (____) = _____

DIMENSION:
EXPECTATIONS:

Initial score (1 2 3 4) X Weighting factor (____) = _____

DIMENSION:
EXPECTATIONS:

Initial score (1 2 3 4) X Weighting factor (____) = _____

Total score [____]

Content-Process-Product

What is it?

A framework for designing assessment criteria that address students' understanding of the *content*, their mastery of relevant thinking *processes*, and the overall quality of their final *products*

What are the benefits of using this tool?

The Common Core State Standards call for a more balanced approach to instruction—one that emphasizes thinking skills and knowledge application in addition to knowledge acquisition. This tool helps us design similarly balanced assessment frameworks by reminding us to consider three distinct dimensions when evaluating students' work: students' understanding of content, their mastery of critical thinking processes, and the quality of their final products.

What are the basic steps?

1. Design an assessment task that challenges students to demonstrate their command of specific content knowledge and thinking skills/processes by creating a product or performance.

   Tip: For general help with task design, or a list of authentic products and thinking skills to choose from, see the Performance Task Designer tool (pp. 197–200).

2. Generate a list of assessment criteria for the task in question by thinking about what you want to see in students' products or performances. Remember to consider content, process, and product. Think:

   - *What CONTENT knowledge should students' completed products demonstrate?* Are there facts that students should recount? Concepts they should explain? Terms they should define?

   - *What will tell you that students have used the requisite thinking skills/PROCESSES?* How will you know, for example, that they "analyzed causes and effects" or "explored alternative solutions"?

   - *What qualities or components should students' final PRODUCTS possess?* Are you looking for clarity? Originality? Correct spelling? Three pieces of evidence to support a thesis?

3. Decide whether all three dimensions (content, process, product) are equally important or if you will count some more than others when calculating students' final grades.

4. Share the assessment criteria (and any weighting information) with students before they begin working. Remind them to use the criteria throughout the process to assess and refine their work.

5. Use the criteria to evaluate and provide students with feedback about their work.

How is this tool used in the classroom?

✔ To develop high-quality assessment criteria that address content, process, and product

✔ To prepare students to produce high-quality work by sharing assessment criteria in advance

The Content-Process-Product framework is extremely versatile in the sense that it can be used to design lists of assessment criteria (see Examples 1 and 2), checklists (Example 3), or rubrics (Example 4).

EXAMPLE 1: Using the tool to generate a list of assessment criteria (first grade)

To expose her students to the kinds of informational texts that the Common Core State Standards recommend, a first-grade teacher made the book *Animals in Winter* the centerpiece of a lesson on the ways that animals prepare for winter. After reading the book aloud and discussing key concepts and terms as a class, she had students summarize their learning by creating colorful and informative posters. She gave students pieces of paper labeled *hibernate*, *migrate*, and *forage*; had students define each term using pictures; and had them draw examples of animals that belonged in each category. The Content-Process-Product criteria she used to assess students' command of the relevant content knowledge and thinking processes are shown here:

ASSESSMENT CRITERIA: <u>ANIMALS IN WINTER</u>

CONTENT

• Students' posters and responses demonstrate an understanding of the following key terms and concepts: hibernate, migrate, forage.

PROCESS

• <u>Defining</u>: Students can explain the key terms in their own words if asked.
• <u>Classifying</u>: Students can classify animals into the appropriate categories.

PRODUCT

• Posters include a "picture definition" of each term.
• Posters include at least two animals per category (animals from the book or from our discussion).

EXAMPLE 2: Using the tool to generate a list of assessment criteria (high school)

An art history teacher assigned the following task: "Research the ways that factors outside the art world (advances in science/technology, a renewed interest in the Classics, humanist philosophy, etc.) influenced the development of Renaissance painting. Create a slide show that you can use to present your findings." The assessment criteria that accompanied this task are shown below.

Assessment Criteria: Influences on Renaissance Painting

CONTENT:
Students should identify and describe at least two factors outside the art world that influenced Renaissance painting.

PROCESS (analysis/explanation):
Students should use specific examples to explain the impact of these factors on Renaissance painting.

PRODUCT:
Slides should be factually accurate and consistent with the purpose of the task. They should include specific examples of art for each factor that students discuss. Text/images should be clear and easy to see. Names of paintings/painters should be indicated.

EXAMPLE 3: Using the tool to generate a checklist for students

The teacher of an early childhood education course used the Content-Process-Product framework to generate a checklist that would help his students understand and meet the requirements for their end-of-unit project. The project description and checklist that he gave them are shown below. (For more on the checklist format, see pp. 47–49.)

THE TASK: "A Toy for Toddlers"

After hearing about your expertise regarding the intellectual development and behavior of toddlers, a toy company has hired you to design a safe, educational, and appealing new toy. Your toy must help toddlers grow in at least one key area of intellectual development: attention, memory, reasoning, imagination, or curiosity. It must also take advantage of one of the four methods of learning that we've discussed in class. Representatives from the company expect to see a sketch of your design in one week's time, and they've asked that you accompany your sketch with an explanation of how your toy will satisfy these design criteria.

THE CHECKLIST

CONTENT: *Cognitive development of toddlers*

- ☐ I reread the relevant sections of my text and reviewed my lecture notes before beginning.
- ☐ I used what I know about how toddlers learn and what engages them to design my toy.

PROCESS: *Designing/Inventing*

- ☐ I designed a completely original toy or I significantly adapted/updated an existing toy.
- ☐ I checked that my design met all the criteria that I was given by the toy company.
- ☐ I examined my design to confirm that it wouldn't pose any obvious safety risks to toddlers.
- ☐ I used the guidelines in my textbook to check that my toy was age appropriate.

PRODUCT: *Sketch and explanation*

- ☐ I drew one or more pictures of what my toy would look like.
- ☐ I labeled my sketch(es) to highlight the key features of the toy.
- ☐ I explained how and why my toy would fulfill the design criteria from the task description.
- ☐ I reviewed my work and corrected it as needed.

SOURCE: Adapted from *Classroom Curriculum Design: How Strategic Units Improve Instruction and Engage Students in Meaningful Learning* (p. 60) by H. F. Silver and M. J. Perini, 2010, Ho-Ho-Kus, NJ: Thoughtful Education Press. © 2010 by Thoughtful Education Press. Adapted with permission.

EXAMPLE 4: Using the tool to generate a rubric

A fifth-grade teacher used the Content-Process-Product framework to create a list of assessment criteria for the following comparative writing task: "Are reptiles and amphibians more alike or more different? Take a position and support it with evidence." She then transformed her list into a rubric by describing what each of the Content, Process, and Product criteria she had generated would look like at three different levels of performance: *excellent*, *almost there*, and *keep working*. A copy of her rubric can be found on p. 52 of the Guiding & Grading Rubric tool.

From Puzzles to Paradoxes

What is it?

A tool for designing assessment tasks that demand real-world thinking, reasoning, and writing skills

What are the benefits of using this tool?

In an effort to prepare our students for the kinds of items they're likely to see on standardized tests, many of us have moved away from using authentic assessment tasks in our classrooms. Since preparing students to succeed in the real world is just as important (if not more so) as preparing them to succeed on standardized tests, it's critical to bring authentic types of assessment tasks back into the picture. This tool helps us do that by outlining twelve different frameworks for designing assessment tasks that engage real-world thinking skills.

What are the basic steps?

1. Identify the content knowledge/thinking skills that you want to develop or assess.

2. Familiarize yourself with the twelve different assessment frameworks. Select a framework that meets your needs.

Note: Guidelines for picking a framework can be found on p. 189; detailed descriptions, instructions, and examples can be found on pp. 190–192.

3. Use your selected framework to create an assessment task for your lesson or unit. Ask yourself the following questions as you develop your task:

- *What* do I want students to produce? (An argument essay? A verbal explanation? A poster?)
- *Why* am I assigning this task? Is the task consistent with my goals and purpose?
- *When* and *where* should students work on it? (During instruction or after? In class or at home?)
- *How* should students work on it? (Alone? In pairs? In groups?)
- *What* criteria will I consider when assessing students' work?

4. Present the task to students. Clarify what the task entails, how students should work on it, and how students' work will be evaluated.

How is this tool used in the classroom?

✔ To deepen and test student learning using authentic types of assessment tasks

✔ To develop and test students' research, writing, and analytical thinking skills

Which Assessment Framework Should I Choose?

Select the **Puzzle** framework to have students demonstrate their content knowledge and reasoning skills by solving a puzzle or logic problem.

Choose the **Mystery** framework to engage students in developing evidence-based explanations of content-related mysteries or discrepant events.

Use the **Historical Investigation** format to deepen and test students' understanding of historically significant people, places, and events—and to develop critical research, writing, and thinking skills.

Use the **Controversy** framework to test students' understanding of a controversial issue and ability to support a position with evidence.

Use the **Personal Dilemma** framework to broaden students' perspective on controversial issues, help students connect with the content on a personal level, and have students express and defend their personal positions.

Select the **Invention** framework to have students apply their content knowledge to the creation of an original product.

Use the **Problem/Solution** framework to test students' ability to analyze problems (real world or fictional), generate solutions, and evaluate the quality of those solutions.

Select the **Decision-Making** framework to have students make or evaluate decisions using a specific set of criteria.

Use the **Informed Prediction** framework to present students with hypothetical scenarios that require them to understand and apply what they've learned.

Use the **Essential Attributes** framework to test students' understanding of important terms and concepts.

Select the **Experimental Inquiry** framework to assess students' ability to generate and/or test original hypotheses.

Choose the **Paradox** framework to boost engagement and test students' understanding of critical concepts by challenging students to explain seemingly contradictory statements or observations.

From Puzzles to Paradoxes: Twelve Assessment Frameworks to Choose From

FRAMEWORK	TO CREATE THIS KIND OF TASK…	CLASSROOM EXAMPLES
Puzzle tasks require students to solve or put the pieces of a puzzle together in a logical way.	**1.** Break a text, process, system, or piece of equipment into parts. **2.** Present the parts to students. **3.** Challenge students to reconstruct the original and explain their reasoning. *Variation:* Give students *any* logic/reasoning problem to solve.	• Can you arrange these pictures to tell a story? • Can you put the steps in this scrambled geometric proof into a logical order? • A copy of Bertrand Russell's "What I Have Lived For" was recently given to us, but the pieces were all out of order. Use what you know about the power of a thesis statement to drive the organization of an essay, the structure of an essay in general, and the function of transitional words to put the pieces back in order. Justify your organization in writing.
Mystery tasks challenge students to solve content-related mysteries by analyzing and synthesizing a set of clues.	**1.** Present a puzzling event/phenomenon ("mystery") to students. **2.** Give students a set of clues (facts, maps, data tables, images, etc.) that will help them solve the mystery. **3.** Encourage students to review the clues carefully, generate plausible solutions, and select the best one. They can do this alone, in pairs, or in groups of three to five students. **4.** Have students present and support their solution with evidence.	• After dominating the earth for over 150 million years, the dinosaurs suddenly disappeared. Can you figure out why? Generate a hypothesis that is consistent with the bits of information ("clues") in your team's envelope. Be prepared to justify your hypothesis. • Over the course of twenty years, more than 80% of the people who settled in Jamestown died. Why might this be? Look for clues in your textbook. Propose an explanation. • A kindergarten mystery: "I live in a den and can roar very loud. In the jungle, I am king—and of that I am proud! Who am I?"
Historical Investigations ask students to research, analyze, and draw conclusions about historically significant events.	**1.** Choose a historically significant event for students to research and explore, either individually or as a class. **2.** Pose a question that requires them to think about the event in an analytical way (e.g., What were its causes? Its effects? How does it compare to another event? Why is it significant?). **3.** Have students present the results of their analysis. *Variation:* Move beyond events. Have students research historically significant people, discoveries, works of literature, and so on.	• Why do athletes from around the world compete in the Olympics every four years? How did this tradition get started? Do the Olympics still matter today? Why? • How did the Space Race affect our country's spending priorities, schools, and achievements? • Where there any silver linings in the sinking of the RMS *Titanic*? • What was Upton Sinclair's purpose in writing *The Jungle*? Did the book have its intended effect? • Can a disease alter the course of world history? Explain using one or more of the examples on the board.
Controversy tasks have students take and defend a position on a debatable or unresolved issue.	**1.** Identify an issue that people have different theories/positions on. **2.** Pose a question that will get students thinking about that issue. **3.** Challenge students to research/consider all sides of the issue, take a position, and justify their position using evidence. If appropriate, have them mention and rebut alternative positions. *Note:* For controversies that revolve around personal values, morals, or feelings, use the Personal Dilemma framework instead.	• Should members of Congress have term limits? • Does "fairness" mean treating everyone the same? • What was President Lincoln's primary motive in signing the Emancipation Proclamation? • Does Pythagoras deserve the credit for the theorem that's named after him? • What's the best way to stimulate the economy during a recession? • Do street artists deserve to be studied alongside art giants like Picasso and Matisse?

Task Type	Description & Steps	Examples
Personal Dilemma tasks are similar to Controversy tasks in that they require taking a position on a controversial issue, but they place more emphasis on personal feelings/values.	**1.** Identify an issue that students will have different views about. **2.** Pose a question that requires students to take a position on this issue. (Dilemma questions often start with the word *should*.) **3.** Have students present and defend their positions. **4.** Clarify that a well-crafted response should reflect factual knowledge as well as feelings; it should also mention the positives and negatives of taking that particular position.	• Should our constitutionally given right to free speech be limited under any circumstances? • Should professional female athletes earn the same as their male counterparts? • Should we be nice to people even when they're not nice to us? • Should a top-notch education include instruction in art and music? • Should animals be used in scientific research? • Should Lenny have shot George at the end of *Of Mice and Men?*
Problem/Solution tasks ask students to analyze a problem, generate possible solutions, and evaluate those solutions.	**1.** Present students with a content-related problem or challenge that could be addressed in a variety of ways. **2.** Have them analyze the problem, generate possible solutions, and select the best one. (This can be done individually or in groups.) *Variation:* Have students examine and evaluate someone else's solution to a problem.	• How might we get the students in this school to care more about recycling? • Can you think of a way to help Frog and Toad solve their cookie-eating problem? [A teacher posed this question after reading part of Arnold Lobel's "Cookies" aloud.] • How could we increase the strength of this paper tube? Explain and support your ideas. • How could we address the issue of low voter turnout? • How effectively did George Washington address the morale problem among his troops?
Invention tasks challenge students to create or invent an original product.	**1.** Challenge students to create or invent something that solves a problem, fulfills a need, or improves an existing product/design. **2.** Encourage them to be creative yet practical and think outside the box. *Note:* This framework differs from Problem/Solution in that it requires students to create something concrete—for example, a drawing or a product rather than an idea or strategy.	• Invent a "study diet" that could improve students' academic performance. • Create a fun name for a healthy snack that would get students more interested in eating it (e.g., "ants on a log" instead of "celery with cream cheese and raisins"). • Invent a fitness routine that people could do in their hotel rooms without any equipment. • The local zoo has hired you to redesign the enclosure for an animal of your choice. The new enclosure should promote the health and happiness of your animal while providing maximum visibility and entertainment for zoo visitors.
Decision-Making tasks require students to analyze different options, pick one, and defend their choice.	**1.** Pose a question that requires students to consider alternatives and make a decision. For example, "Who/what is the best __?" **2.** Tell students what criteria they should use to analyze the various alternatives or let them choose their own criteria. **3.** Ask students to explain and defend their decisions. (What did I decide? How did the criteria guide my decision-making process?) *Variation:* Have students use specific criteria to evaluate someone else's decision (e.g., a politician's or literary character's).	• Imagine that you meet people from another planet who don't know what *friendship* is. Which book from this unit would you pick to help them understand what it is? Why? • Who was the most influential ruler of ancient Egypt? Defend your choice. • If you were the coach, what play would you call in this situation? Why? • Do you agree that bombing Hiroshima and Nagasaki was President Truman's best option for ending the war in the Pacific? Use the criteria on the board to compare the options that were available to Truman and decide what you would've done if you were president. Present, explain, and defend your decision in a letter to the American people.

(continued on next page)

From Puzzles to Paradoxes: Twelve Assessment Frameworks to Choose From (continued)

FRAMEWORK	TO CREATE THIS KIND OF TASK…	CLASSROOM EXAMPLES
Informed Prediction tasks present students with a "what if" scenario and ask them to generate possible outcomes.	**1.** Present students with a "what if" scenario. **2.** Have them describe possible outcomes (or causes). **3.** Make it clear that their predictions should be rooted in their knowledge of the subject matter (i.e., predictions should be logical, not nonsensical).	• What if we had a base-60 number system like the ancient Babylonians instead of base-10? • What if there weren't any oil in the Middle East? • What if the sun stopped shining? • What if Rasputin had never lived? • What if you traveled into the future and found that the United States was no longer the superpower it is today? What might have caused this change in status?
Essential Attributes tasks challenge students to recognize, apply, or define a key concept's essential attributes.	**1.** Select a critical concept that students have learned about. **2.** Test students' understanding of this concept by assigning a task that requires them to recognize, apply, or define its essential attributes/elements. Among other things, you could have students find real-world examples of the concept, list its critical attributes, or explain how it's similar to or different from another concept.	• Show that you understand the key elements of a fable by writing one of your own. • What is an amphipathic molecule? Define it in your own words, draw a real-world example of one, and use the drawing to highlight its essential attributes/parts. • The Notre Dame Cathedral is considered a classic example of Gothic architecture. Why? • Is Willy Loman a true tragic hero? Defend your position using evidence from the text. • What is a rational number? How does it differ from an irrational number?
Experimental Inquiries challenge students to generate and test original hypotheses.	**1.** Ask students to make an educated guess about the outcome of an action, event, or experiment. **2.** Have them generate a plan for testing their guess. **3.** Whenever possible, have them carry out their plans and report their results.	• If you were a plant, do you think the kind of light you got would matter (artificial vs. sunlight)? How could you test your prediction? Let's design an experiment to find out.… • How might using fewer lectures and more hands-on activities affect learning, motivation, and/or engagement? Make a prediction and explain how we could test it as a class. • How might adding resistors affect the current in a series circuit? Make a prediction, generate a plan for testing it, and describe the results of your experiment.
Paradox tasks challenge students to explain seemingly contradictory statements or observations.	**1.** Present students with a seemingly contradictory statement or phenomenon that is nonetheless true. ("How is it possible that __?") **2.** Challenge students to reconcile the paradox by generating possible explanations.	How is it possible that.… • Eating fewer calories can actually prevent you from losing weight? • George Washington lost more battles than he won, yet is one of our greatest war heroes? • Airplanes are extremely heavy, but don't fall out of the sky? • The order of operations can affect your answer? • Burning a forest can be good for its health?

 Teacher Talk

→ Feel free to use the twelve frameworks for instructional purposes as well as assessment purposes (i.e., to help students learn about a topic or issue rather than to test their understanding of it).

→ Can these frameworks be used with very young students? Absolutely! Primary-grade examples have been provided for most of the given frameworks, and the frameworks can be simplified as needed for use with younger students. Among other things, you could have primary-grade students draw or speak their ideas/findings rather than writing them.

→ Giving students choices about their learning can enhance their motivation and success. One option is to give students an assessment framework and let them design a task that interests them. Here's how one teacher did this using the Decision-Making framework: "FDR made a lot of important decisions in his first hundred days as president. Pick one that you want to evaluate, describe the criteria that you'll use to do it, and present the results of your analysis in writing." Another option is to use the different frameworks to create a sampler of assessment tasks (see below for an example) and let students choose which task(s) to complete.

ASSESSMENT SAMPLER: Renewable/Nonrenewable Energy Unit (complete *ONE* of these tasks)		
Controversy	**Investigation**	**Informed Prediction**
Is global warming more a result of natural or human causes? Write an editorial taking a position on this issue. Be sure to define global warming, explain the controversy, and defend your position (rebut the alternative one as well) using relevant evidence.	In *Flat, Hot, and Crowded*, Thomas Friedman contends that the more the United States is dependent on oil from the Middle East, the less democratic the Middle East will be. Why does he believe this to be true? Does our reliance on fossil fuels work against the development of democratic principles in the Middle East?	Prepare a presentation in which you use data charts, mathematical calculations, and other evidence to predict the possible consequences if the causes of global warming aren't addressed and temperatures continue to rise at the same rate they've been increasing over the last 100 years.
Controversy + Investigation	**Decision Making + Problem/Solution**	**Paradox**
Research the pros and cons of nuclear energy, natural gas, and solar energy. Conduct a debate on which form of energy should be expanded to meet rising demands for cleaner energy sources.	Select the form of renewable energy that you believe the United States should pursue most aggressively. Identify a challenge in expanding its use and develop a plan that will address this challenge.	Scientists claim that global warming leads to more severe winters and, at the same time, warms the oceans. How is this possible? Explain.

→ Collectively, the assessment frameworks described in this tool engage the kinds of higher-order thinking skills (e.g., analysis, synthesis, evaluation) that are at the heart of the Common Core State Standards. The frameworks can be used to address specific Common Core Standards as well, some of which are listed here:

- Conduct research projects based on focused questions, and demonstrate an understanding of the subject under investigation (W.CCR.7).

- Construct viable arguments and evaluate the arguments of others (W.CCR.1, R.CCR.8, Standard 3 from the Standards for Mathematical Practice).

- Present information in a way that's clear, logical, and audience appropriate (SL.CCR.4).

More Than Your Usual Multiple Choice

What is it?

A tool for designing multiple-choice tests that require thinking and understanding in addition to recall

What are the benefits of using this tool?

Traditionally, multiple-choice tests have been viewed as vehicles for testing factual knowledge rather than thinking skills—and they've gotten a bit of a bum rap as a result. When designed thoughtfully, however, multiple-choice questions have the capacity to test more than just recall. This tool shows you how.

What are the basic steps?

1. Identify the content knowledge and/or skills that you want to assess. (What should students know, understand, and be able to do at the end of this lesson or unit?)

2. Develop multiple-choice questions that will test students' grasp of the relevant material. Make these questions "more than your usual multiple choice" by designing them around complex thinking skills. Among other things, you could design questions that ask students to

analyze	*compare*	*extrapolate*	*make predictions*
classify	*conclude*	*interpret*	*identify main ideas*
identify evidence	*apply*	*problem solve*	*recognize patterns*

3. Keep these guidelines (adapted from Stiggins et al., 2006) in mind as you write your questions:
   - Use simple, age-appropriate language; avoid including unnecessarily difficult vocabulary terms.
   - Keep test items as short as possible so that reading ability/speed doesn't become an issue.
   - Frame your test items as questions rather than statements that need to be completed. For example, "What can you conclude from the data below?" rather than "The data below suggest __."
   - Emphasize information/instructions that might be overlooked (e.g., "Which of these is NOT...").
   - Check that each test question has only one correct (or best) answer.
   - Aim for answers that are similar in length and parallel in structure.

4. Review your questions to confirm that they require the kind of thinking you intended. For example, check that an *analysis* question will actually require students to conduct an analysis—not remember the results of an analysis you performed in class (in that case, it would be a *recall* question).

5. Confirm that your test is both comprehensive (covers all of the relevant material) and well balanced (includes questions that require a variety of different thinking skills).

How is this tool used in the classroom?

✔ To design multiple-choice tests that require thinking and understanding as well as recall

Representative multiple-choice questions from different grade levels and content areas are shown below. In each case, the thinking skill that's being targeted is indicated in italics.

EXAMPLE 1: A fourth-grade teacher designed this *application* question to test his students' understanding of the structure/function relationship:

> Based on the physical features of this imaginary animal, which of these statements is most likely to be true?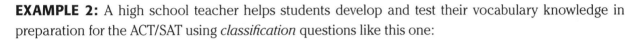
>
> A. It's a plant eater that lives on land in a cold environment.
>
> B. It's a meat eater that lives in the water in a cold environment.
>
> C. It's a meat eater that lives on land in a hot environment.
>
> D. It's a plant eater that lives in the water in a hot environment.

EXAMPLE 2: A high school teacher helps students develop and test their vocabulary knowledge in preparation for the ACT/SAT using *classification* questions like this one:

> Which word is LEAST similar in meaning to the other three?
>
> A. fawning
>
> B. sycophantic
>
> C. philanthropic
>
> D. toadyish

EXAMPLE 3: A third-grade teacher used this *interpretation* question to test students' ability to *identify main ideas*—a Common Core reading skill (RI.3.2) that she had been focusing on for weeks:

> What is the main idea of this passage?
>
> A. Everyone needs food and water to survive.
>
> B. People around the world have different eating habits.
>
> C. An American breakfast may be very different from breakfast in another country.
>
> D. Many different factors influence the kinds of foods people eat.

EXAMPLE 4: A trigonometry teacher used a series of *analysis* questions like the one below to test her students' understanding of trig functions and general characteristics of functions:

> For numbers a and b, where $a < 0 < b$, how often is the function $f(x) = \cos x$ an increasing function?
>
> A. Always
>
> B. Sometimes
>
> C. Never

SOURCE: Adapted from *Math Tools, Grades 3–12: 60+ Ways to Build Mathematical Practices, Differentiate Instruction, and Increase Student Engagement* (p. 56), by H. F. Silver, J. R. Brunsting, T. Walsh, and E. J. Thomas, 2012, Thousand Oaks, CA: Corwin Press. © 2012 by Silver Strong & Associates. Adapted with permission.

EXAMPLE 5: A geography teacher developed this question to test his students' *data analysis* skills:

> Examine the data table that you've been given. Based on the data, where would someone who liked sunshine, hated rain, and enjoyed skiing be happiest living?
>
> A. Washington
>
> B. New Mexico
>
> C. North Carolina
>
> D. Texas

EXAMPLE 6: An English teacher uses this tool to test a variety of Common Core reading skills. An *interpretation* question that he designed around Keats's "To Autumn" is shown here:

> What is the primary purpose of the final stanza?
>
> A. To highlight the key differences between autumn and spring
>
> B. To complete the cycle of the four seasons
>
> C. To celebrate the overlooked beauty of autumn
>
> D. To fill the reader with a sense of loss or mourning

EXAMPLE 7: An AP Biology teacher tested students' understanding of restriction enzymes by asking them to make a *prediction* about the results of a hypothetical experiment:

> Pretend that you've been given a tube with an unknown DNA sample. If you run the sample on an agarose gel both before and after digesting it with EcoRI, how many bands would you expect to see if the sample had been a circular piece of DNA with two EcoRI sites and one HindIII site?
>
> A. Undigested = no band, digested = 2 bands
>
> B. Undigested = no band, digested = 3 bands
>
> C. Undigested = 1 band, digested = 2 bands
>
> D. Undigested = 1 band, digested = 3 bands

Teacher Talk

➔ Since you may inadvertently design a question that has more than one correct answer (it happens to the best of us!), give students an opportunity to justify the correctness of any answers that you've marked wrong. If students present a valid case, be sure to adjust their scores accordingly.

➔ All assessment formats (multiple-choice included) have their strengths and limitations. As educators, we need to be aware of these strengths and weaknesses—and select the formats that are the best fit for our content and goals. *Think:* Is multiple-choice a good fit for what I'm trying to do?

➔ The multiple-choice format can be used for formative as well as summative/evaluative purposes.

➔ Multiple-choice tests can tell us what students got wrong, but they can't tell us why. If we want to understand how and why students went astray, we need to ask follow-up questions (e.g., How did you come to this answer? Can you explain your thinking process?). The more we learn about the sources of students' errors, the better we'll be able to address them.

Performance Task Designer

What is it?

A tool that makes performance assessment tasks easier to design by providing a planning template and a menu of authentic tasks, contexts, and thinking skills to choose from

What are the benefits of using this tool?

Performance assessments—or tasks that ask students to create products or give performances rather than answer test items—offer many benefits: They allow us to include authentic problems and real-world contexts, they engage students in meaningful work and deep thought, and they yield far more insight into how students' minds work than objective test questions can. Yet many of us shy away from using performance assessments, in part because they can be difficult to design. This tool scaffolds the design process, making authentic assessment tasks quicker and easier to create.

What are the basic steps?

1. Establish the purpose of the assessment task you're about to design. To do this, review your standards and/or learning goals and ask yourself the following questions:
   - What content knowledge do I want to assess?
   - What thinking and learning skills do I want to assess? (See Figure 4, p. 198, for ideas.)

   Tip: Use the reproducible Performance Task Planner on p. 200 to jot down your ideas as you work through Steps 1–3.

2. Design an assessment task that's consistent with your purpose. Make it authentic by incorporating a real-world product, context, and skill(s); see Figure 4 for suggestions.

3. Identify the criteria that you'll use to evaluate students' performance on this task. *Think:* How will I assess content knowledge? Thinking skills/processes? What will I look for in a final product?

4. Use your completed planner to present the task to students. Explain what you're trying to assess (the task's purpose), what the task entails, and how you'll evaluate students' work.

Figure 4: Skills, Products, and Contexts

THINKING & LEARNING SKILLS

Procedural/Factual	Logical/Analytical	Original/Speculative	Personal/Social/Emotional
Alphabetizing	Analyzing	Applying	Assisting
Calculating	Classifying	Brainstorming	Coaching
Charting/Mapping	Comparing & contrasting	Creating symbols or icons	Collaborating
Checking & correcting	Constructing arguments	Designing	Communicating with others
Defining	Critiquing	Developing hypotheses	Considering others' views
Describing	Debugging/Error analysis	Elaborating	Discussing
Executing	Drawing conclusions	Experimenting	Empathizing
Fact-finding	Establishing or using criteria	Exploring	Feeling
Goal setting	Evaluating evidence	Expressing ideas via art	Giving opinions
Labeling	Explaining	Extrapolating	Interviewing
Listing	Finding evidence	Free-associating	Listening
Memorizing	Finding out why	Generalizing/Conceptualizing	Personalizing
Note taking	Identifying big ideas	Generating alternatives	Personifying
Constructing	Interpreting	Imagining	Personally prioritizing
Observing	Justifying	Inventing	Reflecting
Organizing	Pattern-finding	Performing	Relating to
Presenting	Problem solving	Predicting	Respecting differences
Recalling	Proving	Speculating – what if?	Role-playing
Recognizing/Locating	Questioning	Synthesizing/Integrating	Seeing different sides
Reporting	Reasoning	Thinking divergently	Sharing
Retelling	Supporting & refuting	Thinking metaphorically	Surveying
Tracing/Sequencing	Testing hypotheses	Using patterns & structures	Team building
Translating	Validating/Verifying	Visualizing	Valuing
Writing (explanatory)	Writing (persuasive)	Writing (creative)	Writing (personal narrative)

PRODUCTS

Analogy	Environmental impact plan	Model	Report (lab, book, police)
Art exhibit	Essay	Movie or music video	Research abstract
Board game	Family tree	Museum display	Research paper
Bulletin board	Flag	Outline	Review or critique
Case study	Flowchart	Painting	Scrapbook
Children's book	Graph, chart, table	Photo album or collage	Sketch or blueprint
Classified ad	Graphic organizer	Picture or poster	Slide-show presentation
Computer program	Instruction manual	Play or puppet show	Slogan
Concept map or web	Interview transcript	Playbook	Song/Musical composition
Dance	Invention	Podcast	Speech
Debate	Lesson plan	Poem	Stock portfolio
Demonstration	Letter or memo	Political cartoon	Summary
Diary, journal entry, blog	Magazine article	Portfolio or e-portfolio	Textbook chapter
Dictionary entry	Map or globe	Problem set & answer key	To-do list
Diet or exercise plan	Memoir/Personal history	Proof	Travel brochure
Editorial	Metaphor	Recipe	Website/Wiki

CONTEXTS

Architecture & design	Current events	Law & criminal justice	Research
Arts & literature	Entertainment	Marketing/Advertising	Science & technology
Communication	Health & medicine	Money & finance	Sociology
Community/Social services	History	Personal history	Sports
Computer science	Industrial arts	Photography	Teaching/Education
Counseling	Invention & manufacturing	Politics & government	Technical writing
Culinary arts	Journalism/Publishing	Radio & television	Travel & tourism

How is this tool used in the classroom?

✔ To design engaging and authentic assessment tasks

EXAMPLES: Two teachers' planners are shown below; see www.ThoughtfulClassroom.com/Tools for additional examples.

CONTENT KNOWLEDGE	**SKILLS**
• Different places have different climates • The climate influences what you wear	• Interpreting data from brochures • Justifying clothing choice with evidence

Packed and Ready to Go...

TASK DESCRIPTION:

Look at the different travel brochures on your group's table. Pick a place that looks like it would be fun to visit. Use the pictures on the brochure to guess what the climate is like in that place. Then look at the pieces of clothing on your worksheet and decide which ones you would pack if you were going to that place for a vacation. Cut those pieces of clothing out and paste them onto your suitcase. Record the name of the place that you're planning to visit and explain why you packed what you packed. What do you think the climate will be like? Why are the clothes that you packed a good fit for this climate?

ASSESSMENT CRITERIA:

- Description of climate is consistent with the pictures in the brochure.
- Appropriate clothing is packed in the suitcase.
- Explanation of why the clothing in the suitcase fits the climate is logical.

CONTEXT	**PRODUCT**
Travel and tourism	Suitcase full of clothing and explanation

CONTENT KNOWLEDGE	**SKILLS**
Probability of compound events	Error analysis and pattern finding

You Be the Teacher!

TASK DESCRIPTION:

On the next page are six probability problems that a student completed for homework. Pretend that you are the student's teacher. Examine the student's work, identify the errors (do you see any patterns?), and correct them. Then identify and explain the flaws in thinking that led the student to make these errors. Finally, design a lesson plan that would help the student understand where he went wrong and how to avoid making a similar kind of mistake(s) in the future.

ASSESSMENT CRITERIA:

- Mistakes have been located and corrected.
- Potential flaws in thinking have been identified and clearly explained.
- Lesson plan explains what the errors were and how to avoid repeating them.

CONTEXT	**PRODUCT**
Teaching/Education	Lesson plan

Lesson/unit topic: _____   Date: _____

Performance Task Planner

CONTENT KNOWLEDGE	SKILLS

TASK DESCRIPTION:

ASSESSMENT CRITERIA:

CONTEXT	PRODUCT

Second-Chance Test

What is it?

A tool that transforms classroom tests into learning opportunities by having students analyze their errors, learn from their mistakes, and take second-chance tests on the same material

What are the benefits of using this tool?

Assessment expert Susan Brookhart (2008) reminds us that "an analysis of test results can be a gold mine of information, but only if students know that they will get a chance to use the information" (p. 66). This tool, which draws on her work, gives students that chance by encouraging them to analyze their tests, learn from their mistakes, and take another test on the same material. Giving students a second chance can boost motivation, learning, and confidence. What's more, the process of taking multiple tests can actually promote retention of the tested material (Pashler et al., 2007).

What are the basic steps?

1. Return a graded test to students. Explain that they'll be given the opportunity to take another test on the same learning goals/material at a later time.

2. Help students analyze and learn from their mistakes:

- Explain why it's important to analyze the types of errors they made: "Once you know what kinds of errors you made, you can figure out how to fix them and avoid making them again."
- Discuss the different types of errors listed on the bottom of the Error Analysis Form (p. 202).
- Have students use the form to indicate which types of errors they made on which questions.

3. Teach students strategies for addressing different kinds of errors—time-management strategies, strategies for writing coherent and well-organized paragraphs, study strategies, etc.

4. Help students generate and record specific plans for improvement on the Error Analysis Form. Remind students that their fix-it plans should reflect the types of errors they made. For example, it wouldn't make sense for a student who forgot to answer part of a question to restudy the material. Instead, that student should plan to read the test questions more carefully the next time around.

5. Give students time to implement their plans. Then administer a Second-Chance Test. (Test questions should be different than the ones on the original test, but target the same material.)

6. Have students reflect on what they've learned about the content, the kinds of errors they tend to make and how to address them, and/or their study habits and how to improve them.

How is this tool used in the classroom?

✔ To help students learn from their mistakes and achieve at higher levels

✔ To boost motivation by giving students multiple chances to succeed

Name: _____ Date: _____

Test topic: _____

• Error Analysis Form •

WHICH question did I get wrong?	WHY did I get this question wrong?	HOW can I avoid making this same type of error the next time around?

TYPES OF ERRORS: Use the suggestions below to help you complete column two.

☐ I didn't check my work (careless error). ☐ I ran out of time.

☐ I didn't know/understand this material. ☐ I knew the material; my writing skills were the problem.

☐ I didn't study this material/didn't think it would be on the test. ☐ I knew this material, but forgot it on the test.

☐ I didn't answer the question that was asked. ☐ I forgot to answer part(s) of the question.

☐ I didn't understand the question or directions. ☐ Other: _____

Show & Share

What is it?

A tool that has students show and share their learning by creating posters or slide-show presentations

What are the benefits of using this tool?

This tool, which has students demonstrate their learning by creating posters or slide-show presentations, provides an engaging and authentic alternative to the traditional culminating assessment test. Having students create these kinds of presentations helps them synthesize (and lets us assess) what they've learned about the content. And having them share these presentations with their classmates helps them develop many of the speaking, listening, and technology skills that are highlighted in the Common Core State Standards.

What are the basic steps?

1. Design an assessment task that requires students to share their learning by creating posters or slide-show presentations.

   Note: You can give everyone the same task or assign different tasks to different students (e.g., "Select the biome that interests you most and create a travel-brochure-style poster that highlights its unique features").

2. Present the task to students. Tell them how to work on it (individually, with a partner, or in a small group), how to present their work (poster or slide show), and how their work will be evaluated.

3. Designate a time for students to present their posters or slide shows to the class.

   Tip: If students are presenting posters, you may want to have them spend half the time standing at their own posters (explaining their work and answering questions) and the other half visiting their classmates' posters. To facilitate this swap, assign students to specific shifts in advance.

4. Discuss roles and responsibilities before students begin their presentations (e.g., "*Presenters* should engage and inform your listeners; *listeners* should engage the speakers in conversation, ask questions, and offer feedback").

5. Use the presentations to evaluate students' command of the content and the sophistication of their presentation skills. Work with students one-on-one or as a class to address any gaps.

6. Use reflection questions like these to help students learn from the experience and improve their future performance: What did you learn as a speaker? What did you learn as a listener? What are the attributes of an effective poster? How could you improve your next presentation?

How is this tool used in the classroom?

✔ To assess student learning at the end of a lesson, unit, research project, or other assignment
✔ To develop and test students' communication, presentation, and/or technology skills

This tool is typically used to evaluate student learning at the end of an instructional unit or research project (see Examples 1–4), but it can also be used to assess students' understanding of a single lesson, concept, or homework assignment. To use the tool in this way, simply pick a less formal and time-consuming presentation format (see Examples 5 and 6 for ideas).

EXAMPLE 1: A first-grade teacher used this tool to evaluate student learning at the end of a unit on adjectives. After taking her students to the zoo, she had them draw their two favorite animals on a piece of poster paper, describe each animal using three different adjectives, and hang their posters around the room. During the poster session, students were encouraged to paste additional adjectives onto each other's drawings using sticky notes.

EXAMPLE 2: A middle school science teacher used the poster session format to have his students share the results of their original experiments. Before students began working, he reviewed the sections that compose an authentic research poster and discussed the criteria by which students' work would be evaluated (experimental originality, depth of data analysis, proper use of all sections, clarity of communication).

EXAMPLE 3: A health teacher used this tool at the end of a unit to reinforce and evaluate students' understanding of the different types of drugs they had learned about—what they look like, how they're used, how they affect the body, etc. He put students into groups, asked each group to develop a slide-show presentation about a different class of drug, and explained that students' work would be evaluated using the following criteria: accuracy of information, clarity and catchiness of presentation, and teamwork.

EXAMPLE 4: After dividing students into teams, a world history teacher had each team research the origin, major doctrines, spread, and impact of a different world religion/belief system. Students then shared their findings with the class by creating engaging and informative slide shows that made strategic use of maps, charts, and other visual displays.

EXAMPLE 5: A geometry teacher used this tool to have teams of students check the logic of each other's proofs. She tacked each team's proof onto a different bulletin board so that students from other teams could tack up comments, questions, suggestions, and/or words of praise. She then gave students time to review and use their classmates' comments to improve their work.

EXAMPLE 6: A US history teacher used the last five minutes of class to check (and have students check) how much they had learned from a lecture on Manifest Destiny. Students created Manifest Destiny "posters" by sketching an image that summed up the philosophy as they understood it. They then left their posters on their desks and walked around the room to see what their classmates had drawn. For homework, they were asked to explain the images on their posters in words.

🎯 Teacher Talk

→ Before deciding which presentation format to assign (poster vs. slide show), think about which one would be a better fit for your content and goals. For example:

- If you're short on time, a poster session might be your best bet. (Poster sessions typically require less time since students present their work simultaneously rather than one at a time.)

- If you're looking to develop large-group oral presentation skills, pick the slide-show format.

- If you're looking to foster the kinds of thoughtful and collegial conversations that the Common Core State Standards encourage, the more intimate and interactive nature of a poster session might be an asset.

→ If you're using the poster session format, you may want to give students sticky notes so they can stick comments, questions, and suggestions right on their classmates' posters. Note that students should only use the sticky notes if the person who created the poster isn't available to talk to them directly (if that person is walking around and viewing other posters, for example).

→ If you're using the slide-show format for the first time, don't assume that all students are expert users of presentation software; some may know nothing, some may only know the basics. Teach students how to create high-quality slides yourself or invite a colleague (e.g., librarian or tech-ed specialist) to give a guest lecture/training session.

→ This tool provides an ideal opportunity to develop many of the speaking and listening skills highlighted in the Common Core State Standards. To address Anchor Standard 5 (SL.CCR.5), for example, teach students how to use digital media (images, videos, sound clips) and visual displays of data to make their presentations more interesting, informative, and understandable.

→ When developing the criteria that you'll use to evaluate students' work, remember to consider *content*, *process*, and *product*. (How will I assess students' understanding of the content material? How will I assess students' use of the requisite thinking skills/processes? How will I assess the quality of students' final products/performances?) For more on using the Content-Process-Product framework to evaluate students' work, see pp. 185–187.

→ To help students understand and internalize the qualities of a successful presentation, select three top-notch examples and challenge them to identify the common attributes. For example, "The students who gave these presentations encouraged and answered questions from the audience."

Note: For more on this approach to helping students identify the characteristics of top-notch work (or to learn about another related approach), see Student-Generated Assessment Criteria, pp. 57–59.

→ While this tool is typically used for summative/evaluative purposes, it can be used formatively as well as illustrated in Example 5.

How Will I Differentiate Assessment to Promote Success for All Students?

If a man does not keep pace with his companions, perhaps it is because he hears a different drummer.

—Henry David Thoreau

Many of the students we are consigning to the dust heaps of our classrooms have the abilities to succeed. It is we, not they, who are failing. We are failing to recognize the variety of thinking and learning styles they bring to the classroom.

—Robert J. Sternberg, *Thinking Styles*

Many teachers have committed themselves to differentiating instruction; fewer, however, have followed through on this commitment when it comes to assessment. Indeed, one-size-fits-all assessment tasks are still prevalent in many classrooms. We believe that differentiating assessment is just as important as differentiating instruction. By designing culminating assessment tasks that speak to all students, we can

- naturally motivate more learners;
- give all students the opportunity to demonstrate their learning in ways that suit them;
- encourage students to make choices and express their unique learning personality;
- increase the depth of student learning by challenging students to think about the content from a variety of perspectives; and
- help all students assess their strengths and weaknesses so they can become better, more flexible thinkers and learners.

In our 35-plus years of helping teachers reach the full range of learners, we have found that the use of learning styles as a differentiation framework is the most practical and effective way to design high-quality assessment tasks that meet the criteria above. Our learning-styles framework (Silver, Strong, & Perini, 2000) outlines four major learning styles, which are described in Figure 5. Each style represents a pattern of thinking, or a set of cognitive strengths that helps explain the ways that different students learn best.

Figure 5: Four Styles of Learners

Mastery learners learn best when they can work in a step-by-step manner and when the focus is on practical skills and information. **Mastery tasks** ask students to demonstrate factual knowledge and procedures.	**Interpersonal learners** learn best when invited to share their feelings and when the content has personal relevance. **Interpersonal tasks** ask students to relate personally to the content and to others.
Understanding learners learn best when encouraged to ask why/how questions and think logically. **Understanding tasks** ask students to reason, analyze, explain, and justify.	**Self-Expressive learners** learn best when challenged to do original, outside-the-box thinking. **Self-Expressive tasks** ask students to create, speculate, and think originally.

In this chapter, we present four tools that use this learning-styles framework to help teachers design culminating assessment tasks that give every student the chance to shine:

1. **Task Rotation** asks students to demonstrate their learning by completing four interrelated tasks, one in each style.

2. **Task Selection** gives students an opportunity to demonstrate their learning in a way that's comfortable for them by letting them choose from four different styles of tasks.

3. **Assessment Menus** offers students a comprehensive menu of tasks to choose from. The tasks in an Assessment Menu are differentiated in two distinct ways: by style and by level of challenge.

4. **A Test Worth Taking** helps teachers craft differentiated tests that engage all styles of learners and that promote learning in addition to evaluating it.

Task Rotation

What is it?

A differentiated assessment framework that uses four different styles of tasks to test students' grasp of critical content

What are the benefits of using this tool?

Well-designed assessment tasks should test the depth and breadth of students' content knowledge. They should also be differentiated so that students with different interests and strengths have an equal opportunity to excel. Using the Task Rotation framework is an easy way to satisfy both of these important criteria.* Task Rotations support students' existing strengths by letting students show what they know in a way that's comfortable for them. They also prepare students to become stronger, more well-rounded thinkers by challenging them to complete assessment tasks that are outside their comfort zone.

What are the basic steps?

1. Identify the content knowledge and skills you want to evaluate. (What should students know, understand, and be able to do?)

2. Familiarize yourself with the four different styles of tasks that compose a Task Rotation:

MASTERY tasks assess students' ability to remember/demonstrate factual knowledge and procedures.

UNDERSTANDING tasks assess students' ability to reason, analyze, explain, and justify.

SELF-EXPRESSIVE tasks assess students' ability to create, speculate, and think originally.

INTERPERSONAL tasks assess students' ability to relate personally to the content and to others.

3. Develop one assessment task in each style (see the Task-Creation Menu on p. 210 for ideas; use the organizer on p. 213 to record your tasks). Each task should test a slightly different facet of the material. Taken together, the four tasks should give you a complete picture of student learning.

Optional: Add descriptive labels that reflect the style of each task (e.g., "summarize the facts task" or "personal connection task") as shown in the examples on p. 212.

4. Check whether your tasks are consistent with the knowledge and skills you're trying to assess. Revise them if needed.

5. Explain how students should work on the tasks (alone vs. with a partner; in a specific order vs. at random; in class vs. at home) and discuss the criteria you'll use to evaluate their work.

6. Review students' completed assignments to evaluate their command of the relevant content/skills.

7. *Optional:* Survey students to find out which styles of tasks they're most/least comfortable completing. This will help them (and you) become more aware of their learning strengths and preferences.

---

*For a more thorough treatment of Task Rotation, see *Task Rotation: Strategies for Differentiating Activities and Assessments by Learning Style* (Silver, Jackson & Moirao, 2011).

Task-Creation Menu: Four Different Styles Of Tasks

MASTERY TASKS
assess students' ability to demonstrate factual knowledge and procedures.

To create a Mastery task, you might ask students to

- Recall important information (facts, formulas, dates, etc.).
- Define terms or concepts.
- Demonstrate, describe, or follow a set of procedures.
- Locate, match, or sequence information.
- Make and label visual displays (charts, maps, diagrams, etc.).
- Perform calculations or procedures with accuracy.
- List or summarize information.
- Describe something or someone (who, what, when, where).

INTERPERSONAL TASKS
assess students' ability to relate personally to the content and to others.

To create an Interpersonal task, you might ask students to

- Share their feelings, reactions, or opinions about the content.
- Connect or apply the content to their personal lives/experiences.
- Teach, work with, or offer advice to other people.
- Personify something. (If you were ___, what would you feel/do?)
- Put themselves in someone else's shoes (real or fictional).
- Prioritize information or make decisions based on personal values.
- Communicate with others (write a letter, blog, diary entry, etc.).
- Role-play.

UNDERSTANDING TASKS
assess students' ability to reason, analyze, explain, and justify.

To create an Understanding task, you might ask students to

- Compare and contrast (items, ideas, events, procedures, people).
- Analyze causes and effects.
- Present a logical argument/give evidence and examples.
- Explain why.
- Classify, categorize, or make connections.
- Test hypotheses.
- Make or evaluate decisions using specific criteria.
- Analyze, interpret, or draw conclusions about data, texts, etc.

SELF-EXPRESSIVE TASKS
assess students' ability to create, speculate, and think originally.

To create a Self-Expressive task, you might ask students to

- Speculate or anticipate consequences. (What if ___?)
- Represent concepts using symbols/images. (Create an icon for ___.)
- Create or invent something original (product, slogan, myth, etc.).
- Visualize or free-associate. (What comes to mind when…)
- Use a simile to illustrate their understanding of a concept.
- Generate alternatives (solutions, endings, approaches, etc.).
- Apply their learning to a new and different context.
- Express their learning in a creative or artistic way.

 Teacher Talk

→ Surveying your students (Step 7) is an informal way to gather information about their learning strengths and preferences. To do a more formal assessment, you might try the Learning Profile System (www.ThoughtfulClassroom.com/lps).

For information on how to develop and support students' learning styles/strengths, see *So Each May Learn: Integrating Learning Styles and Multiple Intelligences* (Silver, Strong, & Perini, 2000).

How is this tool used in the classroom?

✔ To differentiate summative assessment practices and promote success for all students

Task Rotations from three different grade levels and content areas are shown here.

EXAMPLE 1: A kindergarten student completed the Task Rotation below (with some assistance from her teacher) at the end of a unit on plants.

MASTERY TASK	INTERPERSONAL TASK
Draw a flowering plant and label its parts.	If you were a plant, how would you feel on a sunny day?

I am happy. I like the sun cause it grows me up.

UNDERSTANDING TASK	SELF-EXPRESSIVE TASK
Why are plants important to our world? Think of two reasons.	What would life be like if there were no plants?

food

MEDISIN

I was sick because I had no food to eat, or clothes to wear. I had to live on the ground.

EXAMPLE 2: A Task Rotation on Dr. Martin Luther King, Jr.'s "I Have a Dream" speech

"I HAVE A DREAM"	
MASTERY TASK *Summarize the facts task:* Pretend that you are a reporter who was assigned to cover Dr. King's "I Have a Dream" speech. Write an article that describes what you saw and heard. *Criteria for success:* Your article should indicate when, where, and why the speech was given. It should also summarize Dr. King's dream.	**INTERPERSONAL TASK** *Put yourself in someone else's shoes task:* If you had been one of the hundreds of thousands of people on the National Mall that day who had come to hear Dr. King speak, how do you think you would have felt? Share your feelings in a diary entry. *Criteria for success:* Describe how you would have felt and your reasons for feeling that way. Be specific: What aspects of the speech, the crowd, or the overall scene would have triggered those feelings?
UNDERSTANDING TASK *Take a position task:* Has Dr. King's dream been realized? Write a one- or two-paragraph response to this question. *Criteria for success:* Take a clear position and support that position with specific evidence/examples.	**SELF-EXPRESSIVE TASK** *Visualization task:* Dr. King's speech was so rich with images and metaphors that people could see his dream in their minds. What did you see when you listened to his speech? Draw your vision of Dr. King's dream on paper. Identify at least three specific lines or passages that inspired your image. *Criteria for success:* Your completed product should illustrate your understanding of the specific passages that you selected.

EXAMPLE 3: A mathematics teacher's Task Rotation on fractions

FRACTION ACTION	
MASTERY TASK *Definition task:* Define the following terms: fraction, numerator, denominator, divisor, part, whole. Use words, icons, numbers, and/or examples to make your definitions as clear as possible. *Criteria for success:* Define each term clearly and accurately.	**INTERPERSONAL TASK** *Personal connection task:* Think about a typical day in your life. Record how many hours you spend doing each of the activities below. Then figure out what fraction of each day you spend on each. *going to school, watching TV, doing homework, reading, playing an instrument, playing sports, listening to music, using the computer, talking to friends, doing chores, other* *Criteria for success:* Complete all parts of the task. Show your work. Do the calculations properly.
UNDERSTANDING TASK *Analysis task:* Is half of something always more than a quarter of something? Why? *Criteria for success:* Explain your reasoning using examples.	**SELF-EXPRESSIVE TASK** *Speculation task:* Describe how our world might be different if fractions didn't exist. *Criteria for success:* Be creative and think of as many ways as possible.

SOURCE: Adapted from *Math Tools, Grades 3–12: 64 Ways to Differentiate Instruction and Increase Student Engagement* (pp. 229–230), by H. F. Silver, J. R. Brunsting, and T. Walsh, Thousand Oaks, CA: Corwin Press. © 2008 by Thoughtful Education Press. Adapted with permission.

Name: _____   Date: _____

Task Rotation

MASTERY TASK	INTERPERSONAL TASK

TOPIC:

UNDERSTANDING TASK	SELF-EXPRESSIVE TASK

Task Selection

What is it?

A differentiated assessment framework that presents students with four different styles of assessment tasks and lets them choose which task to complete

What are the benefits of using this tool?

Sternberg and Grigorenko (2004) note that students who fail to fulfill their academic potential often fail because we have failed to teach and assess them in ways that are consistent with their individual talents. Task Selection helps all students shine by letting them demonstrate their learning in ways that appeal to them and play to their strengths. Instead of having to complete a one-size-fits-all assessment task, students get to choose the task that fits them best from a menu of options.

What are the basic steps?

1. Determine the purpose of the assessment tasks you're about to design. What specific content knowledge or skills do you want to assess?

2. Familiarize yourself with the four different styles of tasks that compose a Task Selection Menu:

MASTERY tasks assess students' ability to remember/demonstrate factual knowledge and procedures.

UNDERSTANDING tasks assess students' ability to reason, analyze, explain, and justify.

SELF-EXPRESSIVE tasks assess students' ability to create, speculate, and think originally.

INTERPERSONAL tasks assess students' ability to relate personally to the content and to others.

3. Create a Task Selection Menu by designing one task in each style. (For more on the different styles of tasks and how to create them, see the Task-Creation Menu on p. 210.) Note that all four tasks should test the same exact facts, concepts, or skills; the idea is to test the same material in four different ways.

Optional: Add descriptive labels that reflect the style of each task (e.g., "matching task" or "comparing task") as shown in the examples on p. 215.

4. Review the menu with students. Explain that they can complete whichever task they want.

5. Evaluate students' grasp of the relevant material by reviewing their completed assignments.

🎧 Teacher Talk

➜ A blank organizer for recording your tasks is available at www.ThoughtfulClassroom.com/Tools.

➜ Examining students' choices over time can give you clues about their preferred styles of thinking and learning. For ideas about how to support and expand these preferences, see *So Each May Learn: Integrating Learning Styles and Multiple Intelligences* (Silver, Strong, & Perini, 2000).

➜ Teachers often notice the similarities between this tool and the Task Rotation tool (pp. 209–213). So what's the difference? This tool aims to boost confidence and achievement by letting students work within their comfort zones. The Task Rotation tool challenges students to work outside their normal comfort zones so that they develop skills and styles of thinking that come less naturally to them.

How is this tool used in the classroom?

✔ To evaluate students' understanding of critical content

✔ To differentiate assessment by thinking and learning style

Teachers from all grade levels and content areas use this tool in their classrooms. (Example 2 shows how the tool can be modified for use with primary-grade students.)

EXAMPLE 1: A physical sciences teacher created the Task Selection Menu below to test students' understanding of key concepts from a laboratory experiment on phase changes.

TASK SELECTION MENU: Select *one* task to complete.	
MASTERY TASK *Diagram, label, and describe task:* Draw a complete heating or cooling curve for water. Label each phase change, label your axes, and give your graph a title. Describe the behavior of water molecules at all critical points on the curve.	**INTERPERSONAL TASK** *Personification task:* Pretend you're a water molecule. Write a story that describes your trip as you travel along your heating or cooling curve from one end to the other. Be sure to describe what you look like and how you feel at different points on the curve.
UNDERSTANDING TASK *"Explain why" task:* Why does the heating or cooling curve of water have the shape that it does? Explain what is happening at each stage of the curve.	**SELF-EXPRESSIVE TASK** *Speculation task:* What if water froze at 50°C and boiled at 87°C? How would its heating curve look different? Sketch it. Draw pictures to show what's happening to the water molecules at each stage of the curve.

EXAMPLE 2: A kindergarten teacher uses a modified version of Task Selection to reinforce and test students' understanding of critical concepts. Instead of giving his students a menu of tasks, he sets up four activity stations (one for each style of task) and lets students choose which station to go to. The tasks that he developed for a lesson on day and night are described below.

MASTERY TASK *Matching task:* Students will be given two pieces of paper—one labeled *day* and one labeled *night*. They will cut out pictures of day and night activities and paste them onto the appropriate piece of paper.	**INTERPERSONAL TASK** *Sharing task:* Students will share and discuss their favorite daytime and nighttime activities with other students who choose this station.
UNDERSTANDING TASK *Comparing task:* Students will compare their daytime and nighttime activities with those of one of the animals we read about in Katharine Kenah's *Animals Day and Night*. They will identify and tell me about at least two similarities or differences.	**SELF-EXPRESSIVE TASK** *Free-association and drawing task:* Students will draw things they associate with daytime on one piece of paper and things they associate with nighttime on another.

Assessment Menus

What is it?

A tool that provides options for students with different interests, abilities, and learning styles by presenting them with a menu of assessment tasks to choose from

What are the benefits of using this tool?

When it comes to assessment, we need to provide equal opportunities for all students to succeed. Yet designing assessments that accommodate students' different interests, learning styles, and abilities can often be a challenge. This tool addresses that challenge using a differentiated assessment framework called an Assessment Menu. By presenting students with four different styles of tasks at three different levels of difficulty (students select four to complete), an Assessment Menu ensures that there's something for everyone. Since the different styles of tasks test different facets of understanding, having students work their way through an Assessment Menu is also an effective way to evaluate the depth and breadth of their learning.

What are the basic steps?

1. Think about the purpose of the assessment tasks you're about to design. What do you want students to know, understand, and be able to do at the end of the unit you're about to teach?

2. Familiarize yourself with the four different styles of tasks that appear on an Assessment Menu.
   MASTERY tasks assess students' ability to remember/demonstrate factual knowledge and procedures.
   UNDERSTANDING tasks assess students' ability to reason, analyze, explain, and justify.
   SELF-EXPRESSIVE tasks assess students' ability to create, speculate, and think originally.
   INTERPERSONAL tasks assess students' ability to relate personally to the content and to others.

3. Create an Assessment Menu by designing three tasks in each style, each at an increasing level of difficulty. Use the reproducible Assessment Menu on p. 218 to record your tasks.
   Note: For more on the different styles of tasks and how to create them, refer to p. 210.

4. Check if the tasks on your menu are consistent with your purpose. (Will they tell you whether or not students have acquired the necessary knowledge, understandings, and skills?) Revise as needed.

5. Share the Assessment Menu with students at the start of the unit. Explain that they can complete whichever four tasks they want; the only requirement is that they pick at least one task from each style and difficulty level.

6. Have students circle the tasks they want to complete, work on those tasks over the course of the unit (whenever appropriate), and create a portfolio of their completed work.
   Optional: Check in on students' progress and provide feedback along the way.

7. Review students' work at the end of the unit to evaluate their grasp of the relevant material.

How is this tool used in the classroom?

✔ To differentiate summative assessment practices

✔ To assess students' understanding of critical content material

EXAMPLES: One teacher's Assessment Menu for a unit on ecology is shown below. Another sample menu is available for download at www.ThoughtfulClassroom.com/Tools.

ECOLOGY ASSESSMENT MENU

Instructions: By the end of this unit on ecology, you will need to complete four of the tasks on this menu. It's up to you to choose which ones (circle them). The only requirement is that you pick at least one task from each style and difficulty level.

LEVEL	MASTERY TASKS	UNDERSTANDING TASKS	SELF-EXPRESSIVE TASKS	INTERPERSONAL TASKS
1	**Defining Terms** What is ecology? Define the term using three of the techniques from the Defining Knowledge tool.	**Why Bother?** Why is it important to study ecology? Give at least three reasons.	**Scrapbook** Select an ecological problem that interests you. Illustrate the problem in an original and creative way.	**Personal Priorities** Which of the ecological problems that we've discussed do you feel is the most important one to address? Why do you feel that way?
2	**Problems Galore!** Summarize the basic facts about three ecological problems using a visual organizer. The organizer should indicate what each problem is, what its causes are, and how people have proposed to address it.	**No Free Lunches** People often say that when it comes to the environment, there are no free lunches. What do they mean by this statement? Explain using specific examples.	**For Better or Worse** Create an original metaphor, poster, or poem that illustrates the power of humans to change our world for better or worse.	**Express Yourself** Select an ecological issue that you feel strongly about (e.g., global warming). Express your feelings about this issue by creating a newspaper-style editorial, a blog entry, or a podcast.
3	**Extinction Facts** Gather data on an extinct or nearly extinct animal. Summarize and present your findings to your classmates via a slide-show presentation. Use multimedia components and visual displays like charts and graphs to make your presentation more interesting and understandable.	**Making Connections** Explain how at least five of the terms/concepts you've learned about during this unit relate to terms/concepts we've discussed during previous units—terms like *habitat*, *evolution*, *adaptation*, *activism*, and *global economy*. Use any format that you want (diagram, web, paragraph, etc.) to identify and explain these connections.	**Imagine Our World** What might our world be like if we don't do more to stem the loss of biodiversity? Share your vision using any format you want. Your final product or performance should explain what biodiversity is, why it's important, and what our world might be like if we don't preserve it.	**Role-Play** We sometimes forget that there's more than one side to every issue. Select an ecological issue, find a partner to work with, and learn about all sides of the issue. Share what you learn with your classmates by acting out a conversation between two people who feel differently about the issue (for example, a fisherman and an environmentalist discussing commercial fishing).

SOURCE: Adapted from *Classroom Curriculum Design: How Strategic Units Improve Instruction and Engage Students in Meaningful Learning* (p. 60) by H. F. Silver and M. J. Perini, 2010, Ho-Ho-Kus, NJ: Thoughtful Education Press. © 2010 by Thoughtful Education Press. Adapted with permission.

Name: _____ Date: _____

Unit topic: _____

• Assessment Menu •

Instructions: By the end of this unit, you will need to complete *four* of the tasks on this menu. It's up to you to choose which ones (circle them). The only requirement is that you pick at least one task from each style and difficulty level.

LEVEL	MASTERY STYLE	UNDERSTANDING STYLE	SELF-EXPRESSIVE STYLE	INTERPERSONAL STYLE
1				
2				
3				

A Test Worth Taking

What is it?

A framework for designing differentiated assessment tests that promote engagement, learning, and success (adapted from Geocaris & Ross, 1999).

What are the benefits of using this tool?

In thinking about what good assessment should look like, educators Claudia Geocaris and Maria Ross (1999) posed the following questions:

> If our students learn best through a variety of activities, wouldn't they be better able to demonstrate their knowledge and understanding of the content if they had the same avenues for expression? Shouldn't some of our assessments, then, allow students to express their knowledge in ways that best suit their learning styles and intelligences? (p. 29)

Geocaris and Ross answered their own questions with a resounding yes, and redesigned their assessment tests accordingly. Their new and improved "tests worth taking" included different styles of questions and offered students choices about which to answer. These tests promoted learning as well as assessing it by encouraging students to fill in knowledge gaps and reflect on their test-taking experiences. And they brought about "exciting" gains in achievement, "incredible" student responses, and improved attitudes toward classroom testing (p. 32).

What are the basic steps?

1. Learn how to create A Test Worth Taking by reviewing the seven design principles summarized in the table on p. 220. Use these seven principles to help you design your own Test Worth Taking.

2. Before administering your Test Worth Taking, explain how its purpose (to promote learning as well as assess it) and format (two days rather than one; students get a choice of questions to answer) differ from that of a traditional test.

3. Administer the test over a two-day period:
   - *On the first day,* have students review the test to figure out which questions they'll need to answer, which questions they'll choose to answer, and which material (if any) they'll need to revisit. Instruct them to start the test as soon as they finish their review.
   - *Between the first and second days,* encourage students to shore up any gaps in understanding using whatever resources they want.
   - *On the second day,* have students complete the test.

4. Grade students' tests. Use the responses that students generate to assess their understanding of the material, their feelings about the test, and the effectiveness of pre-test activities (your teaching, their studying).

5. Use what you learn to address remaining knowledge gaps and improve future teaching/testing.

Creating a Test Worth Taking: The Basic Principles

The table below identifies and explains the seven basic principles behind A Test Worth Taking. Each principle is illustrated using examples from a test on cell structure and function.

DESIGN PRINCIPLE	SAMPLE TEXT FROM A TEST ON CELL STRUCTURE AND FUNCTION
① Explain why the tested material is important for students to know and understand.	As you know, biology is the study of living things. Since cells are the building blocks of all living things, understanding cell structure and function is critical to understanding biology. The knowledge you have gained during this unit will be the foundation for future units in genetics, heredity, and evolution. It will also serve you well in any future biology classes.
② Explain the purpose of the test, the directions, and the two-day format.	This test will give you a chance to show your understanding of cell structure and function. The goal is to accumulate 100 points. Since I want you to succeed, I'll give you some choices about which questions to answer. The only requirement is that you answer at least one question from each section. Read the directions carefully to see which questions are required and where you have choices. Since the ultimate goal is for you to learn all of the material on the test, you'll get a chance to go home, do some additional studying, and finish the test tomorrow.
③ Craft a narrative that ties the individual questions and the sections of the test together.	In the previous section, you demonstrated your knowledge of various cell structures. Here, we'll examine one of these structures in more detail: the plasma membrane. The first two questions in this section will focus on the properties of the membrane that make it so special. [Questions would appear here. Narrative would resume below.] During class, you learned that molecules move through the membrane via active and passive transport. These next few questions will test your ability to explain and compare these two modes of transport…
④ Include different styles of questions that engage different types of thinking. For help with this principle, see the first Teacher Talk point, p. 222.	*Compare & contrast essay question:* Compare and contrast active and passive transport. *Matching question:* Correctly match the parts of the cell with their functions. *Metaphorical thinking question:* Mitochondria are often called the power plants of a cell. Create an original metaphor for another organelle. Explain your metaphor. *Put-yourself-in-someone-else's-shoes question:* Pretend that you are Anton van Leeuwenhoek. Write a diary entry describing what you see and feel while looking under your microscope one day.

⑤ Give students a choice about how to demonstrate their command of selected concepts/learning targets.	Show what you know about mitochondrial structure and function by completing A <u>or</u> B.
	
	  A. Write a paragraph that describes the structure, function, and significance of mitochondria (why are they important?). Your paragraph should be clearly written and factually accurate. (5 points)
	
	  B. Create a short comic strip that stars a mitochondrion. Your comic strip should be informative as well as engaging. Be sure that it explains what mitochondria do and why they're important. (5 points)

⑥ Give students a chance to share information that they think is important.	Tell me five things you think are critical to know about the cell, its parts, or their functions [first item on the test]. Was there information you studied, but that wasn't tested? Tell me about it below [final test item].

⑦ Include one or more reflection questions.	These questions will help *you* reflect on and learn from your test-taking experience. They will help *me* as well by giving me feedback about the test, the instruction leading up to the test, and your study habits.
	
	  • How do you feel about the two-day test format? Why?
	  • How well did the activities we did in class help you prepare for this test?
	  • How much time did you spend studying? Did this affect your performance in any way?
	  • How might you prepare yourself to do better next time?

How is this tool used in the classroom?

✔ To evaluate and expand students' understanding of critical content

✔ To design differentiated end-of-unit tests that promote learning as well as evaluate it

EXAMPLES: Excerpts from a biology teacher's Test Worth Taking can be found in the "sample text" column of the table on p. 220. Portions of an algebra teacher's test are shown below.

UNIT EXAM: GRAPHS AND FUNCTIONS

We have just completed a chapter on functions and their graphs. This chapter lays the groundwork for most of our studies in algebra. Functions are everywhere in mathematics, and from what you have learned in this chapter, you can see that you have been dealing with functions since pre-algebra. Functions help us predict results, find solutions to problems, and understand the meanings of graphs. The knowledge that you have gained during this unit will prepare you to successfully complete the rest of this class.

On this test, you will need to show me you are capable of gathering data, recognizing functions, and solving problems using functions and their graphs. There are a number of sections on this test. You will be required to complete at least one question from each section. Read the directions carefully to find out which questions are required and where you have a choice about which questions you want to answer. The test is worth 100 points—and you can earn those points however you choose. Good luck to you!

SECTION 1: We learned that graphs are a visual representation of data—and that functions are equations that represent data. In this section, you'll get a chance to show what you've learned about collecting, organizing, and interpreting data.

Question 1 – Pick ONE of the following items (5 points):

A. Listed below are a number of pieces of data. Pair the pieces in columns A & B together in the manner that makes the most sense.

A	B
10 hours worked	140 strikeouts
100 innings pitched	46-inch waist
240 pounds	6 papers typed
6 feet tall	190 pounds

B. At least one of the following four pairs of data is incorrectly paired. Identify this data pair(s) and explain what's wrong.

750 students, 150 minority students   150 women with colds, 240 men with colds

$40,000 income, $5,000 spending money   16-year-old girl, 16-year-old boy

C. List four sets of paired data from your own life. Briefly explain each pair.

SECTION 2: We took what we learned about paired data and began to examine how groups of paired data could be turned into functions and relations. In this section, you'll show your understanding of the differences between functions and relations—and demonstrate why functions and relations are important in the field of mathematics as well as in your daily lives.

Question 4 – Pick ONE of the following items (5 points):

A. Define and give an example of a relation and a function.

B. Use a Venn diagram to depict the characteristics, similarities, and differences between relations and functions.

Question 5 (required question worth 10 points):

How would you convince a friend that it's important to learn about functions? Jot down at least four ideas. Be sure to address the importance of understanding functions both in school and in the real world.

SOURCE: Adapted with permission from the work of Christopher Geocaris, Assistant Director of Educational Technology at Warren Township High School and former Lead Teacher, Mathematics Department (O'Plaine Campus), Gurnee, IL.

🌑 Teacher Talk

→ You may want to review the Questioning in Style and Task Rotation tools before attempting to design A Test Worth Taking. These two tools—particularly the Question Stem Menu on p. 69 and the Task-Creation Menu on p. 210—can help you develop the different styles of test items that this tool calls for.

→ When giving students a choice of questions to answer ("Respond to one of the questions below"), be sure that all options test the same content knowledge/skills. The idea is to give students a choice about *how* to demonstrate their learning (e.g., "Would you rather show your grasp of concept X by writing a summary paragraph or creating and explaining a metaphor?")—not a choice about *what* material they want to be tested on. A well-designed Test Worth Taking should require students to demonstrate the same knowledge/skills regardless of the questions they choose to answer.

→ The narrative format of A Test Worth Taking requires more reading than a traditional test. Keep this in mind when figuring out how much time to allocate for your test—particularly if you have any struggling readers in your class.

→ A Test Worth Taking differs from a traditional end-of-unit assessment test in that it's designed to be used for formative purposes (to inform and improve teaching/learning) as well as summative ones (to evaluate learning).

→ One of the motivational tricks built into A Test Worth Taking is that the two-day testing cycle enables what students view as cheating. (Students get to see the test on the first day and bone up on the relevant material before completing the test the second day.) Since this kind of "cheating" actually helps and motivates students to learn the material, by all means, encourage them to cheat away! Geocaris and Ross (1999) addressed the issue in this way: "Was cheating a problem? The only way for students to 'cheat' was to actively seek assistance from their notes, textbooks, or friends. Any test that inspires students to actively seek knowledge on their own is certainly not a tragedy!" (p. 32).

→ Alternatives to the two-day format: If the two-day test format doesn't fit your goals or schedule, you can have students take the test in one day instead. Another option is to give students more than one day between seeing the test and taking it. (Let them review the test on a Monday, for example, and take it on Friday.) Giving students these extra days affords them more time to review and learn the critical material; rather than trying to cram everything in in one night, they can study the material several times over the course of the week.

→ Test items can be designed to engage different intelligences (Gardner, 1983) as well as different styles of thinking. To engage Gardner's interpersonal intelligence, for example, you could design a *consider-multiple-viewpoints* question. To engage the intrapersonal and verbal-linguistic intelligences, you could design a *write-an-editorial* question.

How Will I Help Students Reflect On, Learn From, and Celebrate Their Achievements?

By three methods we may learn wisdom: first, by reflection, which is noblest; second, by imitation, which is easiest; and third, by experience, which is the bitterest.

—Confucius

If we want students to get in the habit of reflecting deeply on their work—and if we want them to use Habits of Mind such as applying past knowledge to new situations, thinking about thinking (metacognition), and remaining open to continuous learning— we must teach them strategies to derive rich meaning from their experiences.

—Arthur L. Costa and Bena Kallick, *Learning and Leading with Habits of Mind*

Reflection and celebration are critical to the learning process. They allow students to step back from the profusion of details, concepts, and procedures they have learned. From this new vantage point, students are able to see their learning not as a series of isolated episodes but as a connected narrative or journey. Reflection and celebration make learning deeper and ensure that it is continuous.

But as Art Costa and Bena Kallick remind us, reflection is not a reflex; we need to teach students how to look back on their learning—how to examine their learning process, how to think critically about the work they have produced, and how to apply their learning to new situations. This investment in reflection has obvious benefits for students. Not only is reflection critical to the learning process, it is also essential to the development of self-regulation (Zimmerman, 2001). Student reflection also has obvious benefits for teachers, who can use student reflection to tell them how well students are learning and what adjustments may need to be made.

In this chapter, we present seven tools that help students reflect on, learn from, and celebrate their learning:

1. A Job Well Done is a collection of ready-to-use techniques for recognizing students' achievements.

2. **Effort Tracker** helps students understand the importance of effort by having them rate their effort and reflect on the connection between effort and achievement.

3. **Portfolios to Be Proud Of** gives students the chance to select, display, and express pride in their best work.

4. **Reflection Stems** gives teachers a host of simple ways to spark and guide student reflection.

5. **Team-O-Graph** helps students reflect on and improve the productivity of group work.

6. **Test Feedback** makes test-taking experiences more positive by inviting students to reflect on their performance and voice their feelings and reactions to their tests.

7. **What? So What? Now What?** provides students with a simple format for reflecting on what they did, what they learned, and how they can apply that learning.

A Job Well Done

What is it?

A set of quick and easy-to-use techniques for acknowledging and celebrating students' achievements

What are the benefits of using this tool?

When used properly, praise can be motivating and beneficial for students (Cameron & Pierce, 1994; Dweck, 2007). This tool outlines six simple ways to recognize students' efforts and accomplishments. The six techniques are easy to use and encourage active participation by students.

What are the basic steps?

1. Familiarize yourself and your students with the recognition techniques described on p. 226.

   Optional: Invite students to generate some techniques of their own. Add them to the list.

2. Identify an action, attitude, accomplishment, or attribute of a student's work that deserves to be acknowledged.

   For example: Did a student use an appropriate strategy to tackle a task? Exhibit a high degree of effort or persistence? Satisfy specific assessment criteria? Improve upon a previous performance?

3. Acknowledge this "job well done" using the recognition technique of your choice.

4. Accompany the acknowledgement with a specific description of what was done well. ("You did a great job of finding textual evidence to support your position" instead of "Great job.")

How is this tool used in the classroom?

   ✔ To acknowledge and help students learn from their achievements

Recognition Techniques

Oohs and Aahs

Have students acknowledge behaviors or qualities of work that deserve recognition by making "ooh and aah" sounds. Oohs and aahs can be initiated by you (identify something specific that a student has done well and ask the class to ooh and aah in appreciation) or by your students (ask students to ooh and aah when they see or hear something they think is worth praising). In either case, the action, attribute, or attitude that's being acknowledged should be clearly explained as illustrated in the examples below.

Teacher initiated: "Ellen spent a lot of time practicing her waltz, and the improvement in her rise and fall is evident. Let's acknowledge her hard work and progress. Oooh…aaah…"

Student initiated: "I oohed and aahed when I heard Franklin's story because it had a lot of strong verbs and adjectives like a good story is supposed to have."

Shout Out

Identify actions or accomplishments you want to acknowledge, and ask the class to give the appropriate student(s) a "shout out" for those accomplishments. Be specific about what the shout outs are for so that everyone can learn from the experience. For example, "Let's give Ivy a shout out for using our explanatory-writing rubric to review and revise her work."

Round of Applause

This technique is similar to Oohs and Aahs except that students clap their hands in a circular motion instead of oohing and aahing. ("Let's give a round of applause to anyone who has the courage to speak up and say 'I'm lost' during today's lecture.")

Big OK

This technique is similar to Oohs and Aaahs except that students make an "OK" sign with their hands instead of making sounds of appreciation. For exceptionally great work, students can make a "big OK" (touch the fingertips/thumb on their left hands to the corresponding fingertips/thumb on their right hands to create an *O* shape with both hands) instead of a normal OK sign.

Paper Plate Awards

Create awards out of paper plates to acknowledge students' efforts and/or achievements. (If you prefer, you can have students create plates for each other.) In either case, awards should state the recipients' names and explain exactly what behaviors or quality characteristics are being recognized.

This award goes to
JAIME
for his never-give-up attitude on the daily problem set.

Happygrams

If you want to acknowledge a student's actions or achievements in a more private way, you can send that student a HappyGram. To do this, create a form that looks like a telegram, address the outside with the student's name and a happy face, and write a message to the student on the inside explaining what you're happy about. ("Dear Jack: It made me very happy when you offered to help Bobby practice his number facts without being asked. That was very thoughtful of you!") Encourage students to share their HappyGrams with their parents.

Effort Tracker

What is it?

A tool that helps students see the link between effort and achievement by having them rate the amount of effort they put into their assignments and reflect on the way that it impacts their success

What are the benefits of using this tool?

Many students, especially low-achievers, are unaware of the link between effort and achievement; they believe that innate ability is what largely determines whether they succeed or fail (Butkowsky & Willows, 1980). Effort Tracker aims to change this mindset by inviting students to explore the way that effort affects performance, and by using concrete examples to show them that effort really *does* matter. Teaching students that they have the power to improve their academic performance is an extremely valuable lesson—one that can increase their motivation, encourage them to persevere in the face of challenges, and enable them to achieve at higher levels (Alderman, 2008; Dweck, 1975, 2007).

What are the basic steps?

1. Initiate a conversation about the relationship between effort and achievement. Specifically,

- Use personal, fictional, or real-world examples to illustrate and reinforce the effort/achievement relationship; see Teacher Talk for ideas. Then encourage students to share their own examples.
- Ask students what effort looks like in a classroom setting. (Is it always giving 100%? Asking for help if you're stuck? Proofreading work before turning it in?) Record their ideas on the board.

2. Help students understand that effort involves more than spending time working. Teach them to consider these five criteria (adapted from Moss & Brookhart, 2009) when assessing their performance on an assigned task:

- *Degree of effort:* How hard did you concentrate or try?
- *Time spent:* How much time did you spend on this task?
- *Level of care:* How carefully did you check and correct your work?
- *Willingness to seek help:* Did you ask questions or seek help if you were stuck or confused?
- *Use of strategies:* What (if any) strategies did you use while working on this task?

3. Give students a task to work on (e.g., review for a test or make three consecutive free throws).

4. Prepare students to work productively by introducing or reviewing specific strategies that can help them (strategies for writing a focused paragraph, what-to-do-when-stuck strategies, etc.).

5. Have students rate their effort using an Effort Tracker Form (p. 230, Questions 1–5) *before submitting their work*. Have them reflect on the effort/outcome link *after seeing their graded work*.

6. Talk to students whose achievement level doesn't reflect their effort level. Help them identify possible reasons for the discrepancy by posing probing questions like these: What do you mean when you say that you worked hard? Did you use any of the strategies that we discussed?

How is this tool used in the classroom?

✔ To have students reflect on and learn from their classroom experiences

✔ To help students recognize the relationship between effort and achievement

EXAMPLE: The form below was completed by a fourth grader.

EFFORT TRACKER FORM

Name: Sally

Assignment: I was asked to write a book review on Charlotte's Web by E.B. White.

1) How hard did I concentrate or try?

0 (not at all)   5 (somewhat)   10 (as hard as I could)

Explanation:

I really liked the book and wanted to do a good job so I worked very hard.

2) How much time did I spend studying, practicing, or working on this assignment?

0 (none)   5 (a fair amount)   10 (a lot)

Explanation:

I learned how to write a book <u>report</u> last year but I have never written a book review before so I spent a lot of time looking at examples of book reviews so that I would know how to write a good one. I learned a lot by doing that but it still took me a lot of time to write the review because it was something new for me. But I like trying new things so I didn't mind.

3) How carefully did I check and correct my work?

0 (not at all)   5 (somewhat)   10 (extremely)

Explanation:

I spent so much time looking at the sample book reviews and writing my own book review that I hardly had any time left over to proofread my work. I hope that I didn't make too many mistakes.

4) Did I ask questions or request help if I was confused?   Yes ☒   No ☐   I didn't need help ☐

5) Which (if any) strategies did I use? I looked at examples of A+ work to try and learn from them.

REFLECTION: Did my actions (strategies used + amount of effort) affect my success?   Yes ☒   No ☐

My teacher said that I did an excellent job for someone who had never written a book review before. I don't think that I could've done such a good job if I hadn't looked at the sample book reviews, so looking at examples of other people's work turned out to be a good strategy that was worth my time. My grade for grammar and mechanics isn't very good, but I think it is because I didn't spend enough time proofreading. If I spend more time checking my work, I bet I could do better.

 Teacher Talk

→ Seeing concrete examples helps students recognize that their actions and attitudes can actually influence their level of success. The examples that you present in Step 1 can be personal, real world, or fictional:

- *Personal:* Share stories from your own life. (What have you been able to accomplish by working hard? What disappointments or failures do you owe to a lack of effort rather than a lack of ability?)

- *Real world:* Discuss famous individuals (athletes, politicians, scientists, artists, actors) whose work ethic, determination, and perseverance in the face of setbacks enabled them to succeed. Alternatively, identify individuals whose lack of effort prevented them from achieving their full potential.

- *Fictional:* Use familiar stories to illustrate the idea that effort can be more valuable than innate ability (try "The Tortoise and the Hare") or that working hard and believing in yourself can impact your success (try *The Little Engine That Could*).

→ To use this tool with younger students, simplify the reproducible form as needed. Among other things, you can replace the number lines with smiley faces and frown faces as shown here:

→ Head off disappointment by having a discussion about realistic expectations *before* returning graded work. Remind students that hard work won't guarantee them a perfect score, and that success takes time and sustained effort. Use the examples from Step 1 or a tool like GOT It!, which has students examine the impact of effort on achievement over time, to reinforce this point.

→ To encourage regular self-assessment, you can have students complete Effort Tracker Forms on a daily basis (all but the reflection section) rather than just at the end.

Name: _____ Date: _____

Assignment: _____

Effort Tracker Form

1) How hard did I concentrate or try?

|—————————————|—————————————|—————————————|
0 (not at all)   5 (somewhat)   10 (as hard as I could)

Explanation:

2) How much time did I spend studying, practicing, or working on this assignment?

|—————————————|—————————————|—————————————|
0 (none)   5 (a fair amount)   10 (a lot)

Explanation:

3) How carefully did I check and correct my work?

|—————————————|—————————————|—————————————|
0 (not at all)   5 (somewhat)   10 (extremely)

Explanation:

4) Did I ask questions or request help if I was confused?   Yes ☐   No ☐   I didn't need help ☐

5) Which (if any) strategies did I use?

REFLECTION: Did my actions (strategies used + amount of effort) affect my success?   Yes ☐   No ☐

Explain your answer on the back of this worksheet and/or share your ideas with the class.

Portfolios to Be Proud Of

What is it?

A tool that helps students feel proud of what they've achieved by inviting them to select and display their best work

What are the benefits of using this tool?

One of the great rewards of learning is the deep sense of pride and satisfaction that we feel when we recognize our own accomplishments. Unfortunately, students *don't* always feel good about their accomplishments because they compare their work with that of their classmates rather than evaluating it on its own terms. Portfolios to Be Proud Of addresses this problem by helping students identify and celebrate the strengths in their own work. It also increases students' ownership of the assessment process by putting them, rather than their teachers, in charge of evaluating their work.

What are the basic steps?

1. Have students create personal portfolios for storing their work. They can use folders, ring binders, or e-portfolios.

2. Explain that students will fill these portfolios with samples of their best work throughout the year—pieces that they're proud of, that they worked hard on, and that they want to share with others.

3. Give students guidance about what to put in their portfolios. Specifically:

   - *Tell them WHEN they should review their work and select their best piece.* Should they do it at the end of each week? At the end of each month? At the end of a unit?

   - *Tell them WHAT type of work they should choose.* Do you want them to select something specific like their best lab report, poem, or painting? Or can they pick their best piece from any category?

   - *Tell them HOW they should pick (what criteria they should use).* Should they pick their most creative piece? Their most improved piece? The piece with the best supported thesis?

4. Have students attach an explanatory note to each piece of work they select. (Why did I choose this particular piece? What aspects of it am I proudest of?)

5. Review and discuss (or comment on) individual pieces of work or the portfolio as a whole.

6. Encourage students of all ability levels to take pride in their work. Help them understand that everyone's best work is different, and that they should focus on personal achievements.

7. Invite students to share their best work with classmates and parents. One way to do this is to establish a "best-work gallery" and invite different students to display their work each week.

How is this tool used in the classroom?

✔ To have students identify, reflect on, and celebrate their best work

Reflection Stems

What is it?

A fast and easy way to help students reflect on their learning experiences at the end of a lesson/unit

What are the benefits of using this tool?

Inviting students to reflect on what and how they learn can help them get more out of their classroom experiences. Unless students know how to reflect in a productive way, however, "reflection time" can easily become a waste of time. This tool enhances the quality and efficiency of classroom reflection by using sentence stems to spark and guide students' thinking. Having students generate reflective statements at the end of a lesson or unit helps them process and make sense of their learning experiences. It helps you as well by letting you see what students are thinking, feeling, and learning in your classroom.

What are the basic steps?

1. Set aside a few minutes of reflection time at the end of a class period, lesson, or unit.

2. Encourage reflection by inviting students to complete one or more of the sentence stems below. You can either tell students which stem(s) to use or let them choose.

I learned…	*I want to learn more about…*	*I finally understand…*
I wonder…	*I hypothesize/predict…*	*I am proud of…*
I am confused about…	*I see a connection between…*	*I can apply this to…*
I had trouble…	*I would have learned more if…*	*I was fascinated by…*
I feel…	*I tried to be a good student by…*	*I was surprised to learn…*

3. Make it clear that students' responses will be read, but neither judged nor graded.

   Optional: Invite students to share their responses, either in small groups or as a class.

4. Examine students' responses to get a picture of where they are both cognitively and affectively. Use the information that you gather to inform and improve future instruction.

How is this tool used in the classroom?

   ✔ To help students reflect on what and how they are learning

EXAMPLE: At the end of a lecture on the Age of Exploration, a teacher invited students to respond to the reflection stem of their choice. Three students' responses are shown here:

I learned that explorers were looking for more than riches and land. They were also hoping to find new trading partners and new trade routes, especially to the Far East.	I would have learned more if my teacher spoke slower. She talked too fast to take good notes. Showing more pictures and maps would have also made things more interesting and memorable.	I wonder how sailors knew which direction they were sailing in on days when the sun wasn't out.

Team-O-Graph

What is it?

A tool that encourages productive group work by having students use questionnaires called "Team-O-Graphs" to assess their own and their classmates' contributions to group activities and assignments

What are the benefits of using this tool?

In many cases, group work isn't always as productive as we hope it will be. Team-O-Graph addresses this problem by teaching students what effective group work entails—and by having them reflect on their group's performance using Team-O-Graph questionnaires. By providing insight into the workings of each group and the contributions of its members, students' responses prepare us (and our students) to address any problems and make future group work more productive.

What are the basic steps?

1. Develop a small-group activity/assignment that requires students to work cooperatively in order to be successful. Explain the purpose of the task and any ground rules or guidelines.

2. Talk to students about what successful group work entails. Use the criteria on the Team-O-Graph Form (p. 235) as a guide. Make it clear that everyone is expected to contribute (no freeloading!).

3. Teach students strategies that can help them work productively in a group setting—strategies for dividing labor among teammates, giving and receiving feedback, managing conflicts, etc.

4. Encourage students to *informally* assess and improve the functioning of their group as they work. (Does everyone understand the material? Is everyone doing something useful? How can we get this person more involved?) Monitor group performance and offer assistance as needed.

5. When students finish working, have them *formally* evaluate their own and their group members' contributions to their team by completing a Team-O-Graph Form (one form per student).

6. Help students process and learn from the experience by having them discuss their responses as a team. The goal should be to acknowledge strengths, identify problems (individual or group), and develop strategies for improvement.

   Note: Until students are comfortable having these kinds of honest discussions, you may need to act as a moderator or facilitator.

7. Review students' forms to gain insight into the workings of each team and its members. Use what you learn to address any problems and make future group learning experiences more effective.

How is this tool used in the classroom?

✔ To teach students what it takes to be a productive member of a group
✔ To have students reflect on their own and their classmates' contributions to a group task
✔ To gather the kind of feedback that can help make future group work more effective

🌑 Teacher Talk

➜ This tool promotes productivity by reinforcing the critical elements of effective group work outlined by Johnson and Johnson (1994): (a) positive interdependence, (b) individual and group accountability, (c) promotive interaction, (d) use of relevant interpersonal and small-group skills, and (e) processing of current group effectiveness to improve future effectiveness.

➜ The Common Core State Standards stress the importance of preparing students to become productive contributors to collaborative conversations. Having students review and use this tool's criteria for successful group work can help.

➜ Adapt the Team-O-Graph Form as needed depending on your goals and your students' needs. You could, for example, adapt the form to have students reflect on the effectiveness of *partner* work instead of teamwork. Another option would be to simplify the form for use with younger students as shown here:

TEAM-O-GRAPH

My name: Date:

My team members' names:

Activity or assignment:

CRITERIA FOR SUCCESSFUL GROUP WORK	Not Really	Sort of	Yes!
I participated and helped my team succeed.	☹	😐	🙂
Everyone else participated and helped the team succeed.	☹	😐	🙂
I listened quietly when others were speaking.	☹	😐	🙂
Everyone took turns speaking.	☹	😐	🙂
I stayed focused on my work instead of goofing off.	☹	😐	🙂
Everyone stayed focused on our work.	☹	😐	🙂
We worked well as a team.	☹	😐	🙂

What did I do to help my team succeed?

How could my team have done even better?

My name: _____ Date: _____

My team members' names: _____

Activity or assignment: _____

Team-O-Graph Form

Instructions: Review the criteria for successful group work *before you begin working* on the given assignment or activity. Keep the criteria in mind *as you work*. Use the criteria to rate your own and your entire team's performance *after you finish working*.

CRITERIA FOR SUCCESSFUL GROUP WORK	Not really	Somewhat	Mostly	Definitely
I participated.	1	2	3	4
Everyone else on my team participated.	1	2	3	4
I made a major contribution to my team's success.	1	2	3	4
Everyone else made a major contribution to our success.	1	2	3	4
I stayed on task.	1	2	3	4
Everyone else on my team stayed on task.	1	2	3	4
I listened and responded to other people's ideas.	1	2	3	4
Everyone else listened and responded to each other's ideas.	1	2	3	4
I gave people feedback about their work/ideas.	1	2	3	4
Everyone else gave people feedback about their work/ideas.	1	2	3	4
I accepted feedback without getting defensive.	1	2	3	4
Everyone else accepted feedback without getting defensive.	1	2	3	4
I treated everyone the way I'd want to be treated.	1	2	3	4
All of my teammates treated others the way they'd want to be treated.	1	2	3	4
I helped and supported my teammates.	1	2	3	4
All of my teammates helped and supported each other.	1	2	3	4

Some things my group did well…

My greatest challenges when working with this group…

Ideas for improvement…

Test Feedback

What is it?

A tool that makes test-taking experiences more positive by inviting students to demonstrate their knowledge of untested material and express their feelings about their tests

What are the benefits of using this tool?

We require students to take tests all the time, yet we rarely give them a chance to voice their reactions to those tests. This is unfortunate because giving students an opportunity to share their thoughts and feelings about their tests (how well they think they did, what questions they wished we'd asked, how well classroom instruction prepared them to succeed) can be extremely beneficial, both for them and for us. Besides sending the message that students' opinions are valued, inviting students to provide feedback about their tests helps them reflect on their performance in a productive way. Perhaps even more important, the feedback that students generate provides a wealth of information that we can use to improve future teaching, learning, and testing experiences.

What are the basic steps?

1. Prior to administering a test, customize a Test Feedback Form (p. 238) by filling in the blanks in Part 3 (the simile section) with items related to the topic of the test. For example:

- This *English* test was like (a) *a fairy tale* (b) *a horror story* (c) *a mystery novel* (d) *an epic poem*
- This *fitness* test was like (a) *a quick sprint* (b) *a walk in the park* (c) *an uphill run* (d) *a stretching session*

2. After students complete the test, have them respond to the questions on the Test Feedback Form.

3. Assess students' knowledge of untested material by reviewing the backs of their feedback forms. (Making this untested-information section worth five points can help alleviate the frustration of "knowing stuff that wasn't tested.")

4. Review the front side of students' feedback forms. Respond to, use, and help students use the information they've provided to improve future teaching, studying, and test-taking experiences. Here are some suggestions for doing this:

- Meet with students whose perceived level of performance didn't match their actual level of performance (e.g., thought they did great, but failed) and explore reasons for the mismatch.
- Look (and have students look) for a link between study time and test performance. Explore the relationship between focused effort and achievement; see Effort Tracker (pp. 227–230) for ideas.
- Encourage students to reflect on the effectiveness of their studying and study techniques. Teach them specific strategies for studying smarter, not longer (e.g., memorization or note-making strategies).
- Record comments/suggestions on students' completed forms as shown in the example on p. 237.
- Think about ways you could improve test design, test preparation (what you do to prepare students for the test and what students do on their own), and test performance.

How is this tool used in the classroom?

✔ To have students reflect on and share their feelings about their tests and test performance

✔ To assess students' study habits, content knowledge, and self-confidence/perceptions

✔ To gather feedback about the effectiveness of classroom instruction and assessments

EXAMPLE: Here's what an AP Biology student had to say after an end-of-unit test on protein synthesis:

TEST FEEDBACK FORM

Name: Marie   Date: March 14th   Test topic: Protein synthesis

Part 1: How do you feel about your performance on this test? (circle one)

Fantastic!   Great   Pretty good   OK   (Not so good)   I feel sick!

Part 2: Do you think your performance on this test is a good indicator of how well you know/understand this topic? _Sort of_
Why or why not?

Partly I didn't do well because I didn't understand some key concepts, but I also got really nervous and forgot a lot of the material that I did know. I always get really nervous when I take tests.

Marie: Come see me so we can talk about strategies for dealing with pre-test jitters!!

Part 3: This test (or my performance on this test) was like...

(a) _DNA_   (b) _messenger RNA_   (c) _transcription_   (d) _a stop codon_

Explain:

Just like DNA, I have a lot of information stored in me, but that information needs to be expressed in order to be useful and I didn't express it on this test because I got nervous. I also ran out of time.

Part 4: How much time did you spend studying?

WEEKS	DAYS	HOURS	MINUTES
		4	

If you could go back in time and study for this test again, would you do anything differently?

Explain.

I realize now that I was confused about the way that the three different kinds of RNA function in protein synthesis, so I'd review their functions more thoroughly. I'd also spend more time reviewing the problem sets since there were a lot of application questions on the test and I focused more on facts.

Part 5: How well did classroom lessons, activities, and assignments prepare you for this test?

0	1	2	3	4	5
Not at all   Really well!

(2 is circled)

Explain and make suggestions for improvement.

I wasn't expecting so many application questions because we didn't discuss or practice those kinds of questions very much in class.

Part 6: Do you know anything about this topic that wasn't on the test? Tell me about it on the back...

Name: _____ Date: _____

Test topic: _____

Test Feedback Form

Part 1: How do you feel about your performance on this test? (circle one)

| Fantastic! | Great | Pretty good | OK | Not so good | I feel sick! |

Part 2: Do you think your performance on this test is a good indicator of how well you know/understand this topic?_____
Why or why not?

Part 3: This test (or my performance on this test) was like...

(a) _____ (b) _____ (c) _____ (d) _____

Explain:

Part 4: How much time did you spend studying?

WEEKS	DAYS	HOURS	MINUTES

If you could go back in time and study for this test again, would you do anything differently?

Explain.

Part 5: How well did classroom lessons, activities, and assignments prepare you for this test?

0	1	2	3	4	5

Not at all   Really well!

Explain and make suggestions for improvement.

Part 6: Do you know anything about this topic that wasn't on the test? Tell me about it on the back...

What? So What? Now What?

What is it?

A technique that uses three simple writing prompts (What? So what? Now what?) to help students reflect on what and how they learn

What are the benefits of using this tool?

Getting students to reflect on their learning experiences in a thoughtful and meaningful way can sometimes be challenging. This tool increases the productivity and usefulness of classroom reflection sessions by using three simple writing prompts to guide and focus student thinking:

What?	$\longrightarrow$	What did you do during this learning experience?
So what?	$\longrightarrow$	What did this experience teach you about yourself or the content?
Now what?	$\longrightarrow$	How can you apply, extend, or benefit from what you learned?

What are the basic steps?

1. Select a learning experience for students to reflect on (e.g., a lecture, test, homework assignment).

2. Have students reflect on what this experience taught them about the content *or* about themselves and how they learn. Initiate the reflection process by having them do the following:

- Summarize what they did during the learning experience. (*What?*)
- Describe what they learned about themselves or the content material. (*So what?*)
- Explain how they could apply, extend, or benefit from what they learned. (*Now what?*)

How is this tool used in the classroom?

✔ To help students reflect on and learn from their classroom experiences

This tool can be used to have students reflect on what they learn about the content (Example 1). It can also be used to have students reflect on themselves and how they learn (Example 2).

EXAMPLE 1: Here, a student reflects on what he learned from a classroom activity:

> What: We re-enacted the Federalist vs. Anti-Federalist debate over the Constitution.
>
> So what: I realized that the current debate about the rights of individuals vs. states vs. federal government has been going on for centuries!
>
> Now what: I wonder if I can find other examples of conflicts over state/federal/individual rights this semester.

EXAMPLE 2: Here, a student reflects on her experience with a new note-taking technique:

> What: We learned to take notes using pictures as well as words.
>
> So what: It's easier for me to remember stuff after I draw a picture of it.
>
> Now what: I will try using the words and pictures technique to take notes in my other classes.

References

Alderman, M. K. (2008). *Motivation for achievement: Possibilities for teaching and learning* (3rd ed.). New York, NY: Routledge.

Aronson, E., Blaney, N., Stephin, C., Sikes, J., & Snapp, M. (1978). *The jigsaw classroom.* Beverly Hills, CA: Sage Publishing Company.

Ausubel, D. P. (1968). *Educational psychology: A cognitive view.* New York: Holt, Rinehart and Winston.

Blachowicz, C. L. Z. (1986). Making connections: Alternatives to the vocabulary notebook. *Journal of Reading, 29*(7), 643–649.

Black, P., & Wiliam, D. (1998a). Assessment and classroom learning. *Assessment in Education, 5*(1), 7–74.

Black, P., & Wiliam, D. (1998b). Inside the black box: Raising standards through classroom assessment. *Phi Delta Kappan, 80*(2), 139–148.

Brookhart, S. M. (2008). *How to give effective feedback to your students.* Alexandria, VA: ASCD.

Butkowsky, I. S., & Willows, D. M. (1980). Cognitive-motivational characteristics of children varying in reading ability: Evidence for learned helplessness in poor readers. *Journal of Educational Psychology, 72*(3), 408–22.

Butler, A. C., & Roediger, H. L. (2007). Testing improves long-term retention in a simulated classroom setting. *European Journal of Cognitive Psychology, 19*(4/5), 514–527.

Cameron, J., & Pierce, W. D. (1994). Reinforcement, reward, and intrinsic motivation: A meta-analysis. *Review of Educational Research, 64*(3), 363–423.

Chapman, C., & King, R. (2008). *Differentiated instructional management: Work smarter, not harder.* Thousand Oaks, CA: Corwin Press.

Chappuis, J. (2009). *Seven strategies of assessment for learning.* Portland, OR: Educational Testing Service.

Chappuis, J., Stiggins, R., Chappuis, S., & Arter, J. (2011). *Classroom assessment for student learning: Doing it right— using it well* (2nd ed.). Upper Saddle River, NJ: Pearson Education.

Chappuis, S., & Stiggins, R. J. (2002). Classroom assessment for learning. *Educational Leadership, 60*(1), 40–43.

Costa, A. L., & Kallick, B. (Eds.). (2008). *Learning and leading with Habits of Mind: 16 essential characteristics for success.* Alexandria, VA: ASCD.

Dweck, C. S. (1975). The role of expectations and attributions in the alleviation of learned helplessness. *Journal of Personality and Social Psychology, 31*(4), 674–685.

Dweck, C. S. (2007). The perils and promises of praise. *Educational Leadership, 65*(2), 34–39.

Gardner, H. (1983). *Frames of mind: The theory of multiple intelligences.* New York: Basic Books.

Geocaris, C., & Ross, M. (1999). A test worth taking. *Educational Leadership, 57*(1), 29–33.

Guskey, T. R. (Dec 2007/Jan 2008). The rest of the story. *Educational Leadership, 65*(4), 28–35.

Hattie, J. (1999, August). *Influences on student learning.* Inaugural professorial lecture, University of Auckland, New Zealand. Retrieved from http://www.education.auckland.ac.nz/uoa/home/about/staff/j.hattie/hattie-papers-download/influences

Hattie, J., & Timperley, H. (2007). The power of feedback. *Review of Educational Research, 77*(1), 81–112.

Herber, H. (1970). *Teaching reading in the content areas.* Englewood Cliffs, NJ: Prentice Hall.

Himmele, P., & Himmele, W. (2011). *Total participation techniques: Making every student an active learner.* Alexandria, VA: ASCD.

Hunter, M. (1984). Knowing, teaching, and supervising. In P. Hosford (Ed.), *Using what we know about teaching* (pp. 169–192). Alexandria, VA: ASCD.

Johnson, R., & Johnson, D. W. (1994). An overview of cooperative learning. In J. Thousand, R. Villa, & A. Nevin (Eds.), *Creativity and collaborative learning* (pp. 31–44). Baltimore: Paul Brooks Publishing.

Kagan, S. (Dec 1989/Jan 1990). The structural approach to cooperative learning. *Educational Leadership, 47*(4), 12–15.

Marzano, R. J. (2006) *Classroom assessment and grading that work.* Alexandria, VA: ASCD.

Marzano, R. J. (2007). *The art and science of teaching: A comprehensive framework for effective instruction.* Alexandria, VA: ASCD.

Marzano, R. J. (2010). Using games to enhance student achievement. *Educational Leadership, 67*(5), 71–72.

Moss, C. M., & Brookhart, S. M. (2009). *Advancing formative assessment in every classroom: A guide for instructional leaders.* Alexandria, VA: ASCD.

Mosston, M. (1972). *Teaching: From command to discovery.* Belmont, CA: Wadsworth Publishing.

Narvaez, M. L., & Brimijoin, K. (2010). *Differentiation at work, K–5: Principles, lessons, and strategies.* Thousand Oaks, CA: Corwin Press.

National Governors Association Center for Best Practices, Council of Chief State School Officers. (2010). *Common Core State Standards for English language arts & literacy in history/social studies, science, and technical subjects.* Washington, DC: National Governors Association Center for Best Practices, Council of Chief State School Officers.

Pashler, H., Bain, P., Bottge, B., Graesser, A., Koedinger, K., McDaniel, M., & Metcalfe, J. (2007). *Organizing instruction and study to improve student learning* (NCER 2007–2004). Washington, DC: National Center for Education Research, Institute of Education Sciences, US Department of Education. Retrieved from http://ncer.ed.gov

Popham, W. J. (2008). *Transformative assessment.* Alexandria, VA: ASCD.

Reeves, D. B. (2002). *Reason to write: Help your child succeed in school and in life through better reasoning and clear communication* (elementary school edition). New York: Kaplan.

Robinson, F. P. (1946). *Effective study.* New York: Harper & Brothers.

Rowe, M. B. (1986). Wait time: slowing down may be a way of speeding up! *Journal of Teacher Education, 37*(1), 43–50.

Sadler, D. R. (1989). Formative assessment and the design of instructional systems. *Instructional Science, 18*, 119–144.

Schunk, D. H., & Zimmerman, B. J. (Eds.). (1998). *Self-regulated learning: From teaching to self-reflective practice.* New York: Guilford Press.

Schwartz, R. M., & Raphael, T. E. (1985). Concept of definition: A key to improving students' vocabulary. *The Reading Teacher, 39*(2), 198–205.

Shute V. J. (2008). Focus on formative feedback. *Review of Educational Research, 78*(1), 153–189.

Silver, H. F., Brunsting, J. R., & Walsh, T. (2008). *Math tools, grades 3–12: 64 ways to differentiate instruction and increase student engagement.* Thousand Oaks, CA: Corwin Press.

Silver, H. F., Brunsting, J. R., Walsh, T., and Thomas, E. J. (2012). *Math tools, grades 3–12: 60+ ways to build mathematical practices, differentiate instruction, and increase student engagement* (2nd ed.). Thousand Oaks, CA: Corwin Press.

Silver, H. F., Jackson, J. W., & Moirao, D. R. (2011). *Task Rotation: Strategies for differentiating activities and assessments by learning style.* Alexandria, VA: ASCD.

Silver, H. F., Morris, S. C., & Klein, V. (2010). *Reading for Meaning: How to build students' comprehension, reasoning, and problem-solving skills.* Alexandria, VA: ASCD.

Silver, H. F., & Perini, M. J. (2010). *Classroom curriculum design: How strategic units improve instruction and engage students in meaningful learning.* Ho-Ho-Kus, NJ: Thoughtful Education Press.

Silver, H. F., Reilly, E. C., & Perini, M. J. (2009). *The Thoughtful Education guide to Reading for Meaning.* Thousand Oaks, CA: Corwin Press.

Silver, H. F., Strong, R. W., & Perini, M. J. (2000). *So each may learn: Integrating learning styles and multiple intelligences.* Alexandria, VA: ASCD.

Silver, H. F., Strong, R. W., & Perini, M. J. (2007). *The strategic teacher: Selecting the right research-based strategy for every lesson.* Alexandria, VA: ASCD.

Silver Strong & Associates. (2007). *Questioning styles and strategies: How to use questions to engage and motivate different styles of learners.* Ho-Ho-Kus, NJ: Thoughtful Education Press.

Silver Strong & Associates. (2008). *Word works: Cracking vocabulary's CODE* (2nd ed.). Ho-Ho-Kus, NJ: Thoughtful Education Press.

Silver Strong & Associates. (2012). *The Thoughtful Classroom Teacher Effectiveness Framework* (quick guide). Ho-Ho-Kus, NJ: Silver Strong & Associates. Retrieved from http://www.thoughtfulclassroom.com/PDFs/TCTEF_Quick_Guide_02-03-12.pdf

Solomon, G., & Schrum, L. (2010). *Web 2.0 how-to for educators.* Washington, DC: International Society for Technology in Education.

Sternberg, R. J. (1997). *Thinking styles.* Cambridge, United Kingdom: Cambridge University Press.

Sternberg, R. J. (2007/2008). Assessing what matters. *Educational Leadership, 65*(4), 20–26.

Sternberg, R. J., & Grigorenko, E. (2004). Successful intelligence in the classroom. *Theory Into Practice, 43*(4), 274–280.

Stiggins, R., Arter, J., Chappuis, J., & Chappuis, S. (2006). *Classroom assessment for student learning: Doing it right—using it well.* Portland, OR: Educational Testing Service.

Thomas, E. J., & Brunsting, J. R. (2010). *Styles and strategies for teaching middle school mathematics: 21 techniques for differentiating instruction and assessment.* Thousand Oaks, CA: Corwin Press.

Thomas, E. J., & Brunsting, J. R., & Warrick, P. L. (2010). *Styles and strategies for teaching high school mathematics: 21 techniques for differentiating instruction and assessment.* Thousand Oaks, CA: Corwin Press.

Tomlinson, C. A. (2001). *How to differentiate instruction in mixed-ability classrooms* (2nd ed.). Alexandria, VA: ASCD.

Tomlinson, C. A. (2010). *The role of assessment in a differentiated classroom* [PowerPoint slides]. Retrieved from http://caroltomlinson.com/Presentations/Role_of_Assessment.pdf

Tomlinson, C. A., & Imbeau, M. B. (2010). *Leading and managing a differentiated classroom.* Alexandria, VA: ASCD.

Whiting, B., Van Burgh, J. W., & Render, G. F. (1995). *Mastery learning in the classroom.* Paper presented at the annual meeting of the American Educational Research Association, San Francisco, CA.

Wiggins, G., & McTighe, J. (2005). *Understanding by design* (2nd ed.). Upper Saddle River, NJ: Prentice Hall.

Zimmerman, B. J. (2001). Theories of self-regulated learning and academic achievement: An overview and analysis. In B. J. Zimmerman & D. H. Schunk (Eds.), *Self-regulated learning and academic achievement: Theoretical perspectives* (2nd ed., pp. 1–37). Mahwah, NJ: Erlbaum.

Index of Tools

About the Authors

Abigail L. Boutz, PhD, has taught, tutored, and mentored students at the elementary through college levels, most recently at the University of California, Los Angeles, where she served as a lecturer for the Life Sciences Department, a university field supervisor for the Teacher Education Program, and academic coordinator for the Undergraduate Research Center/Center for Academic and Research Excellence (URC/CARE). During her tenure with Silver Strong & Associates, she has designed training modules and workshop materials on teaching tools and strategies, learning styles, and instructional leadership; she also developed and authored a number of titles in the TextWorks! series of curriculum guides.

Harvey F. Silver, EdD, is the president of Silver Strong & Associates and Thoughtful Education Press. He has conducted numerous workshops for school districts and state education departments throughout the United States. With the late Richard W. Strong, he developed The Thoughtful Classroom, a renowned professional development initiative dedicated to the goal of "making students as important as standards." More recently, he has collaborated with Matthew J. Perini to create The Thoughtful Classroom Teacher Effectiveness Framework, a comprehensive system for observing, evaluating, and refining classroom practice. He has also partnered with ASCD to develop The Strategic Teacher Initiative and *The Core Six*, a book of research-based strategies for addressing the Common Core State Standards.

Joyce W. Jackson is a seasoned and practical teacher with over thirty years of classroom experience. Before joining Silver Strong & Associates, she served as a Kentucky Distinguished Educator and worked with the Kentucky Department of Education's Division of School Improvement on closing achievement gaps and improving teaching and learning in low-performing schools. As a senior associate on our Thoughtful Classroom professional development team, she now coaches and mentors educators across the country, helping them make classroom instruction, assessment, and curriculum design more thoughtful, differentiated, and effective. She also works as an educational recovery specialist in a turnaround school for the Kentucky Department of Education.

Matthew J. Perini has served as the director of publishing for Silver Strong & Associates and Thoughtful Education Press for the past decade, authoring numerous books, curriculum guides, and articles on a wide range of topics, including learning styles, multiple intelligences, reading instruction, and effective teaching practices. Most recently, he has collaborated with Harvey Silver, R. Thomas Dewing, and ASCD on *The Core Six*, a book of research-based strategies for addressing the Common Core State Standards. He has also been a driving force in the development of ASCD and Silver Strong & Associates' Strategic Teacher Initiative and The Thoughtful Classroom's Teacher Effectiveness Framework.